VOLUME 675

JANUARY 2018

THE ANNALS

of The American Academy of Political
and Social Science

Developing the Basis for Secure and Accessible Data for High Impact Program Management, Policy Development, and Scholarship

Special Editors:
ANDREW REAMER
George Washington University
JULIA LANE
New York University
IAN FOSTER
University of Chicago
DAVID ELLWOOD
Harvard Kennedy School

⑤SAGE

Los Angeles | London | New Delhi
Singapore | Washington DC | Melbourne

The American Academy of Political and Social Science

202 S. 36th Street, Annenberg School for Communication, University of Pennsylvania,
Philadelphia, PA 19104-3806; (215) 746-6500; (215) 573-2667 (fax); www.aapss.org

Origin and Purpose. The Academy was organized December 14, 1889, to promote the progress of political and social science, especially through publications and meetings. The Academy does not take sides in controverted questions, but seeks to gather and present reliable information to assist the public in forming an intelligent and accurate judgment.

Meetings. The Academy occasionally holds a meeting in the spring extending over two days.

Publications. THE ANNALS of The American Academy of Political and Social Science is the bimonthly publication of the Academy. Each issue contains articles on some prominent social or political problem, written at the invitation of the editors. These volumes constitute important reference works on the topics with which they deal, and they are extensively cited by authorities throughout the United States and abroad.

Subscriptions. THE ANNALS of The American Academy of Political and Social Science (ISSN 0002-7162) (J295) is published bimonthly—in January, March, May, July, September, and November—by SAGE Publishing, 2455 Teller Road, Thousand Oaks, CA 91320. Periodicals postage paid at Thousand Oaks, California, and at additional mailing offices. POSTMASTER: Send address changes to The Annals of The American Academy of Political and Social Science, c/o SAGE Publishing, 2455 Teller Road, Thousand Oaks, CA 91320. Institutions may subscribe to THE ANNALS at the annual rate: $1129 (clothbound, $1275). Individuals may subscribe to the ANNALS at the annual rate: $126 (clothbound, $185). Single issues of THE ANNALS may be obtained by individuals for $39 each (clothbound, $54). Single issues of THE ANNALS have proven to be excellent supplementary texts for classroom use. Direct inquiries regarding adoptions to THE ANNALS c/o SAGE Publishing (address below).

All correspondence concerning membership in the Academy, dues renewals, inquiries about membership status, and/or purchase of single issues of THE ANNALS should be sent to THE ANNALS c/o SAGE Publishing, 2455 Teller Road, Thousand Oaks, CA 91320. Telephone: (800) 818-SAGE (7243) and (805) 499-0721; Fax/Order line: (805) 375-1700; e-mail: journals@sagepub.com. *Please note that orders under $30 must be prepaid.* For all customers outside the Americas, please visit http://www.sagepub.co.uk/customerCare.nav for information.

Printed on acid-free paper

THE ANNALS

Editorial Office: 202 S. 36th Street, Philadelphia, PA 19104-3806
For information about individual and institutional subscriptions address:
SAGE Publishing
2455 Teller Road
Thousand Oaks, CA 91320

For SAGE Publishing: Peter Geraghty (Production) and Mimi Nguyen (Marketing)

From India and South Asia, write to:	From Europe, the Middle East, and Africa, write to:
SAGE PUBLICATIONS INDIA Pvt Ltd	SAGE PUBLICATIONS LTD
B-42 Panchsheel Enclave, P.O. Box 4109	1 Oliver's Yard, 55 City Road
New Delhi 110 017	London EC1Y 1SP
INDIA	UNITED KINGDOM

International Standard Serial Number ISSN 0002-7162
ISBN 978-1-5443-2928-4 (Vol. 675, 2018) paper
ISBN 978-1-5443-2927-7 (Vol. 675, 2018) cloth
First printing, January 2018

Information about membership rates, institutional subscriptions, and back issue prices may be found on the facing page.

Advertising. Current rates and specifications may be obtained by writing to The Annals Advertising and Promotion Manager at the Thousand Oaks office (address above). Acceptance of advertising in this journal in no way implies endorsement of the advertised product or service by SAGE or the journal's affiliated society(ies) or the journal editor(s). No endorsement is intended or implied. SAGE reserves the right to reject any advertising it deems as inappropriate for this journal.

Claims. Claims for undelivered copies must be made no later than six months following month of publication. The publisher will supply replacement issues when losses have been sustained in transit and when the reserve stock will permit.

Change of Address. Six weeks' advance notice must be given when notifying of change of address. Please send the old address label along with the new address to the SAGE office address above to ensure proper identification. Please specify the name of the journal.

THE ANNALS

OF THE AMERICAN ACADEMY OF POLITICAL AND SOCIAL SCIENCE

Volume 675   January 2018

2017 Daniel Patrick Moynihan Lecture on Social Science and Public Policy

IN THIS ISSUE:

Developing the Basis for Secure and Accessible Data for High Impact Program Management, Policy Development, and Scholarship

Special Editors: ANDREW REAMER, JULIA LANE, IAN FOSTER, and DAVID ELLWOOD

Introduction

Section I: Privacy and Confidentiality

Section II: Data Producers

Section III: Comprehensive Strategies

FORTHCOMING

Migrant Smuggling as a Collective Strategy and Insurance Policy:
Views from the Margins
Special Editors: SHELDON X. ZHANG, GABRIELLA SANCHEZ,
and LUIGI ACHILLI

What Census Data Miss about American Diversity
Special Editors: RICHARD ALBA and KENNETH PREWITT

2017 Daniel Patrick Moynihan Lecture on Social Science and Public Policy

Independent Workers: What Role for Public Policy?

By
ALAN B. KRUEGER

I would like to begin by thanking Senator Mark Warner for his kind introduction. I am particularly appreciative that he took the time to come here this afternoon given all the other critical work he is doing. He has taken the leadership in Congress—and I would say in the Nation—on emerging workplace issues. He called me late last year, just after I read the news that he was appointed Vice Chairman of the Senate Intelligence Committee, and I congratulated him on his new position, and he responded by saying something like: "Thanks, but I'd much rather spend my time developing policies that are appropriate for independent workers in the emerging gig economy." I also want to thank Ken Prewitt for his remarks and the American Academy of Political and Social Science for selecting me for this prestigious award and for giving me the opportunity to present the Moynihan Lecture today.[1]

To be associated with Daniel Patrick Moynihan is a tremendous honor. I was inspired by his career and one connection I have always felt that I have with Senator Moynihan is that his career in the federal government began at the U.S. Department of Labor as Assistant Secretary for Policy, Planning and Research. That position was actually created for him. When Bob Reich asked me to be Chief Economist of the Labor Department in 1994

Alan B. Krueger is the Bendheim Professor of Economics and Public Policy at Princeton University. He has published widely on the economics of education, unemployment, labor demand, income inequality, and social insurance. He served as Chairman of President Barack Obama's Council of Economic Advisers and was a member of his cabinet from 2011 to 2013. He was also Assistant Secretary for Economic Policy and Chief Economist of the U.S. Department of the Treasury in 2009–10, and Chief Economist at the U.S. Department of Labor in 1994–95.

Correspondence: akrueger@princeton.edu

DOI: 10.1177/0002716217741109

he told me that what he was hoping to achieve by creating this new position was what was done for Daniel Patrick Moynihan—to bring in scholars who would enrich the government with their work and then go back and enrich the Academy with what they had learned. Daniel Patrick Moynihan was the perfect role model for that process.

There are too many friends, family members, and distinguished colleagues in the audience to acknowledge all of them, but I want to acknowledge that my parents are here. My parents have inspired me throughout my career, but especially for the topic of my lecture today. My dad was a CPA. (I used to say that he is a CPA, but he recently informed me that he finally let his license expire.) He became self-employed in the early 1970s and I remember clearly that when he made that decision we had a family meeting in our living room and he informed my brother, sister, and me that he was going to go out on his own. "Don't worry," he said, "we will still be covered by mom's health insurance." My mom was a public school teacher, with good health insurance. I have thought about that story often in recent years because the Affordable Care Act (ACA) has helped to do for many entrepreneurs what my mom was able to do for my dad, namely, provide access to health insurance. I will have more to say about this later in my talk.

The motivation for my lecture today is that the U.S. job market has been changing for several decades, with steady growth in self-employment. IRS data on Schedule C filings for self-employment income clearly show that self-employment is rising as a share of total employment, while household survey data from the Current Population Survey (CPS) show a downward trend, which suggests to me that the job market has changed so quickly that many workers are fundamentally confused about the nature of their employment relationship (see Figure 1).[2] The distinction between being self-employed and being a traditional employee matters, in part, because self-employed workers are responsible for providing for their own safety net, as well as securing other benefits and work protections, and for assuring that they are paid for work that they complete. The employer-employee relationship and a legal apparatus developed over many years handles these tasks for traditional employees. I think we need to update our labor laws to keep up with the evolving nature of work relationships.

Several factors are fueling the growth in self-employed workers, and one important one is technology. Work is becoming more standardized and more of a commodity. Probably everyone in this room uses Microsoft Office. It is easier to reach out to the external job market and obtain inputs when necessary if work is standardized. More recently, the growth of the gig economy (sometimes called platform work or digitally intermediated work) has boosted the trend toward self-employment. Demographics are also part of the explanation, as older workers are more likely to be self-employed, and our workforce is aging. And, finally, part of the trend is a result of companies misclassifying workers, which Weil (2014) calls a fissuring of the workplace; this trend is unfortunate and needs to be closely monitored and policed.

I suspect the trend toward self-employment will continue. Our labor laws and safety net were developed for a bygone era, when almost all workers could expect continuing employment relationships with companies. I think the question that

FIGURE 1
IRS vs. CPS Data on Self-Employment as a Share of CPS Total Employment

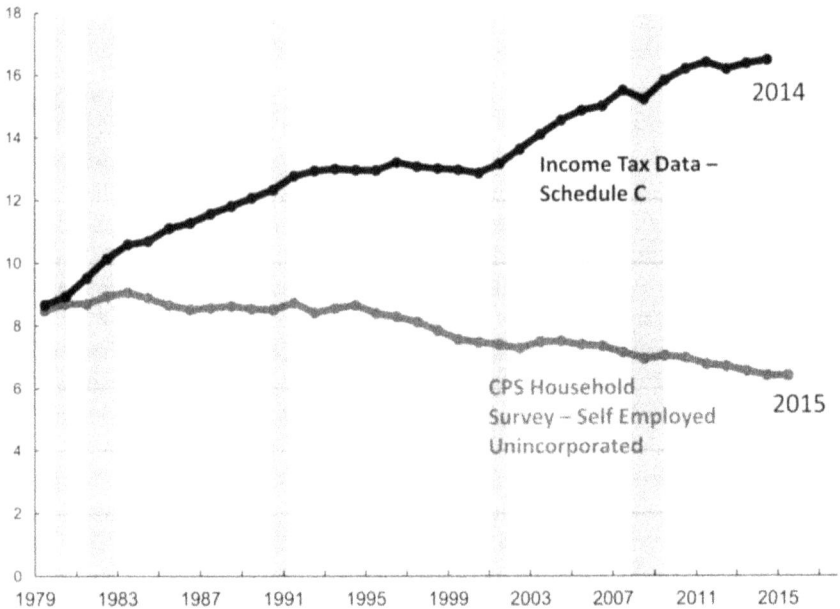

SOURCE: Current Population Survey; IRS Statistics of Income Publication 1304 (Table 1.3).
NOTE: Shading denotes recession.

we face going forward is, How do we extend the safety net to the large and growing group of independent workers, particularly in an age when there seems to be tremendous opposition to universal mandates that compel participation? This is the case even though some of our great advances over the last century—Social Security being a prime example—were only possible because the federal government could pass a universal mandate. And Social Security has passed the test of time; it is the ultimate portable benefit. It applies to workers who are self-employed and to traditional employees who receive W-2 tax forms. It does not matter which employer you work for. I am sure that President Roosevelt and his advisors did not anticipate Uber or TaskRabbit, but Social Security works well even for that sector of the economy. The challenge that we face now is how do we create in our existing system, which has protections and benefits for the roughly 85 percent of the workforce in a traditional job, additional protections and benefits to the rest of the workforce? That is the topic I address today.

I learned when I worked in Washington that when you confront a difficult policy challenge, you basically have three approaches to choose from. First, you could enunciate a set of principles, and challenge others to create policies that satisfy those principles. I will do a little bit of that, I have to confess. Second, you can appoint a commission and hope the commission solves the problem, or at

FIGURE 2
Percent of Workers Who Are Independent Contractors on Their Main Job, by Age

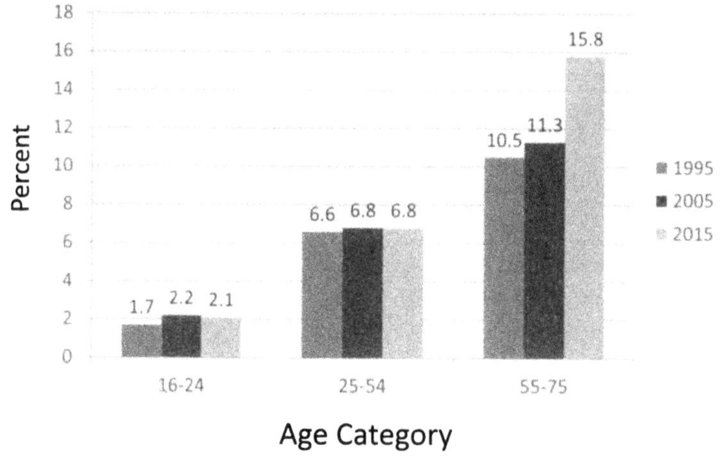

SOURCE: Bureau of Labor Statistics; Katz and Krueger (2016) Rand survey.

least takes the pressure off until a solution could be found. Or, third, you can make concrete proposals to actually solve the problem. I will follow the third approach, but because I am uncertain about the right direction to go, I will also do something else that I learned in Washington: I will report the pros and the cons—arguments in favor, arguments against—my proposals, in an attempt to advance the discussion of policy options concerning independent workers.

Princeton Self-Employment Survey

Figure 2, drawn from Katz and Krueger (2016), shows that older workers are more likely to be self-employed, and there was strong growth in self-employment among older workers over the last decade.[3] Almost one in five workers over the age of 54 is working in self-employment on their main job. Although the Great Recession surely accelerated this trend, the growth in self-employment preceded the recession according to IRS data on 1099 filings and Schedule C filings (see Katz and Krueger 2017).

To better understand the nature and challenges of self-employed workers, I designed the Princeton Self-Employment Survey (PSES). This survey was conducted April 24–April 27, 2017, a week after Tax Day, and I will publicly share the results for the first time in this lecture. This was an online survey of more than ten thousand individuals using Qualtrics software and the Qualtrics panel of respondents. Although the Qualtrics sample does not hold up to the high standards that the Bureau of Labor Statistics and Census Bureau employ, as best I can tell it represents the self-employed population reasonably well. We also

TABLE 1
Question 1: CPS Class of Workers

On your main job last week, were you employed by government, by a private company, a nonprofit organization, or were you self-employed or working in the family business? Or were you not working at all last week?

Type of Work	Count	Unweighted Percent	Weighted Percent
Government	1,650	17.4	14.6
Private for-profit	4,610	52.7	68.2
Nonprofit[a]	940	10.8	7.9
Self-employed	1,549	15.4	7.8
Family business	470	3.7	1.4
Only work last week was filling out surveys	252		
Did not have a job last week	897		
	10,368		

NOTE: Sample size is 8,579 for the percentages because individuals under age 18, nonresidents, and gibberish responders are excluded. Weights are designed to match ACS total.
a. Includes tax-exempt and charitable organizations.

developed sample weights so that on average the sample is representative of the American Community Survey (ACS).[4] One of the features that I built into this survey is an A/B experiment where I asked the same question two different ways to randomly divided groups. Even if one is worried about the representativeness of the overall sample, at least in this survey experiment I had some control and could test the effect of question wording on this group of respondents.

The survey worked as follows. The first question was based on the basic monthly CPS class of worker questions on the main job. The responses are tabulated in Table 1. A total of 10,368 individuals started the survey, and 1,149 were screened out after the first question because their only work in the previous week was filling out questionnaires or because they did not work at all, and another 640 were dropped from my analysis sample because they resided outside the United States, were under age 18, or provided nonsensical (usually typing gibberish to open questions) responses. The remaining 8,579 individuals participated in the A/B experiment. Specifically, half of the respondents were randomly selected and asked the BLS Contingent Worker Survey (CWS) question on self-employment: "Last week were you working or self-employed as an independent contractor, an independent consultant, or freelance worker? That is, someone who obtains customers on their own to provide a product or service." That phrasing, which designates Question A, potentially leaves out much self-employment work. How should an Uber driver, who does not obtain customers on his or her own, respond? And suppose you own your own business and are self-employed, you would be hard pressed to know how to answer that question. So I tried it a second way for the other half of workers, where I first provided a preamble to the BLS question and then asked the CWS Question: "Many people work in

FIGURE 3
A/B Question Test for Subsample That Responded Self-Employed to
Main Job Question ($N = 1,321$)

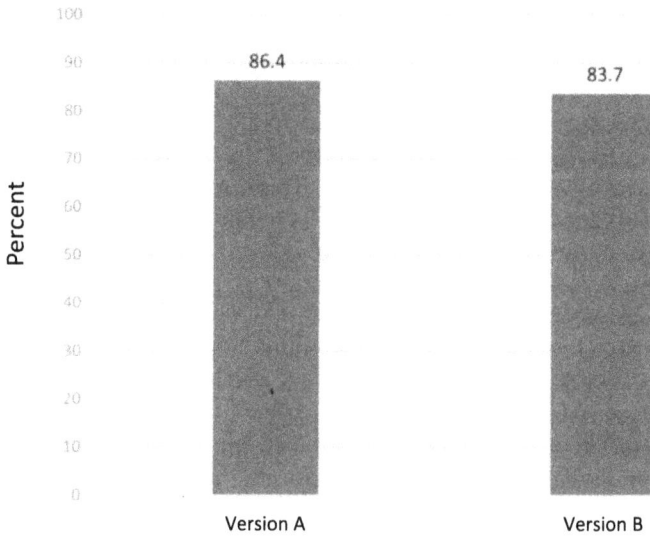

**P-value for difference = 0.17.

self-employment, on either a part-time or full-time basis, doing things such as working on construction jobs, selling goods or services in their businesses, or working through a digital platform or intermediary, such as Uber, Upwork or Avon. Last week, were you working or self-employed as an independent contractor, an independent consultant, or freelance worker? That is someone who obtains customers on their own to provide a product or service?" This version is designated Question B.

Respondents were 4.5 percentage points more likely to be classified as self-employed in Question B than in Question A: 32.2 percent versus 27.7 percent ($p < .001$), which highlights the sensitivity of reporting self-employment status depending on question phrasing.[5] Note also that these percentages are high. Many of these workers are self-employed on secondary jobs, which may go unreported in the CPS. According to the weighted class of worker on the main job question in Table 1, about 8 percent of the workers respond as self-employed. Interestingly when I look at this subset who reported that they were self-employed on their main job, there is not a significant difference in responses to the CWS question asked the A way or the B way. In fact, it reverses order and the Question A phrasing had a slightly higher proportion (see Figure 3). About 85 percent in either question indicated that they were self-employed.

One of the challenges involved in defining self-employment is that many workers combine self-employment activities with traditional employment, while others earn almost all of their income from self-employment. IRS data reported in Jackson, Looney, and Ramnath (2017) show that in 2014 about 60 percent of the self-employed earned virtually all of their income from self-employment, while many others earned a small share of income from self-employment activities. In the rest of my talk I focus on the group that is mainly self-employed—that is, those earning most of their income from self-employment. Specifically, I restrict the PSES sample to the group of individuals who indicated self-employment as their main activity based on the CPS class of worker question in Table 1. Almost one fifth of these individuals have traditional W-2-type jobs in addition to being mainly self-employed. My reason for focusing on those who are mainly self-employed is that workers who are connected to a traditional employer have more access to the safety net and have more access to benefits, such as health insurance coverage, than those who are primarily self-employed. The results of the A/B question experiment also suggest that membership in this group is less sensitive to survey question wording.

Table 2 compares the industry and demographic characteristics of the self-employed in the CPS with the PSES, and with employees in the CPS. Self-employed workers tend to be older than traditional employees. They also tend to be better educated. The self-employed are also over represented in construction and in professional, technical, and scientific positions; they are underrepresented in manufacturing compared with traditional employees. Almost two-thirds of the self-employed are men. The self-employed have higher earnings, on average, than traditional employees, and they have greater dispersion in earnings, highlighting the heterogeneity of the self-employed. The PSES provides some additional details on the self-employed. Most of the self-employed are in unincorporated businesses, and most report that they file Schedule C. About half say they work from home or a home office.

The PSES included a question designed to gauge participation in the gig economy: "Last week, did you find any paying work through a digital platform, such as Uber, TaskRabbit or Handy? This is often called gig work." A total of 14 percent of the self-employed responded yes. To put this figure in context, if you multiply 14 percent by the percent of all workers who are self-employed according to the CPS (about 8.5 percent), you come up with an estimate that a little over 1 percent of the workforce overall is in the gig economy. Of course, there are others who perform gig work who are not mainly self-employed, so that figure understates the total share of workers finding work online. Nevertheless, it is consistent with studies that find that the digitally intermediate labor market is growing exponentially (e.g., Farrell and Greig 2016).

The self-employed as a group are mostly satisfied working in self-employment. When asked, "Would you prefer to work for someone else rather than being self-employed?" a total of 83 percent responded "no." This figure is 63.1 percent for the subset of self-employed workers who simultaneously hold a traditional job, and 63.5 percent for those who find work through a digital platform. Thus, a smaller majority of these workers seem to prefer their employment status.

For those who simultaneously held both a traditional employment job and self-employment position, I asked, "Suppose it was possible for you to work 5 more hours each week. How would you prefer to work: in self-employment at

TABLE 2
Characteristics of Workers by Class of Job

Characteristic	Employed Traditional April CPS 2017	Self Employed April CPS 2017	Princeton Self Employed Survey April 2017
Mean age (years)	41.8	49.4	46.5
Female (%)	48.0	34.0	36.6
Marital status (%)			
Married	52.6	67.7	53.1
Never married	31.8	15.6	24.5
Divorced/widowed/separated	13.5	14.6	22.4
Race/ethnicity (%)			
White	77.8	83.6	84.3
African American	12.6	7.7	9.6
Hispanic	17.4	13.6	13.9
Educational attainment (%)			
Bachelor's degree or higher	36.5	40.7	36.1
Some college or associate's degree	29.4	25.2	29.3
High school graduate	26.7	25.8	28.2
Less than high school diploma	7.4	8.3	6.4
Region (%)			
Northeast	17.9	15.9	19.1
Midwest	21.8	20.2	20.1
South	37.2	35.9	34.3
West	23.1	28.0	26.5
Multiple jobholder (%)	4.8	7.9	18.7
Part-time employment (%)	23.8	30.1	36.8
Industry (%)			
Agriculture, Forestry, Fishing, and Hunting	1.1	5.1	6.2
Mining	0.5	0.2	0.5
Utilities	0.9	0.0	1.3
Construction	5.9	15.6	18.7
Manufacturing	11.2	4.1	2.6
Wholesale Trade	2.4	2.3	2.7
Retail Trade	11.1	8.2	17.3
Transportation and Warehousing	4.3	4.4	3.1
Information and Communications	1.9	1.7	2.7
Finance, Insurance, and Real Estate Rental and Leasing	7.0	8.3	8.6
Professional, Scientific, Technical, Management, and Admin	11.0	23.3	13.7
Educational Services, Health Care, and Social Assistance	24.0	10.1	10.4

(continued)

TABLE 2 (CONTINUED)

Characteristic	Employed Traditional April CPS 2017	Self Employed April CPS 2017	Princeton Self Employed Survey April 2017
Arts, Entertainment, Rec, Accommodation, & Food Services	9.0	7.6	11.9
Other Services (Excluding Public Administration)	4.6	8.8	0.4
Public Administration	5.0	0.2	0.0
Mean hours worked	38.5	40.0	41.6
First job	37.9	38.7	37.7
Second job	13.7	14.1	26.9
Median weekly income ($)	$750	$962	$900
Number of observations	51,322	5,912	1,317

NOTE: All statistics utilize weighted data. Princeton survey weights are based on self-employed in 2011–15 American Community Survey.

your typical hourly rate or in your job as a traditional employee at your current wage rate on that job?" Seventy-two percent responded that they would rather work additional time in self-employment. This finding is consistent with a Gronau (1977)–type model in which self-employed workers first do the most lucrative work available to them, which is self-employment, and then if they cannot find enough work in self-employment they turn to working for an hourly wage in a more traditional job to fill additional hours.

Another finding that is consistent with this interpretation is evidence on "hour constraints." Self-employed workers are often underemployed. In my survey, 40 percent of the self-employed worked less than 35 hours per week in their self-employment job. A third of all self-employed workers said that they would like to have more hours per week. Consistent with this finding, in the CPS the self-employed are more likely than traditional employees to be classified as part time for economic reasons. These findings suggest that one aspect of traditional employment is that it often entails an implicit contract for full-time work. The self-employed, by contrast, take on more risk, and have more volatility in income. Nonetheless, they seem by and large satisfied with this arrangement.

Work-Related Benefits

I consider two types of policies: grand, big ideas, that will not be implemented tomorrow, and incremental policies that could be implemented tomorrow. Both are important to consider. Here is a really ambitious, big idea: Hanauer and Rolf (2015) have proposed the idea of "Shared Security Accounts," in which all workers would be covered by a universal system that provides health insurance, retirement benefits, paid leave, and so on. Employers and online platforms like Uber would contribute 25 percent of their workers' compensation into a fund to pay for those benefits. Workers could choose which benefits they want. Although in practice the plan would be more complicated, which I explain shortly, this is the gist of the idea. I should also note that Shared Security Accounts are not a total head-in-the-sky idea. Washington State and New Jersey have considered legislation along these lines for self-employed workers.

So I asked workers about this proposal in my survey as follows: "Policy-makers have been discussing the idea of creating a fund to help self-employed workers obtain work-related benefits, such as health insurance and retirement savings, that they would be able to receive regardless of where they worked, and they could take with them if they changed jobs. Do you think this is a good idea?" Fully 81 percent thought it was a good idea; only 7 percent thought it was not a good idea. But I did not tell them that they would have to pay for it (or that whoever it was that they were working with would have to pay for it on their behalf), so maybe such strong support is not surprising. Nevertheless, workers seem to like the idea of Shared Security Accounts.

One of the core issues that arises in these proposals is what benefits should be included. The Washington State proposal looks to me like a cafeteria plan, where workers can choose benefits until their account runs out. So I wanted to probe which benefits were most important to the self-employed. Specifically, I gave respondents a list of eight potential benefits to choose from: life insurance, paid sick leave, paid family leave, retirement savings, disability insurance, unemployment insurance, workers' compensation insurance, and health insurance. I randomly changed the order of these benefits across respondents and asked them to select and drag the benefits listed on the screen to put them in order from the ones that are most important to them to least important.

What did I find? Simply put: health insurance. More than 50 percent listed health insurance first, and another 15 percent put health insurance second. Retirement savings was a distant second in terms of desired benefits (see Figure 4 for the full results).

If I look at those who do not have health insurance versus those who do have health insurance, the picture looks about the same. This not surprising because in earlier work with Ilyana Kuziemka, we found that a large share of those who lacked health insurance pre-ACA had been turned down for health insurance because of pre-existing conditions, and they said they wanted health insurance.[6] So what I take away from this exercise is that the consensus of the self-employed is that they want assistance obtaining health insurance.

In the PSES, 78.6 percent of the self-employed were covered by health insurance. That is close to estimates from the CPS and IRS. Using IRA tax data, Jackson, Looney, and Ramnath (2017) find that 75 percent of the self-employed had health insurance in 2014, while 90 percent of W-2 workers had health insurance. This gap takes on added significance, and suggests a market failure, if you bear in mind that median income is 25 percent less for W-2 workers than for the self-employed.

FIGURE 4
Ranking of Various Benefits by Self-Employed Workers

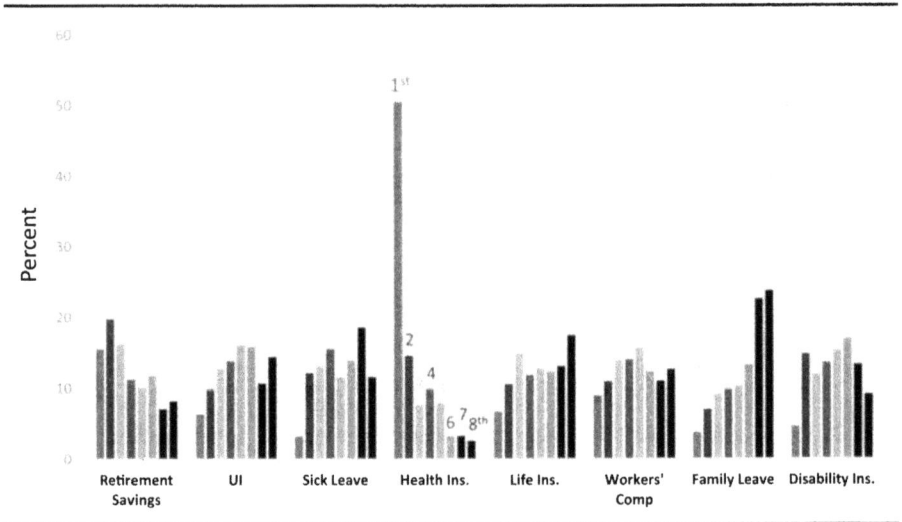

I explored how the self-employed obtained their health insurance in the PSES. Almost 20 percent of the self-employed with health insurance reported that they obtained their insurance from healthcare.gov or a state exchange. Since these exchanges were only up and running for a few years at this time, this is a remarkable success story. Another 24 percent said they obtained health insurance from "the government or state (e.g., Medicaid or Medicare)," which is probably related to the expansion of Medicaid under the ACA. These findings are consistent with other evidence suggesting that health insurance coverage has increased significantly more for the self-employed than for the employed since the ACA took effect.

Job Training and Taxes

Next consider job training. Just 36 percent of self-employed workers in my survey said they received training in the last year. Interestingly, this figure was much higher (55 percent) for the subset of workers who had a traditional job in addition to being self-employed. Higher educated workers were also more likely to report having received training in the last year.

Across all self-employed workers, 16 percent participated in continuing education and 19 percent had skills training. Those were the two most popular forms of training. Only 8 percent of self-employed workers said they had safety training in the last year. This is a broader point, but if you look at some of the major safety disasters we have had in the last decade, such as the BP Oil Spill or the Gold King Mine catastrophe in Colorado, contractors have played a central role in causing safety and environmental hazards. I think these incidents and my survey finding of relatively little safety training raise the question of whether self-employed contractors are receiving enough safety training.

Most (62 percent) self-employed workers paid for their training themselves or had a family member pay for it. Only in 6 percent of cases was training paid for by a hirer or a customer, which again highlights the risk that contractors are not provided adequate safety training.

Taxes

Because the survey was conducted the week after taxes were due I asked, "Is the amount that you have to pay in income taxes more than you planned for this year, about the same as you planned for this year or less than you planned for this year or hadn't paid taxes yet?" The good news is that only 6 percent admitted that they had not paid taxes yet. Fifty-six percent said they paid about the same amount as they planned for. Now I thought if I gave them a chance to complain about their taxes, more would have said they paid more rather than less than expected, but the remaining cases were close to symmetric: 17 percent said they paid more than they planned and 14 percent said they paid less than planned. I was surprised that more were not surprised by their tax bill.

I also asked if they had any unreimbursed expenses. A majority (56 percent) had no expenses over the year. Among those with positive unreimbursed expenses, the median expense was $50 and the 90th percentile was $600.

Policy Options for Benefits, Training, and Taxes

As background for discussing policy options, I feel obliged to first report my objectives for policies for independent workers. These are listed below, not necessarily in order of priority:

- Policy should be neutral with respect to self-employment vs. traditional W-2 employment (e.g., tax treatment of health insurance should be equivalent).
- Policy should avoid creating incentives for employers to convert W-2 jobs into self-employed jobs.
- Policy should be economically efficient, which implies that policy for the self-employed should take advantage of scale economies and risk pooling, and avoid adverse selection.
- Self-employed workers should be covered by the same essential protections and benefits as W-2 employees (i.e., social compact applies equally).
- Policy should minimize administrative burdens and overcome well-established behavioral biases (e.g., status quo bias and hyperbolic discounting).

These objectives stem from a desire for economic policy to be efficient and fair. You will notice, however, that the objectives can sometimes be in conflict with each other. I do not view that as a fatal flaw, however, because in economics we think about trade-offs, so we can think about trade-offs when it comes to these objectives.

The desire for policy to be economically efficient is particularly challenging in this area, because, when it comes to insurance, markets often break down because of adverse selection and moral hazard problems, as Joe Stiglitz, a previous Moynihan Winner, showed in his path-breaking work with Michael Rothschild. A standard solution to these problems in insurance markets is to have universal coverage enforced by a mandate. Given political obstacles, the way we often solve these problems in practice is to pool risks within groups, which is what employer-provided insurance does.

With these objectives in mind, let us consider Shared Security Accounts. First consider the pros. The goal of Shared Security Accounts is to provide independent workers with the same safety net as traditional employees. In the Washington State bill the accounts would only apply to self-employed workers who work through a broker, such as Uber, or some other type of intermediary that connects workers to their customers. But, as I noted, one can think of applying the policy more broadly. Shared Security Accounts would have the benefit of taking advantage of scale economies since they pool workers across eligible intermediaries.

Shared Accounts also prevent free riding, which can be a major problem with our existing laws. The ACA helps to minimize this problem with health insurance, but a company like Uber is arguably free riding on other employers who provide health insurance benefits to Uber drivers, either because they have another job in addition to driving on the Uber platform or because their spouse is employed and they obtain coverage through their spouse's employer. Another major pro is that it offers a comprehensive solution. And it maintains flexibility in that workers can take their benefits wherever they work; they are portable like Social Security.

What about the cons? I think the workers are likely to ultimately pay for this benefit because the costs of providing benefits are often shifted from firms to workers in the form of lower wages, so the next time I do this survey I will ask, "If you have to pay for this do you think it is a good idea?" Another con is that there is a risk of adverse selection if workers can choose their benefits from a cafeteria plan. In the Washington State bill there is also a significant problem with hours proration, meaning that if you work 20 hours a week as opposed to 40 hours a week, you qualify for only half the benefits. But the concept of work hours worked is ill-defined for many self-employed workers. An Uber driver, for example, could be reading a book or taking care of personal tasks while waiting for a customer (and can turn down the customer), so it is difficult to ascertain how much he or she worked in a given time period. The concept of work hours is quite different for the self-employed, and proration would be difficult or impossible to administer. Moreover, the Washington State proposal, while very important and in a way path breaking, only addresses a small portion of the population that struggles to obtain benefits. As mentioned, only 14 percent of independent workers are connected to a digital intermediary.

Another conceptual issue is that part of the compensation an independent contractor receives is a return on capital. If you are driving a car for Uber or Lyft, part of the income you are making is a return on the investment in your car, yet we would be requiring a contribution on that investment for your benefits.

Next consider health insurance. I think the most important lesson from my survey is that we should take steps to ensure that the health insurance exchanges work if we want the self-employed to continue to have access to health insurance, particularly when they are foreclosed from other options. Given that the debate on the ACA is hopefully settled for now, I will skip to the idea of a safe harbor.

One policy proposal that has gained some traction is to have a carve out for intermediaries that permits them to provide benefits without risk that their contractors will be deemed employees. Indeed, my sense is that many of the new online intermediaries would like to provide some benefits to their workers, but they refrain from doing so because they are worried that they will be classified as an employer if they provided access to benefits, such as life insurance.

Another, less extreme, solution to this problem is to support greater use of third parties to provide benefits. Stride and the Freelancers Union are examples of such third parties. There is a risk of adverse selection when it comes to third parties: an enterprising third-party benefit provider might deploy strategies to help only the healthy people, for example. This is a con.

Nevertheless, especially when I think about a group such as the Freelancer's Union, I think that having more representation and voice for workers are positive outcomes in their own right, and my personal view is that I would be willing to sacrifice some economic efficiency from adverse selection to provide workers with greater representation and voice at work. Senator Warner has proposed the sound idea of supporting the states to have pilot projects—to experiment—on alternative ways of providing benefits. In an area where we have much to learn before going to a national scale, this seems quite safe and sensible.

One of the main concerns policy-makers have about self-employment is their enormous tax gap. The IRS estimates that about 65 percent of the income taxes owed by self-employed proprietors are not paid.[7] One way of addressing the tax gap is to have intermediaries assist with filing tax information with the IRS. For example, Uber could populate their drivers' tax forms. Another idea worth considering is to have a standard deduction for the self-employed. If most self-employed workers have very low expenses, you can have a standard deduction like 10 percent or 5 percent of people's income and most would be better off. This could help to increase tax compliance. It would certainly reduce record keeping. Such a proposal has been implemented in France.

The tax treatment of health insurance for the self-employed is disadvantaged compared to that of traditional employees in that the cost of providing health insurance for employees is excluded from their income, so it is not covered by the income tax or by payroll taxes. For the self-employed, however, health insurance expenses are excluded from income taxes but not from payroll taxes. With payroll taxes of around 15 percent, this creates a significant additional tax on the self-employed. That could easily be rectified through tax policy.

FIGURE 5
Perceived Discrimination, Selected Groups

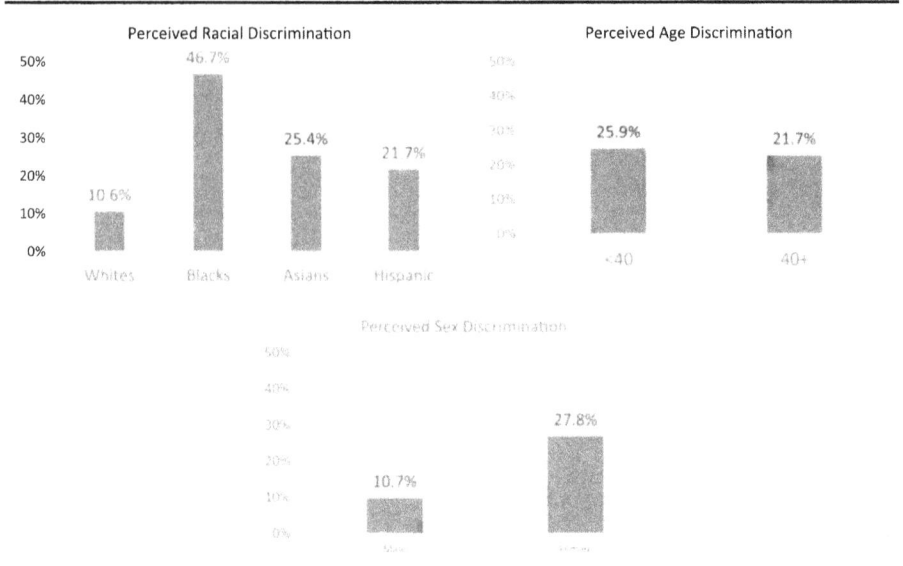

As mentioned, the self-employed receive relatively little job training. The IRS is tough on the deductibility of training expenses for the self-employed. Particularly when it comes to safety-related training, it would make sense for the IRS to be more permissive in allowing training deductions as a business expense. Congress could also enact tax credits to encourage job training, particularly for safety training, for self-employed workers.

Discrimination and Contract Enforcement:
Findings and Policy Proposals

Two of the most interesting findings came from my survey related to discrimination against minority self-employed contractors and contract enforcement. The survey asked: "Have you ever felt that you were discriminated against by a client or customer because of your race, sex, age, ethnicity or religion?" Respondents had the opportunity to mark yes or no for each category. The key findings are summarized in Figure 5 for selected subgroups. The most disturbing result is that 47 percent of self-employed African Americans indicated that they had felt discriminated against because of race.[8] The corresponding figures were 22 percent for Hispanics and 25 percent for Asians; only 11 percent of whites said they had felt they had been discriminated against because of race. Looking at the other groups, young people (40 years old and below) were slightly *more likely* to say that they felt discriminated against than older workers, and that may well be related to the reason why young people are less likely to be self-employed. Last,

28 percent of women said they had felt discriminated against based on sex, compared to just 11 percent of men.

These findings lead to an obvious policy proposal: *Extend coverage under Title VII of the Civil Rights Act of 1964 to independent contractors*. The self-employed currently have few options if they face discrimination. The arguments in favor of this proposal are obvious: (1) it would extend protections that already exist for employees to the self-employed; (2) discrimination is plainly unfair and economically inefficient if it originates from personal animus or ignorant stereotypes; and (3) there is an administrative system in place to enforce the policy. On the con side, one could argue that self-reported survey responses do not prove that workers were actually discriminated against, even if they report feeling discrimination. Relatedly, one could also argue that extending protection under the Civil Rights Act to self-employed workers could lead to frivolous lawsuits.

If you go back to the objectives for policy that I laid out, I think one could make a strong case for extending Title VII protections against discrimination to the self-employed.

Contract enforcement

I will conclude by talking about contractual issues. By coincidence, New York City this very week began implementing a law called the Freelance Isn't Free Act that the City Council enacted at the end of last year to require that contractors be paid on time. Consequently, I asked in the survey, "Have you had an incident in the last year where someone hired you to do a job or project and you were not paid on time?" A total of 36 percent of respondents indicated "yes" that they had not been paid on time.

In about two-thirds of these cases contractors were paid within two months of when they thought payment was due, and in more than 10 percent of cases it took more than six months for the contractors to receive payment. The survey also asked, "Have you had an incident in the last year where you were not paid the full amount that you were owed for a job or project that you completed?" Some 27 percent of all self-employed workers said "yes" that they had had an incident in the last year when they were not paid in full. And among those who said they had a late payment, more than half reported that they had an instance when they were not paid the full amount they were owed.

New York City's new law follows common sense contracting practices. It requires a written contract for any contract involving more than $800 in goods or services. The contract must contain (1) a list of services or products to be provided, (2) the rate and mechanism of compensation, and (3) the date at which the hiring party must pay the contractor or a mechanism for determining the date. There is a mechanism to try to resolve contract disputes and there can be penalties—up to two times damages, injunctive relief, and legal fees—if there is evidence of a pattern or practice of violations.

Arguments in favor of the Freelance Isn't Free Act are that it addresses an important market failure and imbalance in the contractor market, it enshrines good contract practice into law, and it protects freelancers from exploitation and against retaliation. On the other side, critics could argue that the law is burdensome for the parties to administer, that it interferes with private contracts, and that it can make it harder for the hiring party to seek redress for substandard work. New York's experience under this new law will provide valuable evidence for research going forward that should be of interest to other towns, cities, and states around the United States.

Conclusion

One of Daniel Patrick Moynihan's famous sayings was, "Everyone is entitled to his own opinion, but not to his own facts." The research reported in this lecture was an attempt to develop a base of facts that could be used to devise and debate policy for independent workers. The challenge of modernizing our labor and employment laws to address independent workers will likely grow in the future with the advent of digitally intermediated labor markets and the aging of the workforce. As a result, we will continue to have a sizable and growing share of the workforce that is left to its own devices when it comes to securing their safety net, obtaining training, preventing discrimination, and enforcing contracts. A key challenge for policy-makers and researchers in coming years is to develop policies tailored to independent workers to address the imbalances between the self-employed and traditional employees, and make the labor market operate more fairly and more efficiently. I am not sure if the policies that I considered in my lecture today are the best path forward, but I am convinced in the spirit of Daniel Patrick Moynihan that we need to develop a base of facts to advance the quality and outcome of the policy debate.

Notes

1. This is a revised version of the Moynihan Lecture that I delivered on May 18, 2017, in the Kennedy Caucus Room of the Russell Senate Office Building, Washington, D.C. I have benefited from helpful discussions with Al Fitzpayne, Ed Freeland, Bill Gale, Seth Harris, Richard Hinz, Sara Horowitz, and Mark Mazur, who are free to disagree with any and all of the ideas in this lecture. Kevin DeLuca provided excellent research assistance. The Sloan Foundation provided funding for the survey of self-employed workers conducted for this lecture.

2. See Abraham et al. (2015) for related evidence.

3. Specifically, we asked a set of questions based on the 1995 and 2005 BLS Contingent Worker Survey to a national sample that was part of the Rand American Life Panel. Figure 1 includes those who indicated they were "working or self-employed as an independent contractor, an independent consultant, or a freelance worker" on their main job.

4. Two sets of weights were developed based on the 2011–15 ACS: one for the full sample and one for those who were self-employed based on the class of worker question. The weights were based on sex, race, Hispanic ethnicity, age, education, and income categories.

5. These are weighted differences. The sample size is 8,579.

6. See Krueger and Kuziemko (2013).

7. See www.irs.gov/pub/irs-soi/p1415.pdf.

8. Comparable figures for traditional employees are unavailable from the PSES, but Gallup did a survey in 2005 that found that 12 percent of whites and 26 percent of blacks (non-Hispanic) felt discriminated

against. The percentage for whites is virtually the same as I find, whereas for blacks it was lower in the Gallup survey. This suggests that the perception of discrimination among African Americans in self-employment is at least as great, if not greater, than it is for African Americans in traditional employment relationships.

References

Abraham, Katharine G., John C. Haltiwanger, Kristin Sandusky, and James R. Spletzer. 2015. *Measuring the "gig" economy*. Washington, DC: U.S. Census Bureau. Available from http://www.sole-jole .org/16375.pdf.

Farrell, Diana, and Fiona Greig. 7 March 2016. *The online platform economy: What is the growth trajectory?* New York, NY: JP Morgan Chase & Co. Available from https://www.jpmorganchase.com/corporate/institute/insight-online-platform-econ-growth-trajectory.htm

Gronau, Reuben. 1977. Leisure, home production, and work: The theory of the allocation of time revisited. *Journal of Political Economy* 85 (6): 1099–1123.

Hanauer, Nick, and David Rolf. 2015. Shared security, shared growth. *Democracy* 37. Available from https://democracyjournal.org/magazine/37/shared-security-shared-growth/.

Jackson, Emilie, Adam Looney, and Shanthi Ramnath. 2017. The rise of alternative work arrangements: Evidence and implications for tax filing and benefit coverage. Office of Tax Analysis Working Paper 114, Washington, DC.

Katz, Lawrence, and Alan Krueger. 2016. The rise and nature of alternative work arrangements in the United States, 1995–2015. National Bureau of Economic Research Working Paper No. 22667, Cambridge, MA.

Katz, Lawrence, and Alan Krueger. 2017. The role of unemployment in the rise in alternative work arrangements. *American Economic Review: Papers and Proceedings* 107 (5): 388–92.

Krueger, Alan B., and Ilyana Kuziemko. 2013. The demand for health insurance among uninsured Americans: Results of a survey experiment and implications for policy. *Journal of Health Economics* 32 (5): 780–93.

Weil, David. 2014. *The fissured workplace*. Cambridge, MA: Harvard University Press.

Introduction

Keywords: evidence-based policy; data infrastructure; roadmap

A Roadmap to a Nationwide Data Infrastructure for Evidence-Based Policymaking

By
ANDREW REAMER
and
JULIA LANE

Throughout the United States, there is broad interest in expanding the nation's capacity to design and implement public policy based on solid evidence. That interest has been stimulated by the new types of data that are available that can transform the way in which policy is designed and implemented. Yet progress in making use of sensitive data has been hindered by the legal, technical, and operational obstacles to access for research and evaluation. Progress has also been hindered by an almost exclusive focus on the interest and needs of the data users, rather than the interest and needs of the data providers. In addition, data stewardship is largely artisanal in nature.

There are very real consequences that result from lack of action. State and local governments are often hampered in their capacity to effectively mount and learn from innovative efforts. Although jurisdictions often have treasure troves of data from existing programs, the data are stove-piped, underused, and poorly maintained. The

Andrew Reamer focuses on federal policies that support U.S. economic competitiveness, particularly the role of the federal statistical system. Before joining the George Washington Institute of Public Policy at The George Washington University, he was a fellow in the Brookings Institution's Metropolitan Policy Program and cofounded two economic development consulting practices.

Julia Lane is an elected fellow of the American Association for the Advancement of Science, the International Statistical Institute, and the American Statistical Association. She cofounded such data infrastructures as the LEHD program at the Census Bureau, Patentsview at the Patent and Trademark Office, the NORC/University of Chicago Remote Access Data Enclave, and the Institute for Research on Innovation and Science.

Correspondence: areamer@gwu.edu

DOI: 10.1177/0002716217740116

experience reported by one large city public health commissioner is too common: "We commissioners meet periodically to discuss specific childhood deaths in the city. In most cases, we each have a thick file on the child or family. But the only time we compare notes is after the child is dead."[1] In reality, most localities lack the technical, analytical, staffing, and legal capacity to make effective use of existing and emerging resources.

It is our sense that fundamental changes are necessary and a new approach must be taken to building data infrastructures. In particular,

1. Privacy and confidentiality issues must be addressed at the beginning—not added as an afterthought.
2. Data providers must be involved as key stakeholders throughout the design process.
3. Workforce capacity must be developed at all levels.
4. The scholarly community must be engaged to identify the value to research and policy.

There is substantial interest in building a data infrastructure that effects such changes. In a very high-profile example, Congress established the federal Commission on Evidence-Based Policymaking (CEP; 2017) through the bipartisan Evidence-Based Policymaking Commission Act of 2016 (Public Law 114-140), jointly sponsored by Speaker Paul Ryan (R-WI) and Senator Patty Murray (D-WA), and signed by President Barack Obama on March 30, 2016. On September 7, 2017, the CEP released its final report, "The Promise of Evidence-Based Policymaking," laying out a series of recommendations regarding approaches to building the capacity of the federal government to generate and make effective use of evidence for public policy purposes while fully protecting privacy and confidentiality.

There is also an emerging opportunity to build such an infrastructure at scale. Recent years have seen dramatic growth in the technological capabilities to organize, link, integrate, and analyze enormous volumes of data from multiple, disparate sources. The new data make it possible to gather more information from a larger population (of people, households, or businesses) at a far lower cost.

To develop a roadmap for the creation of such an infrastructure, the Bill and Melinda Gates Foundation, together with the Laura and John Arnold Foundation, hosted a day-long workshop of more than sixty experts to discuss the findings of twelve commissioned papers and their implications for action. This volume of *The ANNALS* showcases those twelve articles. The workshop papers were grouped into three thematic areas: privacy and confidentiality, the views of data producers, and comprehensive strategies that have been used to build data infrastructures in other contexts. The authors and the attendees included computer scientists, social scientists, practitioners, and data producers.

This introductory article places the research in both an historical and a current context. It also provides a framework for understanding the contribution of the twelve articles.

BOX 1
A Brief History of Statistical Capacity for Evidence-Based Policymaking

- 1662—John Graunt publishes "Observations on the Bills of Mortality," the first time that British health statistics are collected and used for public health policy design.
- 1690—William Petty and Charles Davenant invent "political arithmetic" to calculate optimal British tariffs and taxation.
- 1751—Benjamin Franklin writes and privately circulates "Observations Concerning the Increase of Mankind, Peopling of Countries, Etc," laying the groundwork for demographic analysis for the purpose of public policy. The next year Franklin creates the first successful fire insurance company in the colonies.
- 1790—Congress approves Representative James Madison's proposal to add questions to the First Census so that Congress could "adapt the public measures to the particular circumstances of the community." Madison's idea lives today as the Census Bureau's American Community Survey.
- 1791—Sir John Sinclair publishes the first comprehensive survey-based statistical study in the English-speaking world. Sinclair adopted new German "statistical" methods (the "science of dealing with data about the condition of a state") to measure the "quantum of happiness" that existed in Scotland and identify ways of improving this.
- 1884—Carroll D. Wright proposes in an address to the American Social Science Association that tariffs be set "scientifically," based not on politics, but on data. Congress takes up the cause, expanding the federal capacity to collect data, and in so doing created the foundations of today's federal economic statistical agencies.
- 1946—The Employment Act of 1946 establishes the infrastructure for data-driven macroeconomic (fiscal and monetary) policy.
- 1966—As part of efforts to measure the impact and improve Lyndon Johnson's Great Society programs, the White House proposes a National Data Center, essentially a federal data clearinghouse, but Congress does not approve the proposal because of broadly voiced concerns about the potential of the center to invade personal privacy.

The Historical Context of Evidence-Based Policymaking

While the term *evidence-based policymaking* is of recent origin, the notion of designing public policies based on data analysis has been practiced in the English-speaking world since the 1600s (see Box 1).

A perennial problem—overcoming decision-makers' penchants for ignoring or ridiculing evidence—must be addressed, but that is beyond the scope of this volume. What we propose here is a path toward capitalizing on advances in information technology (IT) that make it possible for policy to be more evidence-based than ever before.

Current Context

Recently, multiple disparate efforts have been initiated to promote data infrastructure development for evidence-based policymaking. These efforts are

---

BOX 2
Examples of Current Data Centers and Networks

- Centers
  - Federal
    - Federal Statistical Data Research Center Program—partnerships between federal statistical agencies and leading research institutions. (This program has one database and multiple access points for qualified researchers.)
    - Census Bureau's Administrative Records Clearinghouse for the Evaluation of Federal and Federally Sponsored Programs (funded by Congress; $10 million annually)
    - Commission on Evidence-Based Policymaking (2017)—created by Congress to ascertain desirability and design of federal data clearinghouse
  - Nonprofit
    - NORC Data Enclave
    - Private Capital Research Institute
    - Health Care Cost Institute
  - University
    - Institute for Research on Innovation and Science (IRIS), University of Michigan
    - Inter-university Consortium for Political and Social Research, University of Michigan
    - Institute for Research in the Social Sciences, Stanford University
    - Dataverse, Harvard University
    - Massive Data Institute, Georgetown University
    - Minnesota Population Center, University of Minnesota
- Networks (associations of centers)
  - Actionable Intelligence for Social Policy—organized by University of Pennsylvania
    - The network consists of twelve sites, providing data on five states (Florida, Michigan, South Carolina, Washington, Wisconsin) and seven counties or cities (Allegheny County [Pittsburgh], Cook County [Chicago], Cuyahoga County [Cleveland], Los Angeles County, Mecklenburg County [Charlotte], New York City, and Philadelphia)
    - Made possible by a grant from the MacArthur Foundation
  - Administrative Records Data Network—initiative of the Sloan Foundation
  - National Neighborhood Indicators Partnership, The Urban Institute
  - Civics Analytics Network—national peer network of urban Chief Data Officers, funded by the Arnold Foundation and managed by Harvard University

---

housed in governments at all levels, in nonprofits, and in universities. Many have been supported by philanthropic foundations (see Box 2).

Operators of data repositories and systems may include nonprofit organizations, universities, state governments, local governments, federal governments, think tanks, and industry associations. Data repositories and systems may be accessed by researchers and analysts employed by universities, governments, think tanks, other nonprofits, and for-profits. They may receive technical assistance—in business operations and data management and methods—from network organizations (via network staff or peers), universities and other non-profits, and for-profit consultants.

Data can have either a geographic or topical focus. They can be held by (1) *individual government programs*, particularly administrative records (e.g., Social Security); (2) *corporate and nonprofit* providers of their own data (e.g., Uber or Mastercard); (3) *data repositories* that bring together data from multiple sources without attempting to integrate them (e.g., data.gov); (4) *enterprise data systems* that bring together, and make compatible, data from multiple programs (e.g., the Census Bureau's enterprise data system); (5) *integrated data systems* that bring together, and make compatible, data from multiple enterprises, for example, state- or county-wide (e.g., Data Share in Milwaukee); and (6) *nationwide networks* of programs, data repositories, enterprise data systems, or integrated data systems (such as Chapin Hall at the University of Chicago), which are networks of organizations and typically do not (as yet) involve data-sharing among members.

Building a Robust National Data Infrastructure

The articles commissioned for this project make clear that while there are considerable barriers to the development of a robust data infrastructure ecosystem, it is possible to address these barriers. The articles point to five areas in which progress can be made: legitimacy, public data providers, law, transaction costs, and data protection.

Legitimacy

It is important to treat data subjects as a stakeholder group and offer an opportunity for input on data infrastructure uses and operations. Rare disease research consortia provide a model for doing this. Notions that may prove useful include "collective consent" and "social license."

The legitimacy of data infrastructure organizations could also be called into question if stakeholders have concerns about other dimensions of trustworthiness, such as capabilities and practices. To address this issue, some project participants suggested that a process be created by which organizations are certified by a national authorized body as having the desired capabilities and practices.

Also, it is important for data infrastructure proponents to have the capacity to disentangle concerns expressed about protecting subjects' privacy from political concerns, say about the proper role of government programs in a market economy. Sometimes, project participants said, their experience suggests that political concerns are raised in the guise of a desire to protect privacy, for example, in the case of the Family Education Rights and Privacy Act (FERPA). Particularly important to legitimacy is identifying means to institutionalize the use of evidence in policymaking in the executive and legislative branches. In this regard, it is helpful, but certainly not sufficient, that the Evidence-Based Policymaking Commission Act of 2016 passed both Houses of Congress with strong bipartisan support.

Public data providers

Data infrastructure development and evidence-based policymaking can be successful only if public data providers, particularly public program managers, are invested in making their data available and usable and acting on the results of analysis. Project participants identified a number of challenges that need to be addressed in any design, including individual agencies' willingness to be evaluated and give up control of their data. In addition, public data providers suffer from lack of staff trained to document, extract, and transmit data and lack of capacity to establish data standards and IT capacity. Projects that are inordinately long term in nature are unlikely to succeed, since providers do not have the budget or the mandate to take on long-term data-driven performance improvement projects. Project participants found that rather than bemoaning these problems, it is essential to identify projects that provide short-term wins while moving toward a long-term goal.

Law

Project participants found that laws regarding data access and privacy serve as a barrier to data infrastructure development in multiple ways. Most obviously, laws are complex and siloed. At the federal level, data access is governed by numerous laws, including the Health Insurance Portability and Accountability Act (HIPAA), Family Educational Rights and Privacy Act (FERPA), Video Privacy Protection Act (VPPA), Children's Online Privacy Protection Act (COPPA), and regulations concerning personally identifiable information (PII). Similar complexity exists at the state level. Some laws unnecessarily restrict data access, and some laws are difficult to clearly interpret. Many states restrict federal reuse of their data. Many lawyers are risk averse, choosing to serve as gatekeepers rather than problem solvers. Many government agency lawyers do not have proper and adequate training in privacy and confidentiality law.

To address these issues, project participants proposed a number of steps. These include conducting a systematic review and analysis of existing laws to facilitate greater consistency, clarity, and legitimate data access; creating a roster of qualified legal experts; and creating training curricula in data privacy and confidentiality, which include legal toolkits in data privacy and confidentiality, such as model legislative and legal agreement templates. The political approaches include passing federal and state laws that require use of data for analysis.

As an example of efforts in the field, the State Data Sharing Initiative (SDS), funded by the Arnold Foundation, works in a number of states to reduce the extent to which law and regulation are barriers to data access.

Transaction costs

Successful expansion of the nation's data infrastructure for evidence-based policymaking requires a substantial reduction in the transaction costs now borne by data providers, repositories, systems, and networks.

At present, due to the artisanal nature of most efforts, organizations too often need to re-create what others have already developed and put much time and effort into crafting standards, templates, methods, practices, and laws that enable legitimacy and good organizational, project, and data management. Project participants proposed the following approaches for reducing transaction costs: (1) carry out ecosystem-wide efforts to develop, adopt, and disseminate widely affirmed and "evidence-tested" standards, templates, methods, practices, and laws; (2) establish repositories of technical assistance and coaching talent that would be available to eligible organizations; (3) facilitate information sharing through peer learning and executive education; (4) create laboratories for testing new methods; and (5) learn lessons from existing federal-state cooperative data programs.

Organizations also face significant transaction costs in data management. To address this, they suggested that the new capacity in computer science could be used to develop (1) processes for automated data stewardship and (2) cloud-based data enclaves for shared data, methods, results, and expertise.

Data protection

Trustworthy, effective data protection is essential for successful infrastructure expansion. While data protection challenges are numerous and ever-growing, good practices have been identified and can be built upon. These include (1) statistical disclosure prevention techniques, such as de-identification, fuzzy data, synthetic data, simulation, and differential privacy algorithms; and (2) access management mechanisms, such as interactive query systems, two-factor authentication, unforgeable query logs, and secure data enclaves. Concerted efforts should be made to enhance, test, standardize, and disseminate good data protection practices and technologies.

Conclusion

Examples are now frequently emerging of artisanal efforts to build data infrastructures. Too often, however, one individual must work tirelessly to overcome the legal and bureaucratic barriers to linking and using existing administrative or survey data on a one-off basis. Often the system is built on the trust of a few key actors, and unique rules and workarounds are developed. Enough has been learned to build a new approach. It is clear that to move from artisanal integrated data systems to professional, routinized and sustainable systems requires starting with the value propositions to data owners and other stakeholders.

Achieving long-term useable and sustainable integrated systems will require focusing on creating standardized systems for creating access while ensuring privacy; secure data centers; and useable standards for key elements such as identifiers, core data structures, and metadata. It will be important to make investments that demonstrate the impact of innovations on a large scale and provide blueprints and frameworks that make it possible for other localities to create capacity far more effectively.

Any approach should focus on building sustainable, coordinated, and scalable data infrastructures built around state-of-the-art technology with effective and safe privacy protections. In so doing, this effort will be a valuable partner to many existing efforts, starting with highly motivated state and local programs, and moving on to inspire other jurisdictions. It is possible to build a national framework for sharing and learning both about effective policies and programs and a highly useable data infrastructure.

Note

1. David Ellwood, Opening remarks, Roadmapping workshop, 25 January 2017.

Reference

Commission on Evidence-Based Policymaking. 2017. *The promise of evidence-based policymaking: Report of the Commission on Evidence-Based Policymaking*. Washington, DC: Commission on Evidence-Based Policymaking.

Keywords: statistical data; administrative records; standards; quality

Standards and Guidelines for Combined Statistical Data

By
NANCY POTOK

A consensus has formed within the federal statistical data community that a proactive approach is needed to make use of new sources of data to supplement data collection through random sample surveys and censuses. Data collected through surveys are challenged by less cooperation from survey respondents, which results in both lower response rates and greater expenditures. Data users want more complex data faster and with greater geographic specificity without sacrificing quality.

However, funding constraints on federal agencies make it unfeasible for the agencies to keep pace with the increasing costs of addressing these issues. Major technology-enabled methodological changes, requiring additional research and development, need to be incorporated quickly into ongoing data collection and production efforts. Under the Paperwork Reduction Act (PRA), the U.S. Office of Management and Budget (OMB) is required to ensure the integrity, objectivity, impartiality, utility, and confidentiality of information collected for statistical purposes. This charge, assigned in the PRA to the chief statistician, is central to the maintenance of high-quality data as the federal statistical system moves to put in place significant and necessary changes to our national data infrastructure in coming years.

Many nonsurvey sources of data could be used to reduce costs and meet the growing

Nancy Potok is chief statistician of the United States and chief of Statistical and Science Policy at the U.S. Office of Management and Budget. Previously, she served as the deputy director and chief operating officer of the U.S. Census Bureau. She is also an adjunct professor at The George Washington University.

Correspondence: nancy.a.potok@omb.eop.gov

DOI: 10.1177/0002716217737247

needs of data consumers. Although data are widely available from multiple sources on the Internet and through purchase from private sector companies, numerous problems arise when these data are the sole source of important policy decisions and government and business planning activities. The lack of transparency in how these data are produced can lead to a lack of user understanding when companies change proprietary models or have a vested interest in data results. Because businesses are interested in profitability, their business models may change or companies may change hands, eliminating sources of data and creating uncertainty around long-term availability. Open data scraped from the web may be biased in ways the casual user may not detect. By contrast, federally produced statistics are transparent, reliable, high quality, and objective. Nonetheless, if agencies that produce these valuable statistics cannot respond to today's challenges, data users may turn to suboptimal solutions to meet their evolving needs.

Data sources that federal statistical agencies can make more use of include administrative records (federal and state records collected for program administration), curated commercial data (such as aerial photos, aggregated credit card records, etc.), and limited researched and analyzed open source data (such as consumer goods prices scraped from retail store websites). These data may be combined with survey data, used in lieu of survey data, or used to create new products. Although some statistical data have a long history of coming from multiple sources, the uses of combined data are still being developed.

OMB fulfills its statistical data quality responsibilities under the PRA through the development of policies, principles, standards, and guidelines concerning statistical collection procedures and methods, among other things. To this end, the OMB has issued multiple statistical directives. In particular, *Statistical Policy Directive No. 2: Standards and Guidelines for Statistical Surveys* (OMB 2006) contains in-depth guidance on how to conduct a rigorous and methodologically sound random sample survey to gather federal statistical data. However, no standards or guidelines have been issued by OMB that address statistical data generated from combining administrative, commercial, and survey data. The lack of a standard leaves producers and users with little consistent information about assessing the quality and utility of future combined federal statistical data. For the OMB to issue such guidelines, additional research is needed to examine the different dimensions of quality around combined data. These are briefly described here.

Transparency: How can an agency openly inform data users about how the data were collected and for what purposes? What are consistent ways of creating and providing such documentation? How can the strengths and limitations of the data be conveyed to the data user? As recommended by the National Academy of Sciences, Engineering and Medicine (2017), *openness* also means that a statistical agency should describe how decisions on methods and procedures were made for a data collection program and provide ready access to research results that entered into such decisions. Such transparency is essential for credibility with data users and trust of data providers.

Fitness for various purposes: How can a determination be made about whether various datasets are appropriate for specific uses? Data may be good enough for some purposes but not for others. Should there be a quality rating system developed to guide the user? As we know from survey data, some surveys have too small of a sample size to be used to develop estimates for small populations or small geographic areas. Similarly, nonsurvey data may not be suitable for certain uses. For example, aggregated credit card data may be missing commodities that are not normally purchased with a credit card. Depending on what research or policy questions you are trying to answer, missing data could make some datasets unsuitable.

Privacy: Data may have been collected for particular program purposes. Are additional permissions needed from providers to combine that information with other data for different purposes? When data are available commercially does permission for use come from the vendor? How can the government do a better job of making sure that de-identified data collected from individuals and businesses cannot be reidentified once the statistical data are released to the public? Private sector companies collect a lot of data about individuals through mechanisms such as store frequent buyer programs, app terms of service agreements, bank loans, and other interactions with customers. What sort of consent from those customers would be needed if the government were to start buying data from these companies to create new statistical products?

Disclosure avoidance: When data are combined and then used for multiple purposes, what new techniques are needed for protecting privacy and confidentiality, especially when researchers want to replicate research results? It is very important to make sure that statistical data cannot be easily linked to other data that is publicly available to reidentify businesses or individuals whose data have been aggregated to produce the datasets.

Microdata: What type of access can be granted to microdata coming from multiple sources, some of which may be proprietary? How are privacy and legal agreements protected? Microdata are the individual records of people and businesses, whether they have been collected through surveys or through program records. Some examples are Social Security payment records, tax filings, registrations for programs such as the Supplemental Nutrition Assistance Program (SNAP) or housing assistance, as well as individual responses to statistical surveys or censuses. The confidentiality of the information contained in these sources needs to be vigorously protected while giving limited access for approved statistical purposes.

Ownership: What rights do original owners, including statistical agencies conducting surveys and governments providing administrative records, retain for future uses? What happens when commercial data are procured under a licensing agreement?

Quality: How does one measure traditional aspects of quality such as accuracy, coherence, comparability, reproducibility, bias, and coverage when combining data from multiple sources with varied collection methods?

Break in series: What is the responsibility of and appropriate methodology for the statistical agency to bridge a break in a longitudinal data series when the sources of data are dramatically changing? For example, monthly retail sales are currently calculated using sample survey data collected each month from businesses. If, instead, the information were to be gathered using consumer spending records, such as aggregated credit card purchases, that would change the retail sales number going forward. The gap in the data series would need to be bridged in an understandable way for researchers and others looking to understand changes that occur over time.

Risk: What are the mitigation procedures needed for an agency to reduce the risk of discontinued availability of commercial or other data that it is acquiring but not responsible for collecting?

Postcollection processing: What changes in methodology are needed in production activities such as editing, imputation, weighting, and modeling when data are coming from multiple sources? To what extent do these methods need to be consistently applied across sources?

As research in these areas proceeds, more issues will certainly be identified. They must be addressed if the federal statistical system is to continue as the gold standard for providing high-quality statistical data. As more statistical data are derived from combined data sources, new research-driven OMB standards and guidance will help to ensure that data continue to be available for business and civic purposes, as well as for evidence-driven policymaking arising out of federal and state program evaluation and academic research.

The research on statistical methodologies and quality control moving forward will require extensive collaboration between federal statistical agencies and program agencies, academia, states, and other stakeholders to expeditiously advance our learning on combined statistical data. Such collaboration should take many forms. Intergovernmental projects that bring together city, state, and federal partners can be especially valuable, particularly when universities can assist with training, data analytics, and meaningful insights. Many such pilot projects are currently underway, funded by foundations interested in evidence-based policy at all levels of government. For example, the State of Rhode Island has been working with Brown University to enhance the analytics applied to state data to improve state program operations.

Private sector data providers can work with federal partners in statistical agencies to increase the transparency of commercial data, as well as to identify ways to standardize legal and operational approaches to incorporating commercial data into official statistics.

In addition, the Federal Committee on Statistical Methodology (FCSM) could sponsor multiple workshops on some of these research topics and invite members of the National Academy of Sciences Committee on National Statistics (CNSTAT) and other academics to participate. Academic researchers are also making contributions to the field. These are just a few of the opportunities available for collaboration, and the OMB can play a critical role in coordinating and corralling the learning to develop new, much-needed standards governing combined datasets. Although much work is already under way, much remains to be done. Exciting times indeed.

Note

1. Paperwork Reduction Act of 1995 (44 U.S. Code 3504 (e)).

References

National Academies of Science, Engineering and Medicine. 2017. *Principles and practices for a federal statistical agency*, 6th ed., ed. Connie Citro. Washington, DC: Committee on National Statistics, The National Academies Press.

Office of Management and Budget (OMB). 2006. *Statistical policy directive no. 2: Standards and guidelines for statistical surveys*. Washington, DC: OMB. Available from https://obamawhitehouse.archives.gov/sites/default/files/omb/inforeg/statpolicy/standards_stat_surveys.pdf.

Keywords: Illinois State government; multiagency data infrastructure; data-analytic skills; evidence-based policymaking; employment outcomes; career information

Building an Infrastructure for Evidence-Based Policymaking: A View from a State Administrator

By
JEFFREY MAYS

During the last 35 years, I have served as a five-term state legislator and chief House sponsor of the Illinois state budget, leader of two statewide business associations dedicated to shaping public policy, and, currently, director of a state agency (the Illinois Department of Employment Security). In these diverse roles, I have gained an appreciation for joining on-the-ground subject matter expertise with cutting-edge research and technical practice to more fully inform policy, toward the goal of effective outcomes. More often, I, and those with whom I have worked, have tried to formulate policy when critical information to make an informed decision has not been available.

Certainly, the ways in which legislation is crafted and enacted (often with legal restrictions, and spending and regulatory imperatives) has abetted the development of state governments that are siloed and less inclined to do work across agencies. While I recognize the need for distinct missions among state agencies and their unique capacities to serve Illinois citizens, I argue for a comprehensive perspective as it relates to evidence-based policymaking. Many state agencies have in-house research

Jeff Mays was appointed as director of the Illinois Department of Employment Security (IDES) by Governor Bruce Rauner on January 12, 2015. He has extensive experience working in state and federal government and is an advocate of education and workforce development in Illinois. He is a former five-term Illinois state legislator and also served both as president of the Illinois Business Roundtable and executive vice president of the Illinois State Chamber of Commerce.

Correspondence: Jeff.Mays@illinois.gov

DOI: 10.1177/0002716217739275

offices charged to respond to legislative requests. A multiagency data infrastructure, coupled with the enhancement of data-analytic skills among agency staff, would establish an important precedent for policymaking based on a comprehensive context. Siloed government mitigates the range of considerations for key questions that should be asked of every policy proposal: What's the value statement? Who does this impact? What benefit or harm does this change present?

For example, one of the most pressing legislative budgetary issues during the 1980s was building new capacity to house the growing population of people incarcerated in prisons and jails. This legislative discussion would have benefited from a comprehensive contextual understanding of this population. In retrospect, an integrated multiagency effort to investigate demographic trends of the at-risk population, training opportunities for the incarcerated, their postrelease employment outcomes, attributes of recidivism, and community impacts could have lent important insight to the pertinent discussions and to the legislation. Recent initiatives in the direction of evidence-based policymaking are critical, but in my experience, such efforts need to be undergirded by linking sources of information that lends a comprehensive analytical perspective. In the aforementioned example, linking data from training/education, employment and earnings, corrections, and community/place would have vastly improved the contextual understanding for deciding then-current and future prison capacity requirements.

In my role as a leader of business associations, I became acutely aware of the number one concern voiced by Illinois businesses year after year—the need for a workforce with relevant workplace skills. Business executives often make the case that the very skills needed to grow the Illinois economy do not receive sufficient attention in the state education curriculum. A significant amount of my time was spent advocating on behalf of the business community with education institutions, as well as with high school students and parents to consider careers in industries experiencing shortages of skilled labor, such as manufacturing, that may not require a four-year degree. A key information gap in my conversation with these stakeholders was systematic evidence on employment outcomes for individuals in credential/training programs compared to those who complete a four-year degree.

And now, as director of a state agency charged to help people find employment, and to align multiple agencies to this charge, I have focused agency resources to support the value proposition of framing and answering policy questions on employment outcomes. To that end, we have begun linking our employment and earning records on Illinois workers to data compiled by the education/training community (Illinois Board of Higher Education, Illinois Community College Board, Illinois Department of Commerce and Economic Opportunity, and Illinois Student Assistance Commission). We have produced employment outcomes on job stability, career earning, and mapping of career pathways for high school students, community college students, and four-year degree students by program of study. Currently, we are developing visualizations of these outcomes for institutional researchers, students, and parents to be included in career information systems. We work closely with our data-sharing partners to develop data-rich products to inform both institutional policymaking and decision-making by students and their parents on career choices. This augmentation of our career information, to be released in fall 2018 through our career website and mobile apps, will include more than ninety postsecondary institutions and cover their student graduating cohorts from 2012 forward.

The strategic vision for employment outcomes needs to look beyond school administrators, parents, and students. We are committed to use these outcomes to serve as a context for fuller involvement of the business community and the state legislature in discussions on postsecondary curriculum priorities. We envision the context for policy formulation to be inclusive of both statewide and local considerations. Moreover, we expect this cross-section of stakeholders to challenge us to develop more effective measures for their deliberation, such as employer networks and their links to job placement initiatives. The organic nature of this endeavor encourages more effective decision support tools for stakeholders and deepens the empirical footings for policy formulation.

Section I: Privacy and Confidentiality

Privacy Protective Research: Facilitating Ethically Responsible Access to Administrative Data

Companies and government entities collect substantial amounts of administrative data through the Internet; mobile communications; and a vast infrastructure of devices and sensors embedded in healthcare facilities, retail outlets, public transportation, social networks, workplaces, and homes. They use administrative data to test new products and services, improve existing offerings, conduct research, and foster innovation. However, the lack of a clear legal framework and ethical guidelines for use of administrative data jeopardizes the value of important research. Concerns over legal impediments and ethical restrictions threaten to diminish productive collaboration between researchers and private sector businesses. This article provides strategies for organizations to minimize risks of reidentification and privacy violations for individual data subjects. In addition, it suggests that privacy and ethical concerns would best be managed by supporting the development of administrative data centers to lower transaction costs and increase the reproducibility of research conducted on administrative data.

Keywords: administrative data; data research; data protection; big data; privacy; ethics

A secret isn't invalidated by its disclosure, it's defined by its disclosure. What makes a secret a secret is simply the operating instructions that accompany its movement from one person to the next.

—Malcolm Gladwell (2016)[1]

By
DANIEL GOROFF,
JULES POLONETSKY,
and
OMER TENE

Researchers in academic institutions and private sector businesses seek to repurpose a variety of sources of organizational data ("administrative data") to pursue projects that promise great

Daniel Goroff is vice president and program director of the Alfred P. Sloan Foundation.

Jules Polonetsky is CEO of the Future of Privacy Forum (FPF).

Omer Tene is a senior fellow at FPF.

Correspondence: otene@iapp.org

DOI: 10.1177/0002716217742605

societal benefits. Companies collect massive amounts of administrative data through the Internet, mobile communications, and a vast infrastructure of devices and sensors embedded in healthcare facilities, retail outlets, public transportation, social networks, workplaces, and homes. They use administrative data to test new products and services, improve existing offerings, conduct research, and foster innovation. For example, in an article recently published in the *Journal of Oncology Practice*, a group of Microsoft scientists demonstrated that by analyzing a large sample of search engine queries, researchers could in some cases identify Internet users who were suffering from pancreatic cancer even before those users were diagnosed with the disease (Paparrizos, White, and Horvitz 2016). In its 2014 report on big data, the White House referred to an example of a research project synthesizing millions of data samples from monitors in a neonatal intensive care unit to determine which newborns were likely to contract potentially fatal infections. The White House reported, "By analyzing all of the data—not just what doctors noted on their rounds—the project was able to identify factors, like increases in temperature and heart rate, that serve as early warning signs that an infection may be taking root. These early signs of infection are not something even an experienced and attentive doctor would catch through traditional practices" (Executive Office of the President 2016).

Increasingly, the collection and analysis of large-scale administrative data drives advances in the measurement and tracking of economic activities. While compelling from a societal standpoint, such data-intensive research projects face formidable transaction costs, including real and perceived legal and ethical challenges. Too often, data remain locked in corporate coffers weighed down by concerns about individuals' privacy, data security, and reidentification risk, as well as by corporate incentives to protect trade secrets and intellectual property and a general inclination to avoid risk by keeping data close. These challenges affect all links of the data chain, including access to administrative data and its protection, analysis, sharing, and linking. Yet as Malcolm Gladwell suggests, secrets are best addressed with appropriate information disclosure controls, not with absolute limits on use of information.

The lack of a clear legal framework and ethical guidelines for use of administrative data jeopardizes the value of important research, either because the public perceives it as ethically tainted or because research outputs remain hidden from public view. Concerns over legal impediments and ethical restrictions threaten to diminish productive collaboration between researchers and private sector businesses, restricting funding opportunities, and potentially locking administrative data and research projects behind corporate walls. Further complicating matters, companies struggle to define the line between scientific research projects and A/B (split) testing for marketing or product improvement.

Similarly, data held by government agencies, as well as by entities such as universities, school districts, or other quasi-governmental institutions, are also

NOTE: Opinions or errors expressed here are the authors' and do not necessarily represent those of the Sloan Foundation or its grantees. Work on this project benefited from generous support from the Rockefeller Foundation in the form of a Bellagio Center Writer's Residency and from a grant to FPF from the Bill and Melinda Gates Foundation.

often inaccessible for important analysis by researchers. Data use benefits can include everything from improving official government statistics using corporate transactions records to rigorously testing causal hypotheses about policy improvements by using randomized controlled experiments. Despite important steps to make data available, which have been advanced by open data movements, by efforts to use data to encourage accountability in education systems, and by smart city efforts and other programs, the ability of researchers to access significant government datasets is often limited by a range of concerns, in large part consisting of privacy and security objections.

This article provides strategies for organizations to minimize risks of reidentification and privacy violations for individual data subjects. In addition, we suggest that privacy and ethical concerns can be most effectively managed by supporting the development of administrative data centers. These research centers would operate in academic institutions, facilitating researchers' use of administrative data by lowering transaction costs and increasing the reproducibility of research conducted on administrative data. They will serve as centers of expertise for de-identification, to certify researchers, provide state-of-the-art data security, organize ethical review boards, and support best practices for cleansing and managing datasets. Such centers have demonstrated success in Europe and are emerging in various sectors in the United States.

Given the multiple issues that need to be addressed to manage privacy concerns and the general trust deficit that strains society when research is viewed skeptically and risks are magnified, well-resourced and trusted centers can provide a path forward for different sectors of the economy. Such centers would be part of a data environment with the requisite data governance, accountability, and enforcement mechanisms to ensure accuracy, privacy, and efficacy of data-driven research. Ideally, a network of these centers would develop expertise on solving data sharing privacy and ethics problems. This expertise would be leveraged across different centers to further enhance their capabilities. In an age where data are used as currency and as raw material of production, establishing new data intermediaries follows logically from the existence of financial intermediaries that, in another context, have streamlined and regulated market practices for many years.

Privacy, Ethics, and Evidence-Based Policymaking

Policy-makers have long grappled with the need for evidence-based decision-making. In the words of Speaker of the House of Representatives Paul Ryan, a lead sponsor of the bipartisan National Commission on Evidence-Based Policymaking, "You always hear people in Washington talk about how much money was spent on a program, but you rarely hear whether it actually worked. That has to change."[2]

A policy is "evidence-based" when it is informed and created by a process relying on data-driven research. In many cases, evidence-based policies rely on data about individuals, known in law and policy circles as personally identifiable information (PII). Often the data used by researchers contain private or sensitive information about individuals, including about their health, education, financial condition, race, or ethnicity. How can researchers continue to access and use the data necessary to support evidence-based policymaking while at the same time ensuring individuals' privacy? This article addresses challenges and opportunities associated with balancing the benefits of evidence-based policymaking against the costs potentially imposed on individual data subjects.

Such challenges arise when researchers access organizational data for a purpose different from the one for which the data were originally collected. We refer to such repurposed organizational data as "administrative data,"[3] including, for example, the online search logs researchers examine to identify telltale signs of users' pancreatic cancer. The information, which a search engine provider collected and aggregated in the course of providing online search capabilities, could be repurposed and used to advance a compelling public policy goal. Research into administrative data is fundamentally different from traditional research on "made" data, typically assembled with hard opt-in consent from the individuals who agreed to participate in an experiment or survey. Over the past few years, the great explosion in volume, velocity, and variety of administrative data has led commentators to herald the arrival of "big data," which encompasses government, company, and other organizational records. Big data of this sort holds great promise for evidence-based policymaking but, at the same time, raises privacy and ethical concerns. Often performed without affording individuals with meaningful choice, research to support policymaking should only take place when the benefits of evidence-based policymaking outweigh the costs to individuals.

Concerns Limiting Research Access to Administrative Data

This section introduces the main roadblocks impeding the sharing of administrative data between the public and private sector and researchers. Organizations considering sharing administrative data about citizens, consumers, patients, and employees face privacy concerns and ethical challenges that strain the existing regulatory frameworks and require new, innovative solutions to protect privacy and enable data sharing while complying with laws and ethical mandates.

Privacy risk

Traditionally, de-identification was the primary method for enabling researcher access to administrative data while protecting individuals' privacy. Organizations viewed de-identification as the silver bullet that allowed them to reap data benefits while at the same time avoiding operational risks and legal requirements. The applicability of legal frameworks governing privacy and data management in the United States and European Union (EU) turned on whether the data were personally identifiable (Schwartz and Solove 2011; see also Polonetsky, Tene, and Finch 2016).

However, in recent years, scientists have repeatedly demonstrated that datasets that had been claimed to be de-identified were in fact vulnerable to reidentification attacks. Critics argued that real-world demonstrations of reidentification undermined the validity of de-identification techniques (Ohm 2010). They cast doubt on the extent to which de-identification remained a credible method for using and deriving value from large datasets while protecting privacy. They claimed that de-identification methodologies lacked rigor, failed to reliably distinguish between identifiable and de-identified information, and were not based on formal mathematical models that apply similar parameters across different contexts (Dwork and Roth 2014).

Other experts, particularly practitioners who have long implemented de-identification of health data on the ground, vigorously disputed the claim that anecdotal demonstrations of successful reidentification undermined the validity of de-identification techniques writ large (El Emam and Alvarez 2015). They noted that in some of the cases, the attacked datasets were not anonymized in a credible manner to start with or that the de-identification attacks were limited in scope, proving only the possibility of reidentifying public figures for whom extensive exogenous data were available. They claimed that despite the theoretical and demonstrated ability to mount such attacks, the likelihood of reidentification for most datasets remained minimal.

The de-identification debate continues, unresolved, and introduces obstacles to research access to critical data. Clearly, reidentification risks will continue to grow as computing technologies become ever faster and the data economy emits more and more data for linkage and analysis over time. We discuss a number of de-identification solutions and their relative attributes for different types of research.

Ethical uncertainty

The ethical framework applying to human subject research in the biomedical and behavioral research fields dates back to the Belmont Report, which was drafted in 1976 and adopted by the United States government in 1991 as the Common Rule (U.S. Department of Health, Education, and Welfare 1979).[4] The Belmont principles were geared toward a paradigmatic controlled scientific experiment with a limited population of human subjects interacting directly with researchers and manifesting their informed consent.

These days, researchers in academic institutions as well as private sector businesses not subject to the Common Rule analyze a wide array of data, from massive commercial or government databases to individual tweets or Facebook postings publicly available online. In doing so, researchers have little or no opportunity to engage human subjects directly to obtain their consent or even inform them of the research. The challenge of fitting the round peg of data-focused research into the square hole of existing ethical and legal frameworks may end up determining whether society can reap the tremendous opportunities latent in administrative data of governments and cities, health care institutions and schools, social networks, and search engines, while at the same time protecting privacy, fairness, equity, and the integrity of the scientific process.

These difficulties weigh down the application of the Belmont principles to even the academic research that is directly governed by the Common Rule. In many cases, the scoping definitions of the Common Rule are strained by new data-focused research paradigms. For starters, it is not clear whether research on large datasets collected from public or semipublic sources even constitutes human subject research, as data-driven research often leaves little or no footprint on individual subjects, such as in the case of search query analysis or automated testing for security flaws (see, for example, Narayanan and Zevenbergen 2015).

Unlike experiments with "made" data, which requires active recruitment of participants and direct engagement with them to obtain their informed consent, research can be performed on administrative data without any prior communication with data subjects. Indeed, one of the hallmarks of big data research is its promise to find previously hidden and unanticipated correlations in large unstructured datasets.

The definitional contours of the Common Rule and the Belmont principles themselves require reexamination in this context. The first principle, *respect for persons*, is focused on individual autonomy and its derivative application, informed consent. While obtaining individuals' informed consent may be feasible in a controlled research setting involving a well-defined group of individuals, such as a clinical trial, it is untenable for researchers experimenting on databases that contain the footprints of millions, or indeed billions, of data subjects. The second principle, *beneficence*, requires a delicate balance of risks and benefits that not only respects individuals' decisions and protects them from harm but also secures their well-being. Difficult to deploy even in traditional research settings, such cost-benefit analysis becomes daunting in a data research environment where benefits could be probabilistic or incremental and diffuse, and where the definition of harm is subject to constant wrangling between minimalists who reduce privacy to pecuniary terms and maximalists who view any collection of data as dignitary injuries.

Competing Objectives

Before assessing possible solutions for privacy and ethics concerns, it is necessary to discuss on what basis a data-access system for researchers would be successful. We suggest three criteria:

a. **Accuracy objective:** The system should enhance utility by promoting *research reliability*. That is, the results should be robust, unbiased, fully documented, and easily contestable or validated by other researchers. Judgment on this criterion rests with academic editors, referees, and other gatekeepers.
b. **Privacy objective:** The system should *protect privacy*. That is, the studies undertaken should be publicly defensible with respect to privacy protection. Judgment on this criterion rests with the public generally, but especially with anyone whose data may be under study.
c. **Efficacy objective:** The system should promote *practical sustainability*. That is, the framework's demands should not be too burdensome in terms

of the financial, legal, or bureaucratic support necessary to maintain smooth operations. Judgment on this criterion rests with system funders and managers as well as with data donors and users.

Of course, with multiple objectives, pursuing any one objective could adversely affect the others. For example, there is a fundamental trade-off between utility, measured by research accuracy and privacy. Increasing privacy protection necessarily entails additional data obfuscation or reproducibility obstructions. These two goals are inherently at odds. While technological advances may change and improve the options available, they will not entirely obviate the need for some trade-offs. One consideration when deciding how to supply data for a given research project is, therefore, the appropriate balance between the privacy and utility/accuracy objectives. This will depend on the nature of the study and the type of administrative data along with other factors. Another kind of consideration involves familiar constraints on time, funding, and attention. Because supplying data entails certain monetary and nonmonetary costs, policy-makers must establish priorities among projects.

How should policy-makers weigh such competing objectives? When considering a request to access data for research purposes, there may be many ethical, practical, or other considerations. But to the extent privacy per se is the focus, we suggest the following three steps:

Step 1: **Admissibility**. First, compile a menu of all the protocols available that would govern how administrative data are released and used. Options could range from de-identification to nondisclosure agreements and data management plans. Next, rank each protocol twice, once according to the privacy it affords and separately according to the accuracy it affords. A protocol will be admissible if (1) there is no other protocol available that would provide at least as good privacy, at least as good accuracy, and do better in one respect or the other (i.e., there is no *pareto superior* solution); and (2) both the privacy protection and the accuracy exceed a minimum acceptable threshold.

Step 2: **Appropriateness**. From among the admissible protocols, some might be more appropriate for certain kinds of data than others. For example, Internal Revenue Service information, which is multidimensional and highly sensitive, would typically be studied only under the strictest privacy protections. In contrast, scanner card data about individuals' grocery purchases is already sold and studied by corporations. Before making such datasets available for academic research, there may be little point in manipulating the information other than replacing names with random identifiers.

Step 3: **Affordability**. While the marginal cost of providing data to one more researcher may be small, there are also high fixed costs associated with infrastructure, legalities, bandwidth, and documentation. Besides weighing down budgets, each additional research study necessarily leaks some privacy and accuracy, so it is neither practical nor desirable to make a particular dataset containing sensitive information accessible to everyone who might ever be interested. Priority should be given to projects that stand to provide the greatest net benefit to society by advancing scientific knowledge and understanding. Of course, this cannot be predicted with certainty ahead of time—if we knew what the answers would be in advance of conducting a study, we would not call it research—but academic panels, funders, and researchers already make judgments about such matters regularly.

The minimum admissibility levels may vary from time or place depending on prevailing societal norms. We offer that any protocol that could be overcome in a few days by a skilled adversary should be ruled out as providing substandard protection. For example, "white hat" teams could be charged with randomly mounting reidentification attacks to test a system's resilience.

As for minimal utility, some critics argue that exploratory research projects are so inaccurate and unreliable that they should never warrant *any* sacrifice of privacy (Gelman and Loken 2013). Where this is feasible, such preliminary work could be performed on synthetic datasets rather than sensitive ones. Access to actual data should be reserved for confirmatory research that tests a specified hypothesis using a preregistered analysis plan. This would prevent "p-hacking," that is, dredging through data until a researcher sooner or later finds coincidences that can masquerade as statistical significance (Simonsohn, Nelson, and Simmons 2014).

Protecting Private Administrative Data

Common research protocols sometimes purport to deliver accuracy or privacy that in fact they do not. One useful way to classify proposed protocols is according to the stage in the research process that data obfuscation occurs: during input, computations, or output (Goroff 2015). Applying or relaxing restrictions at each stage gives rise to eight possible states (see Table 1). Illustrations of each state follow, starting with the traditional methods whose shortcomings motivated more recent approaches.

No restrictions: Open data

Consider, for example, a researcher who wishes to study state university faculty wages. Some states publish names, salaries, and other information about university employees in downloadable formats. In this case, there are no restrictions on data collecting or sampling, linking or analyzing, or release and reuse.

This is the ideal supported by "open data" advocates. It facilitates accuracy but, of course, not confidentiality. Individuals who care about keeping their salaries private should at least know about such a disclosure policy before they decide to accept a position.

TABLE 1
The Research Stages at Which Protocols Impose Restrictions

	Input	Computation	Output	State / Protocol
1				Open data
2			X	Data enclave
3	X		X	Nondisclosure agreement
4		X		Anonymization
5	X			Randomized response
6	X	X		Multiparty computation
7	X	X	X	Fully homomorphic encryption
8		X	X	Differential privacy

Restricted output: Federal data enclaves

Next, consider the example of a researcher who wishes to study U.S. wage and employment trends more broadly. The most comprehensive datasets are compiled from state and federal administrative records under the Longitudinal Employment and Household Dynamics Program (LEHD). Academics can apply for access to personal information at one of several "research data centers" run by the U.S. Census Bureau.[5] If approved, a researcher's "special sworn status" makes him or her subject to prosecution for misuse of private information under the same terms as a government official. Computations typically take place on-site, in a "data enclave" that is both physically and digitally disconnected from the rest of the world. To protect against improper disclosures, the resulting research papers must be approved by the Census Bureau before they can be released.

Typically, the Census Bureau checks that any information reported is aggregated to obfuscate the identity of individuals. This is akin to pixelating faces in photographs to hide identities, a strategy that works well for unfamiliar people but not so much for those who an adversary has additional information about. Such procedures have produced no known security breaches to date and are gradually becoming less cumbersome. At the same time, this strategy prevents the replication of research results obtained at a data enclave.

Restricted input and output: Commercial nondisclosure agreements

Companies often draw inferences about online users' salaries and other characteristics based on their web behavior. This method can involve inaccuracies at the input stage because of its indirect, obscure, and irremediable nature, as well as potential sample bias. Researchers rarely gain access to such datasets without signing nondisclosure agreements that give a company control over what private or proprietary details may be released.

This arrangement usually precludes replication of the results or reuse of the data. The *American Economic Review*, a premier academic journal whose authors are required to post the data they use, reported having to waive this requirement for nearly half the empirical papers published in 2014 because of nondisclosure agreements (see Einav and Levin 2014).

Restricted computation: Anonymization

In 2014, New York City released "anonymized" data about every taxi ride taken in the city in 2013. Hackers quickly reidentified the data by exploiting weak techniques used to encode the information and by linking with other publicly available datasets. Not only is it now possible to track the earnings of each taxi driver by name, but a researcher can also trace the times, fares, and tips of trips made by celebrities or map all the precise GPS coordinates on the other end of trips to or from The Hustler Club, for example (Neustar Research 2014).

This privacy fail joined several other famous examples of datasets that were initially released with assurances of de-identification, yet were nevertheless linked with other public information to leak private confidences. More generally, Latanya Sweeney has claimed that 87 percent of the U.S. population can be uniquely identified by just three pieces of information: gender, zip code, and date of birth.[6] Once this information is out, an adversary can search for or purchase the names, social security numbers, and additional categories of sensitive, sometimes intimate, data about individuals in a dataset (O'Neil 2016).

In most of these cases, while reidentifying individuals from a de-identified dataset alone would be extremely difficult, privacy violations arose by linking the anonymized data with other publicly available datasets. The possibility of such linkage attacks makes safety guarantees of de-identification dependent on knowledge of all the current and future datasets that could ever conceivably emerge to be used to reidentify individuals. Clearly, this is not a practical approach to rigorous privacy protection. That is one of the reasons that—despite creative efforts to aggregate, average, edit, adjust, or otherwise impose obfuscation at the computational stage—experts are now concluding that "sanitizing data doesn't" and "de-identified data isn't" (Dwork 2014; see also El Emam 2013).

Restricted input: Randomized response

Consider, for example, a researcher who wants to estimate what percentage of individuals in a group have incomes below the poverty line yet do so without compromising any individual's confidentiality. One approach yielding a privacy protective response would be to give each individual in the group a coin to flip without anyone else seeing the outcome. If the coin lands on heads, the individual must truthfully answer whether her or his income level is below the poverty line. If the coin lands on tails, she or he must flip the coin again. If the second toss is a head, the individual again should answer truthfully; but if the second toss is a tail, he or she should lie—that is, respond that his or her income level is above the poverty line if it really is not—and vice versa. Under this method, to arrive at a good estimate of the fraction of the group that is actually below the poverty line, the researcher would compute twice the number of yes responses minus 0.5.[7]

Even if the researcher knows who answered what, he or she cannot tell who is poor without seeing the result of the coin toss. The usefulness of this technique depends on having participants who are all willing to follow instructions and do not cheat or collude. Other privacy-preserving variants are more efficient estimators, but some accuracy is sacrificed in any case.

Restricted input and computation: Multiparty computation

Consider, for example, a researcher who would like to calculate the average salary of a group of individuals without any individual ever communicating her or his own salary. Surprisingly, this can be done quite precisely as long as everyone cooperates. If, for example, there are three individuals in the group, each individual would generate two random numbers and give one number to each of the other two participants. Next, each individual would add the two random numbers he or she generated to his or her own salary, subtract the two numbers he or she was given, and report the result. Adding all those results and dividing by three would give the average salary, without revealing any individual's number.[8]

Although no one's salary was ever communicated, this protocol does not necessarily protect the privacy of those who participate. If, for example, all but one of the participants collude by using the same method to compute their average salary, that new group could easily deduce the salary of their additional colleague.

Applications of blockchain technology[9] have been proposed to make deviations from agreed protocols more easily detectable (Zyskind, Nathan, and Pentland 2015). Similarly, more complicated computations can secretly carry out operations beyond just taking averages (Prabhakaran and Sahai 2013; see also Abbe, Khandani, and Lo 2012).

Restricted input, computation, and output: Fully homomorphic encryption

Banking and other sensitive information routinely travels over the Internet without interception. Suppose that an individual could not only send salary information to a researcher using similar or stronger encryption, but that the researcher could perform computations and return the encrypted results to the individual without ever being able to decrypt either the inputs or the results. Long thought impossible, methods for such "fully homomorphic encryption" have now been devised (Gentry 2009). Though practical applications are coming online, many algorithms remain still too slow to operate in real-world settings. Proposed protocols would perform regressions and other analyses on encrypted data supplied by survey participants, for example, but only allow the statistics to be decrypted if those participants verify that the calculations have been done properly and to their satisfaction (Lopez-Alt, Tromer, and Vaikuntanathan 2012).

Once practical, fully homomorphic encryption could have profound implications for the privacy of numerous applications, including cloud computing, search engines, tax preparation, and "personal data lockers." But even effectively hiding inputs to research will not necessarily preserve the privacy of participants, especially if the statistical findings are subject to linkage or "differencing" attacks. As an example of the latter, consider that asking two simple questions—how many employees of a company make more than $1 million in salary, and how many employees of a company who are not the CEO make more than $1 million—could reveal whether the CEO makes more than $1 million.[10]

Restricted computation and output: Differential privacy

Consider, for example, a dataset D that contains an individual's personal information in one "row" and another dataset D' that is missing that row but is otherwise identical. Two datasets are said to be adjacent if they differ by only a single row like this. A research protocol would be considered privacy preserving if it could not distinguish between D and an adjacent D'. Alas, it also would not be very useful because too many different datasets would all look the same. But what if the protocol could barely make such a distinction? Specifically, consider the probabilities that it generates a given answer to a given question when applied to D as compared to D'. The ratio of those two probabilities should be as close as possible to one. In fact, the log of that ratio measures the loss of privacy incurred when the protocol answers the given question.[11] If the log of that probability ratio is always less than ε for any adjacent datasets, the protocol is said to provide ε-differential privacy.

Cynthia Dwork and her colleagues not only formulated this definition and showed that it captures basic intuitions about privacy loss; they also devised explicit research protocols that provide ε-differential privacy (Dwork et al. 2006). In this system, data are held by a trusted curator who accepts only certain questions from an investigator. Calculations are performed behind a firewall, and answers are returned only after injecting a small amount of carefully calibrated noise.[12] There is a limit on the number of questions that can be allowed; however, since each question depletes the given "privacy budget" by an amount that depends on ε.

Conceptually, choosing a parameter ε for a differentially private protocol determines how a research project will trade accuracy for privacy. The smaller the ε, the less leakage of information, but this comes at a cost of more noise and less accuracy. As a practical matter, how to provide differential privacy by designing, implementing, or combining various algorithms is the subject of intense research.[13] Increasingly, scientists are devising real-world systems that implement differential privacy to enable data research with minimal accuracy-privacy losses.

Summary

In assessing the privacy protecting research protocols presented above, it is useful to distinguish between those that affect the *collection* of data and those that deal with *computations* and *output*. The former protocols, if built into a data project from the start, can help to ease privacy concerns later. Researchers should therefore be aware of techniques such as secure multiparty computation or fully homomorphic encryption before setting out to collect data, and should be encouraged to use them when appropriate.

In many cases, however, researchers are eager to work with datasets that have already been compiled for other purposes. For such administrative datasets, privacy protecting protocols can be applied only at the computational and output stages. Because so much of the evidence base for policymaking derives from administrative data, it is worth focusing in more detail on comparing and contrasting postcollection protocols, such as data enclaves, de-identification, and differential privacy.

For these postcollection scenarios, the main privacy concern involves risk of reidentification, since information is not obscured or protected when initially recorded. De-identification is controversial among scientists and policy-makers. If performed carefully, de-identification is often considered acceptable in many practical applications. But as discussed above, there have been numerous actual and potential examples of reidentification. In contrast, research protocols that enforce differential privacy effectively rule out the identification of individuals altogether, no matter what postprocessing or linkages might ever be attempted. Data enclaves have similarly proven quite safe. Reidentification is unheard of, but the theoretical possibility remains that the release of precise statistics—even if aggregated, averaged, or otherwise sanitized—would allow linkage, differencing, or other attacks to compromise privacy.

At the end of the day, society must decide what the trade-off is between privacy concerns and research potential.[14] How well society understands, facilitates, and regulates privacy-preserving research will, in turn, determine whether the public will benefit from advances in empirical behavioral and social science or whether that value will flow strictly to those private interests that hold enormous and ever growing stores of sensitive information.

Building Institutions

One type of institution that already addresses data privacy in research settings is the academic institutional review board (IRB). However, IRBs, which were initially conceived to address research ethics generally, remain anchored in a paradigm that involves direct engagement with individual study participants, which is untenable in the context of administrative data research. New institutions, including recent kinds of research facilities and networks, offer a promising path toward ethical, privacy-aware data sharing between organizations and researchers.

IRBs

In federally funded human subject research, IRBs are the institution responsible for evaluating whether a research project comports with ethical frameworks. Yet in today's data economy, research using administrative data is increasingly taking place outside of universities and traditional academic settings. With information becoming a raw material for production, organizations are regularly exposed to and closely monitoring vast quantities of administrative data about citizens, consumers, patients, and employees. This includes not only companies in industries ranging from technology and education to financial services and healthcare, but also nonprofit entities, which seek to advance societal causes, and even political campaigns.

Whether the proposed revisions to the Common Rule address some of these new concerns or exacerbate them is hotly debated. But whatever the final scope of the Common Rule, while raising challenging ethical questions, a broad swath of academic research will remain neither covered by the rules nor subject to IRB review. Currently, gatekeepers for ethical decisions range from private IRBs to journal publication standards, association guidelines, and peer reviews. Whether there is a need for new principles as well as new structures for review of academic research that is not covered by the current or expanded version of the Common Rule is a key question for future debate (National Research Council 2014).

To be sure, privacy and data protection laws provide a backstop in cases involving commercial uses of data, and in setting boundaries like consent and avoidance of harms. But in many cases where informed consent is not feasible and where data uses create both benefits and risks, legal boundaries are ambiguous and rest on vague concepts such as "unfairness" (in the U.S.)[15] or the "legitimate interests of the controller" (in Europe).[16] An uncertain regulatory terrain jeopardizes the value of important research, which could be perceived as ethically tainted or become hidden from the public domain to prevent scrutiny.[17] Concerns over data ethics could diminish collaboration between researchers and private sector entities, restrict funding opportunities, and lock research projects in corporate coffers contributing to the development of new products without furthering generalizable knowledge (Polonetsky, Tene, and Jerome 2015).

To address ethical questions about corporate data research, Ryan Calo foresaw the establishment of "Consumer Subject Review Boards" (Calo 2013). Calo suggested that organizations should "take a page from biomedical and behavioral science" and create small committees with diverse expertise that could operate according to predetermined principles for ethical use of data (Polonetsky and Tene 2013). The idea resonated in the Obama White House's legislative initiative, the Consumer Privacy Bill of Rights Act of 2015, which required the establishment of "Privacy Review Boards" to vet noncontextual data uses.[18]

In Europe, the European Data Protection Supervisor announced the creation of an Advisory Group to explore the relationships between human rights, technology, markets, and business models from an ethical perspective, with particular attention to the implications for the rights to privacy and data protection in the digital environment.[19] A number of organizations are working to advance new types of review boards, but these efforts are still nascent. Supporting the development of these entities would help to ensure ethical oversight over research data that are not subject to IRBs.

In "Beyond IRBs: Ethical Guidelines for Data Research," Omer Tene and Jules Polonetsky (2016) discussed possible guidelines for industry-wide or corporate IRBs. They offered suggestions as to what projects would be subject to review, how a review board would be structured, when review would be conducted, and which principles would apply. They argued that even research initiatives that are not governed by the existing ethical framework should be subject to clear principles and guidelines. They noted, "As the field of data ethics develops and grows, policy-makers should seek to harmonize the principles and procedures governing academic research, corporate research, and corporate product development using personal data, as well as research projects affecting individuals in real ways" (Tene and Polonetsky 2016, 471).

Administrative data research facilities

Because IRBs primarily examine research ethics before a project starts, they can recommend a broad range of precollection and postcollection protocols for data privacy. Yet as noted above, more and more information is compiled by agencies, offices, or companies for purposes other than research. Such administrative data, which comprises a by-product of standard enterprise activity, stands in contrast to the results of surveys, lab experiments, and field trials that are designed by academics and approved by IRBs to test specific hypotheses.

If handled properly, administrative datasets can nevertheless be hugely valuable for research. Yet using data for secondary purposes, such as research or program evaluation, can entail high transaction costs. When faced with a collective action problem with high transaction costs such as this, economists seek institutional solutions—especially ones that engender trust (Williamson 1996). In this vein, we suggest setting up a network of trustworthy data intermediaries called Administrative Data Research Facilities (ADRFs) to allay transaction costs that impede data-driven research. Each ADRF would develop expertise to solve data-sharing privacy and ethics problems for a given industry sector. In addition to setting forth procedures to enhance accuracy, privacy, and efficacy at the data input, computation, and output stages, an ADRF would institute accountability measures for auditing and monitoring compliance with data-sharing rules.

While an ADRF could go a long way to lowering transaction costs for both data suppliers and users, setting up multiple ADRFs is only the first phase of a comprehensive plan. The next phase would involve organizing an Administrative Data Research Network (ADRN) whose members are ADRFs committed to sharing best practices and high standards. Such an association of data intermediaries would, for example, create working groups on topics such as compliance and legal matters, researcher credentialing, ADRF accreditation, data security, systems and operations, private and proprietary data protections, government and public relations, research and reproducibility standards, corporate relations and contracting, data interfaces and linking, and more. Any researcher or facility found to be jeopardizing the ADRN's reputation for trustworthiness would lose their status, privileges, and data access, presenting a forceful deterrent to misbehavior.

A similar model has already been tried and tested in the UK. According to a 2012 report, *The UK Administrative Data Research Network: Improving Access for Research and Policy*, an interagency administrative data taskforce headed by Sir Alan Langlands recommended to set up an independent organization that would help social and economic researchers to gain access to administrative data in a safe and lawful way (UK Administrative Data Taskforce 2012). The goal was to create a single point of access for researchers who want to use administrative data: an institution that would screen researchers, make sure that they are properly trained to handle potentially sensitive information, provide safe rooms for the researchers to access data, and take on the task of negotiating for data access as well as find safe ways to link different datasets together without compromising the privacy of any individual.

Consequently, the UK Economic and Social Research Council decided to fund an ADRN to facilitate access to government-sourced administrative data. The ADRN not only provides de-identification services—using a trusted third party to link administrative datasets without leaking identifying information about the individuals involved—but also helps researchers to prepare their proposals before they go to an IRB ("approvals panel"), which determines whether their research project is lawful, ethical, feasible, of high scientific merit, and of potential benefit to society. The ADRN then provides a secure environment where researchers can access the linked de-identified data. Before researchers can remove their final results from the secure environment, ADRN staff check that their findings are relevant to the approved research project and do not contain directly identifying personal information that would allow any individual to be identified.

The ADRN-UK comprises an administrative data service, which coordinates the network, as well as four ADRCs, one in each country in the UK: England, led by the University of Southampton; Northern Ireland, led by Queen's University Belfast; Scotland, led by the University of Edinburgh; and Wales, led by Swansea University. Other parties to the network include national statistics authorities, government departments and agencies (the data custodians), the ESRC (the funder), and the UK Statistics Authority, which leads the ADRN Board that reports directly to Parliament.

The ADRN-UK focuses especially on government datasets and is especially notable for its facilities and procedures that can link such datasets in straightforward and timely but secure ways. Laws and traditions vary from country to country, of course, but there are also others and potential partners set up by governments in Germany and Denmark, for example.

In the United States, the Census Bureau runs a network of Federal Statistical Research Data Centers (FSRDCs) where data from a dozen different agencies can be made available to qualified researchers. Some states and localities participate in similar schemes. Access to data is carefully regulated before, during, and after any calculations are performed. At the federal level, researchers must obtain Census Bureau special sworn status that makes them subject to prosecution for breaking confidentiality restrictions. On one hand, this limits privacy risks, so much so that there has never been a reported breach of confidentiality. On the other hand, this also limits the replicability and reliability of research results since it is nearly impossible for anyone other than the original investigator to verify the accuracy of the data or the calculations.

The United States also has several data centers and archives that are not run directly by the government but serve the needs of researchers interested in evidence-based policy. For example, the National Opinion Research Center (NORC) at the University of Chicago runs a "data enclave" as one of its signature data governance solutions. This is a system that allows the sharing, among a closed community of researchers, of datasets that are too sensitive to be shared broadly.[20] In addition to archiving, curating, and indexing the data, NORC provides extensive privacy protection by restricting access. The Inter-University Consortium for Political and Social Research (ICPSR) is another example of a data intermediary.[21] "Virtual data enclaves" can also be used to enable remote access by qualified researchers (Abowd and Lane 2004).

In contrast to these institutions, which have a broad purview, there are examples of data intermediaries that focus on a given industry sector. In the UK, for example, the Consumer Data Research Centre based at the University College London works specifically with high street retailers; the Urban Big Data Centre based at the University of Glasgow works with smart cities.[22] Because researchers and managers associated with each such facility know the data and the data providers, they build up a reputation for trust and expertise as data intermediaries in their space. The Administrative Data Service provides an overall framework of standards, procedures, training, and other forms of support for their operations.

Sector-specific data specialists already exist in the United States as well. For example, researchers interested in exploring supermarket scanner data can consult the Kilts Center at Chicago Booth, which acts as an ADRF for this category of administrative data. Those interested in university data can turn to the Institute for Research on Innovation and Science (IRIS) at the University of Michigan. To study cities' administrative data, experts, datasets, and systems meet at the Center for Urban Science Progress (CUSP) at NYU. With these institutions in place, a researcher who needs data held in an ADRF does not have to renegotiate a new data access agreement with original data producers every time he or she wants to access the data.

Yet the U.S. landscape still lacks facilities in numerous industries. And American ADRFs could benefit from an ADRN-U.S., modeled after the UK network and charged with accrediting ADRF members and providing a staff of experts in law, ethics, technology, research methodology, and government relations to support them. Such coordinated support for data intermediaries would facilitate evidence-based policymaking.

Ultimately, at least one ADRF would cover each major data-producing sector in the economy, including, for example, online retailers; traditional retail chains; credit card companies; financial services; automotive companies; payroll processors; as well as all levels of state, local, and federal agencies. An ADRF with a given specialization would negotiate a standard data use agreement with each industry member on behalf of researchers. The ADRF would then be responsible for preparing each dataset for study by creating the necessary documentation, metadata, basic data hygiene and versioning, approximate summary statistics, citation information, and archiving services. This would include scrutinizing data-sets to flag and minimize selection bias such as excluding vulnerable populations or reflecting preexisting societal biases (see Sanfilippo 2016). For credentialed researchers with sound research plans, access to the data would be granted using admissible privacy protecting protocols as appropriate.

While it is natural to think of an ADRF as an institution hosted at a university, other organizations could play that role, including NGOs, corporations, or government agencies—especially those that, like the Census Bureau, are not only actively engaged in generating data but also in facilitating its use by independent researchers. Of course, this will require establishing robust and transparent accountability mechanisms to foment trust in entities that lack the institutional tradition of academic establishments. Having received funding to establish a clearinghouse for government and other administrative data, for example, the Census Bureau would be an important partner. This would be especially significant since all network members would abide by explicit and streamlined procedures for sharing, linking, and protecting datasets.

Whereas the FSRDC system and the ADRN-UK system were created by government, in the United States, sector-specific ADRFs and the ADRN-U.S. could coordinate closely with federal agencies without necessarily depending on them for initiation, governance, or even financing. As is often the case in the United States, there is an important role for private philanthropy. Indeed, some of the existing ADRFs have been established by grants, and some ADRFs are beginning to develop long-term sustainability plans to make themselves self-sufficient. Both IRIS in Michigan and the CDRC in the UK, for example, deliver services that data donors are willing to pay for, such as data cleansing, linking, archiving, and analysis. In this way, the private benefits that ADRFs supply can help to pay for the public benefits they provide by facilitating evidence-based policymaking.

Conclusion

To promote policymaking based on evidence derived from private or public administrative data, at least four stakeholder groups must cooperate: government agencies, private sector corporations, independent researchers, and philanthropic funders. Academics such as Gary King, Director of the Institute for Quantitative Social Science at Harvard University, have long discussed the need for a "grand bargain" among these groups with respect to administrative data. Lowering the transaction costs associated with studying data would benefit all. Led by the Census Bureau, government agencies at all levels are beginning to work more seamlessly with academics. At the same time, private sector corporations continue to encounter repeated and disparate data requests from a steady stream of academics or government agencies. In many cases, businesses and government agencies already realize that outside researchers can add enormous value by cleaning, compiling, archiving, and analyzing administrative data in ways that could not be performed internally.

Researchers, in turn, have been slow to organize facilities or networks to deal with access to administrative data. Certain researchers who have gained such access through personal connections or otherwise may not be eager to share the wealth and are less concerned about the difficulties their colleagues face when trying to access administrative data. More generally, academics, who are laser-focused on what is needed to publish their next article, spend little time finding ways to cooperate with colleagues to create more streamlined processes for granting access to data or generating reliable evidence. Journal editors, while troubled by reproducibility requirements, continue to offer waivers liberally.

At their best, philanthropies can provide incentives to help solve such collective action problems. Some already do so through support of ADRFs, which in the long run can be structured to generate self-sustaining revenue. Besides launching more ADRFs, foundations should work on establishing governance mechanisms, offices, working groups, and membership criteria for an ADRN.

In the end, there is no single solution to the problems limiting researchers' access to private data. But the technical and institutional solutions discussed above would greatly facilitate access and reduce transaction costs. Enabling data science to improve policymaking while also protecting privacy is well within reach.

Notes

1. Gladwell writing in *The New Yorker* about the work of sociologist Beryl Bellman, December 19, 2016.

2. Speaker Paul Ryan, press release, *Evidence-Based Policy Commission Gets to Work*, July 26, 2016; see http://www.speaker.gov/press-release/evidence-based-policy-commission-gets-to-work.

3. Other common terms are transactional, observational, or "found" data.

4. See also https://www.hhs.gov/ohrp/regulations-and-policy/regulations/common-rule/index.html.

5. U.S. Census Bureau, Center for Economic Studies (CES), https://www.census.gov/ces/rdcresearch/.

6. See http://aboutmyinfo.org/.

7. If r is the reported fraction of yes responses and p is the true fraction, then the expected value of r is $E(r) = \dfrac{p}{2} + \dfrac{p}{4} + \dfrac{(1-p)}{4}$.

8. In other words, let S_i denote the secret salary of person i, and let R_{ij} denote the random number generated by person i and given to person j. Then person i reports the result X_i where

$$X_1 = S_1 + \left(R_{12} + R_{13}\right) - \left(R_{21} + R_{31}\right)$$

$$X_2 = S_2 + \left(R_{21} + R_{23}\right) - \left(R_{12} + R_{32}\right)$$

$$X_3 = S_3 + \left(R_{31} + R_{32}\right) - \left(R_{13} + R_{23}\right).$$

9. Blockchain is a technology for creating secure and transparent distributed ledgers. The blocks are added and protected using cryptographic methods to ensure that they remain secure and meddle-proof. Transactions create a permanent record that cannot be changed. A record's authenticity can be verified by the entire community using the blockchain instead of a single centralized authority.

10. It may seem straightforward for a system to simply rule out lines of questioning like this. Provably, however, no algorithm can reliably determine whether a given set of questions that seem to inquire only about statistical aggregates would nevertheless yield answers that, taken together, reveal private information (see Dwork 2014).

11. For a protocol M that yields research result $\gamma = M(D)$ when applied to database D, Dwork (2014) defines the loss of privacy as $L = \ln \dfrac{\Pr[M(D) = \gamma]}{\Pr[M(D') = \gamma]}$, where D' is adjacent to D.

12. It suffices, for example, to draw that noise from a Laplace distribution with parameter $1/\varepsilon$ when responding to a counting query. Other aggregate statistics, including regression coefficients and contingency tables, can be handled similarly.

13. One promising example is the Census Bureau's OnTheMap Project, which provides probabilistic differential privacy. A "synthetic database" has been constructed by carefully perturbing and aggregating actual payroll tax records in each state. By querying this dataset, members of the public can receive approximate but quite accurate answers to a large class of counting and geographic questions. See http://onthemap.ces.census.gov.

14. This choice differs from any individual's choice between, for example, taking an expensive vacation or buying a new car. Whereas that decision affects only the specific individual concerned, privacy or validity leakages can affect other researchers and their subjects. Indeed, the reliability of privacy protection and of scientific research are *public goods*, which, like national security or lighthouses, are neither excludable nor rival.

15. FTC Policy Statement on Unfairness, Appended to International Harvester Co., 104 F.T.C. 949, 1070 (1984). See 15 U.S.C. § 45(n).

16. Article 29 Working Party, WP 217, Op. 06/2014 on the notion of legitimate interests of the data controller under Article 7 of Directive 95/46/EC, Apr. 9, 2014, http://ec.europa.eu/justice/dataprotection/article-29/documentation/opinion-recommendation/files/2014/wp217_en.pdf.

17. The Common Rule's definition of "research" is "a systematic investigation, including research development, testing, and evaluation, designed to develop or contribute to *generalizable* knowledge" (emphasis added).

18. Consumer Privacy Bill Of Rights §103(c) (Administration Discussion Draft 2015), https://www.whitehouse.gov/sites/default/files/omb/legislative/letters/cpbr-act-of-2015-discussion-draft.pdf.

19. European Data Protection Supervisor, Ethics Advisory Group, Dec. 3, 2015, https://secure.edps.europa.eu/EDPSWEB/edps/site/mySite/Ethics. See also Naser (n.d.).

20. See http://www.norc.org/Research/Capabilities/Pages/data-enclave.aspx.

21. See http://www.icpsr.umich.edu/icpsrweb/content/ICPSR/access/restricted/enclave.html.

22. The term "smart city" is used to describe the transformation of the urban environment into a landscape of data collection, analysis, and use by a network of always-on devices typically referred to as the Internet of Things. See Finch and Tene (2014).

References

Abbe, Emmanuel, Amir Khandani, and Andrew Lo. 2012. Privacy-preserving methods for sharing financial risk exposures. *American Economic Review* 102 (3): 65–70.

Abowd, John M., and Julia Lane. 2004. New approaches to confidentiality protection: Synthetic data, remote access and research data centers. In *International workshop on privacy in statistics databases*, eds. Joseph Domingo-Ferrer and Vicenc Torra, 282–89. New York, NY: Springer.

Calo, Ryan. 2013. Consumer subject review boards: A thought experiment. *Stanford Law Review*. Available from https://www.stanfordlawreview.org/online/privacy-and-big-data-consumer-subject-review-boards/.

Dwork, Cynthia. 2014. Differential privacy: A cryptographic approach to private data analysis. In *Privacy, big data, and the public good: Frameworks for engagement*, eds. J. Lane, V. Stodden, S. Bender, and H. Nissenbaum, 296–322. New York, NY: Cambridge University Press.

Dwork, Cynthia, Frank McSherry, Kobbi Nissim, and Adam Smith. 2006. Calibrating noise to sensitivity in private data analysis. In *Theory of cryptography conference (TCC)*, eds. Shai Halevi and Tal Rabin, 265–84. New York, NY: Springer.

Dwork, Cynthia, and Aaron Roth. 2014. The algorithmic foundations of differential privacy. *Foundations and Trends in Theoretical Computer Science* 9 (3–4): 211–407.

Einav, Liran, and Jonathan Levin. 2014. Economics in the age of big data. *Science* 346 (6210). doi:10.1126/science.1243089.

El Emam, Khaled. 2013. *Guide to the de-identification of personal health information*. Boca Raton, FL: CRC Press.

1

El Emam, Khaled, and Cecilia Alvarez. 2015. A critical appraisal of the Article 29 Working Party Opinion 05/2014 on data anonymization techniques. *International Data Privacy Law* 5 (1): 73–87.

Executive Office of the President. 2016. *Big data: Seizing opportunities, preserving values*. Washington, DC: Executive Office of the President.

Finch, Kelsey, and Omer Tene. 2014. Welcome to the metropticon: Protecting privacy in a hyperconnected town. *Fordham Urban Law Journal* 41 (5): 1580–1615.

Gelman, Andrew, and Eric Loken. 2013. The garden of forking paths: Why multiple comparisons can be a problem, even when there is no "fishing expedition" or "p-hacking" and the research hypothesis was posited ahead of time. Available from http://www.stat.columbia.edu/~gelman/research/unpublished/p_hacking.pdf.

Gentry, Craig. 2009. Fully homomorphic encryption using ideal lattices. In *STOC '09: Proceedings of the forty-first annual ACM symposium on theory of computing*, 169–78. New York, NY: ACM.

Goroff, Daniel. 2015. Balancing privacy versus accuracy in research protocols. *Science* 347 (6221): 479–80.

Lopez-Alt, Adriana, Eran Tromer, and Vinod Vaikuntanathan. 2012. On-the-fly multiparty computation on the cloud via multikey fully homomorphic encryption. In *STOC '12: Proceedings of the forty-fourth annual ACM symposium on theory of computing*, 1219–34. New York, NY: ACM.

Narayanan, Arvind, and Bendert Zevenbergen. 2015. *No encore for Encore? Ethical questions for web-based censorship measurement*. Available from https://papers.ssrn.com.

Naser, Curtis. n.d. *The IRB sledge-hammer, freedom and big-data*. Available from https://bigdata.fpf.org/papers/the-irb-sledge-hammer-freedom-and-big-data/.

National Research Council. 2014. *Proposed revisions to the Common Rule for the Protection of Human Subjects in the Behavioral and Social Sciences*. Washington, DC: National Academies Press.

Neustar Research. 15 September 2014. *Riding with the stars: Passenger privacy in the NYC taxicab dataset*. Available from http://research.neustar.biz/2014/09/15/riding-with-the-stars-passenger-privacy-in-the-nyc-taxicab-dataset.

Ohm, Paul. 2010. Broken promises of privacy: Responding to the surprising failure of anonymization. *UCLA Law Review* 57 (1701): 1717–23.

O'Neil, Cathy. 2016. *Weapons of math destruction: How big data increases inequality and threatens democracy*. New York, NY: Crown Publishing Group.

Paparrizos, John, Ryen W. White, and Eric Horvitz. 2016. Screening for pancreatic adenocarcinoma using signals from web search logs: Feasibility study and results. *Journal of Oncology Practice* 12 (8): 737–44.

Polonetsky, Jules, and Omer Tene. 2013. Privacy and big data: Making ends meet. *Stanford Law Review* 66:25–33.

Polonetsky, Jules, Omer Tene, and Kelsey Finch. 2016. Shades of gray: Seeing the full spectrum of practical data de-identification. *Santa Clara Law Review* 56 (3): 593–629.

Polonetsky, Jules, Omer Tene, and Joseph Jerome. 2015. Beyond the Common Rule: Ethical structures for data research in non-academic settings. *Colorado Technology Law Journal* 13 (2) 333–67.

Prabhakaran, Manoj, and Amit Sahai. 2013. *Secure multi-party computation*. Amsterdam: IOS Press.

Schwartz, Paul, and Dan Solove. 2011. The PII problem: Privacy and a new concept of personally identifiable information. *New York University Law Review* 86:1814–94.

Simonsohn, Uri, Leif Nelson, and Joseph Simmons. 2014. P-curve: A key to the file-drawer. *Journal of Experimental Psychology: General* 143 (2): 534–47.

Sanfilippo, Madelyn Rose. 2016. An unequal information society: How information access initiatives contribute to the construction of inequality. PhD diss., Indiana University, Bloomington, IN.

Tene, Omer, and Jules Polonetsky. 2016. Beyond IRBs: Ethical guidelines for data research. *Washington and Lee Law Review Online* 72 (3): 458–71.

The UK Administrative Data Taskforce. 2012. *The UK Administrative Data Research Network: Improving access for research and policy*. Essex: The UK Administrative Data Research Network.

U.S. Department of Health, Education, and Welfare. 1979. *Belmont report: Ethical principles and guidelines for the protection of human subjects of research*. Washington, DC: U.S. Department of Health, Education, and Welfare.

Williamson, Oliver E. 1996. *The mechanisms of governance*. New York, NY: Oxford University Press.

Zyskind, Guy, Oz Nathan, and Alex Pentland. 2015. Enigma: Decentralized computation platform with guaranteed privacy. arXiv:1506.03471 [cs.CR]. Available from https://arxiv.org/abs/1506.03471.

Turning the Law into a Tool Rather than a Barrier to the Use of Administrative Data for Evidence-Based Policy

By
JOHN PETRILA

"The law" is too often viewed as an impenetrable barrier to the use of administrative data to create and evaluate evidence-based policy. There are various reasons for this, including complexities of the law, organizational and cultural norms in government agencies that restrict data sharing, a lack of adequate legal expertise among potential data providers, and a lack of political support for the use of administrative data. However, an emerging political consensus on the importance of the use of administrative data, growing interest among funders, and efforts to create resources for lawyers working in this field provide a foundation for a fundamental shift in attitude about "the law," making the law an essential tool to data sharing and use, rather than a barrier to these efforts.

Keywords: law; privacy; administrative data; policy

In 1984, Charles Murray published his critique of the social policies adopted as part of Lyndon Johnson's Great Society (Murray 1984/2015). While Murray's conclusions about how to address the social needs of American citizens were controversial, he observed that those constructing social policies in the 1960s had little data or even practical experience to draw on. In the introduction to the 2015 reprint of his book, he writes:

> For someone born in the decades since then, it is hard to realize the degree to which planners of the Great Society were starting from scratch. ...

John Petrila is vice president of adult policy at the Meadows Mental Health Policy Institute (MMHPI) and was a member of the founding Board of the Policy Institute. He is an attorney with 40 years of experience in mental health law and policy. Before joining MMHPI, he chaired the Department of Health Policy & Management at the University of South Florida College of Public Health.

NOTE: The views expressed in this article are those of the author and do not represent the views of the Meadows Mental Health Policy Institute.

Correspondence: petrilajohn@gmail.com

DOI: 10.1177/0002716217741088

> The reaction when the programs didn't work was bewilderment and confusion. … I hope my narrative conveys how little social policy planners understood what they were up against. They had a limited body of historical examples of government social programs to draw upon, [and] assumptions about the nature of poverty and disadvantage that were compassionate but empirically dubious. (1984/2015, xv)

Today there is nearly boundless information and data available to policy-makers, and it is difficult to argue that "the data simply don't exist" for sound analysis of social policy or evidence-based policymaking. Administrative data should be an essential tool in implementing and augmenting the core functions of government. For example, administrative data can be used to determine whether government-funded interventions work as intended (Liebman, this volume), to improve government operations and processes at federal agencies such as the Census Bureau (O'Hara, this volume) and the Social Security Administration (McNabb et al. 2009), to provide the foundation for social sciences research on programs and populations (Culhane et al., this volume; Goerge, this volume), and to inform the development of policy.[1]

Government officials of course are not the only ones interested in the productive use of administrative data. Many researchers have turned to administrative data as a virtual laboratory for their work, though the use of such data in research is new enough that there is no consensus yet on even the meaning of "administrative data" or "big data" (Connelly et al. 2016). Citizen advocates increasingly seek data from the government, which can lead to clashes over access. Data mining is at the core of the explosive growth of some of the most successful businesses in the world, such as Amazon and Facebook.

However, as this article and others in this volume suggest, administrative data are often not used to their potential, with serious consequences:

- Policy-makers who ignore or do not have access to administrative data may be more likely to make decisions based on whim, personal preference, or untested assumptions. While such decision-making has always been a feature of policy design, the rejection of or unwillingness to test available data is particularly difficult to rationalize in an era in which society is awash in data.
- Researchers deprived of data cannot empirically test the success or failure of government programs.
- The public is uninformed about whether governmental programs and social policies "work."
- Problems of discrimination and inequity in the allocation of resources or the imposition of punishment (as happened in the strengthening of penalties for drug possession) may be exacerbated. Murray (1984/2015) was one of the first to point out that a lack of empiricism can lead to unintended consequences, and his caution applies perhaps even more forcefully in a society in which stark differences in political views make achieving consensus on nearly any social policy difficult.

In the current political climate, one could ask whether agreement could even be achieved within government that the use of administrative data could be beneficial.

Perhaps surprisingly, though, a growing political consensus at the highest levels of government has emerged over the last decade that the use of administrative data should be accelerated and that data from different sources must be integrated to maximize their utility. For example, the Obama administration urged executive agencies to expand the use of administrative data to create evidence-based policy and evaluation strategies. In 2013, the director of the Office of Management and Budget (OMB) in a memo to federal agency heads wrote, "Agencies are encouraged to allocate resources to programs and practices backed by strong evidence of effectiveness while trimming activities that evidence shows are not effective" (OMB 2013, 2). The directive went on to state that "proposals should enable agencies and/or researchers to access and utilize relevant data to answer important questions about program outcomes while fully protecting privacy" and noted that linking "administrative data … can be a valuable resource for program improvement" (OMB 2013, 3,6).

On the legislative side, the bipartisan congressional agreement to create the Commission on Evidence-Based Policymaking showed broad legislative support for the use of data to improve public policy.[2] In September 2017, the commission issued its final report; among its recommendations is a recommendation to Congress and the president to create the National Secure Data Service "to facilitate data access for evidence building while ensuring transparency and privacy" (Commission on Evidence-Based Policymaking 2017, 40). There have also been significant national efforts to link researchers to policy-makers through the use of administrative data, such as the Actionable Intelligence for Social Policy (AISP) initiative (Culhane et al., this volume; see also AISP 2017).

However, while the use of administrative data for purposes described in the articles in this volume has increased, the use of such data has not necessarily been maximized; nor does it mean that there is a consensus on whether the benefits from using different types of administrative data outweigh their costs, primarily because of concerns over improper use and intrusions into privacy.

One barrier to the use of administrative data is "the law." This barrier can be articulated in different ways, from "the law won't let me share information" to "the law will punish me if I share information" to "the law is too complicated to figure out how to share information." There are situations in which each of these may be true, but too often "the law" becomes the default rationale for permitting little or no use of administrative data. The law does not exist in a vacuum, however, so before moving to the different issues raised when specifically considering the law and administrative data, I consider a number of contextual factors that influence how we think about law.

Contextual Factors That Influence Opinions Regarding "the Law" and Administrative Data

Culture

Factors other than the text of the law create the context in which legal interpretation occurs. One such factor is culture. Cultural barriers may be organizational. Amy O'Hara (this volume) observes, "It is not typically an actual legal barrier that curtails sharing and access. Rather, there are perceived legal barriers and actual financial constraints limiting progress." She includes among cultural factors the long tradition in government agencies of not sharing administrative data and their reluctance to begin to do so. This reticence may be reinforced by political calculation—sharing administrative data within government or beyond government may reveal that government is not performing well. It is better not to provide the public with information that "could be used against us." Some governments may withhold information and data from public disclosure even when the law seems to clearly mandate release, a phenomenon that exists in many countries even as more nations adopt formal freedom of information laws (Banisar 2006).

Distrust of government. Beyond organizational culture and history, there are other larger cultural factors at play that can have an impact on the ability of policy-makers to gather or use data. One is the ingrained and growing distrust of government. The Pew Research Center conducted a survey a year before the 2016 presidential election and found that only 19 percent of respondents said that they could trust the government always or most of the time, a figure Pew reported was among the lowest levels of trust in the prior half century (Pew Research Center 2015). Just as government may not wish to release information to the public, a growing number of citizens may wish to withhold information from the government. This widespread distrust and its causes need not be belabored here, but it creates concerns over using administrative data derived from individually identifiable information. The widespread hacking of governmental and private business databases has undoubtedly exacerbated this distrust. A hack of U.S. government databases in 2014 exposed personal information, including information about security clearances of 22.1 million people (Nakashima 2015), a story that at the time seemed shocking but that has been dwarfed by subsequent stories about Russian efforts to hack voting machines and the massive intrusion into personal records in the breach of Equifax security, which may have affected 143 million people in the United States (Bernard et al. 2017). Blogs now exist to keep track of data breaches. These blogs provide a common good in informing the public about intrusions into data, but they may also reinforce distrust of those institutions and organizations that collect individual data.[3]

Privacy. Another cultural factor is the principle of privacy. However widely debated the meaning and application of privacy are in political and legal spheres, privacy has deep value in American life. Privacy as a legal concept evolved primarily as a means of limiting government control of or intrusion into the autonomy of the individual, particularly though not exclusively in sexual matters (for an early and a more recent review, see Rubenfeld [1989] and Siegel [2015]). But it also is a principle that influences individual and group attitudes about the use of data, and it is increasingly recognized that individual concerns over invasion of privacy unrelated to law are relevant to whether individuals (and by extension the broader public) are even willing to share information that might generate administrative datasets (Phelps, Nowak, and Ferrell 2000). The desire to keep private information *confidential* is also a critical issue: "confidentiality" as used here refers to the legal duty of an entity holding or with access to information about individuals to ensure that information is not available to other parties except when permitted or mandated by law. When confidentiality is breached, it can have a significant impact on public trust.

Technological evolution

Another important contextual factor is the technological evolution that has made collecting, storing, and mining enormous amounts of individual data possible. Because the broader discussion about privacy and confidentiality is often informed by the latest news over hacking and the compromise of data held in massive electronic databases, technology is often seen as a massive threat to privacy. Too often, discussions regarding the question, "Does the law let administrative data be shared?" occur without reference to advances in technology that can allay concerns over privacy and confidentiality. However, Garfinkel (this volume), while noting the many ways in which individual information can be inappropriately accessed, concludes that advances in technology and research methods will make it possible for researchers to access millions of records from multiple databases while ensuring the security of those records. He concludes, "computer science is up to the task, with a wide range of techniques that have been developed over the past decade that can protect data while unlocking its potential" (see also Szalay [this volume] for a discussion of emerging technology). These developments may provide the basis for thinking more broadly about the application of law.

Beyond Culture: Are There Ways in Which Law Does Create Barriers to the Use of Administrative Data?

While law can be misinterpreted, misunderstood, and used as the default excuse by those who simply do not wish to share data, it would be naïve to pretend that law did not create any practical barriers to the use of administrative data. These barriers stem in part from the law itself and in part from the complexities of knitting together the legal framework necessary to permit the sharing and use of administrative data in a secure manner.

Complexity of the law

One barrier to the use and integration of administration data is simply the complexity of the multiple laws that affect data use and integration. In a 2016 white paper (OMB 2016), the OMB noted the "patchwork nature" of the various federal and state laws that govern the use of administrative data. The OMB's characterization of the "state of the law" is worth quoting at some length:

Various federal and state laws govern the use of administrative data in the U.S. on a program-by-program basis. In some cases, statutes authorizing programs permit use of administrative data for only a narrowly prescribed purpose that does not include evidence-building activities. Other authorizing statutes prohibit the development of certain datasets. More often, the patchwork nature of these statutes at both the state and federal level inadvertently makes matching administrative data and survey data impractical or impossible. (OMB 2016, 1)

One of the reasons the law in this area is so complicated is because there is so much of it from different sources and from different eras. If the use of administrative data were simply governed by federal law, the complexities of the legal landscape might be softened, or if each state had only its own statutory scheme, differences in the treatment of administrative data could be reconciled within the state. However, federalism plays a significant role in shaping the legal parameters in which data may or may not be shared, with both federal and state governments having the authority to enact rules for some types of activities that generate vast amounts of data. An excellent example of the impact of federalism can be found in the myriad federal and state laws governing the confidentiality (and therefore use) of information generated in health care. The Health Insurance Portability and Accountability Act (HIPAA) of 1996 and the body of administrative regulations establishing federal rules governing protected health information, which became effective in 2005, did not create rules that all states must follow. Rather, the standards established by HIPAA create a floor for protecting health information, which the states may exceed—if state law is *more* protective of privacy than the federal law, then the state law prevails.

This can create practical difficulties in determining whether state or federal law is more protective. For example, in the 1999 report of the Surgeon General on mental health, written as various federal proposals to protect health information were being considered, one can find this passage:

Determining whether a state's mental health law provides more or less protection than a national standard may be difficult in at least some cases. For example, in one state, the law permits disclosures without consent to some but not all types of providers. One of the proposals to establish a national standard would permit disclosures to be made to other providers without the consent of the individual, but would give the individual the opportunity to "opt out" of disclosures to specified providers. In this example, it is difficult to determine whether the state law in question is more or less protective than the proposed national standard. On the one hand, the state law in this example is more restrictive than the reform proposal because it limits the types of providers that can receive information without consent. On the other hand, it is weaker than the reform proposal because it does not provide the individual with an opportunity to decline permission to disclose to those providers. (U.S. Department of Health and Human Services 1999)

The HIPAA rules that were eventually enacted did create this analytic dilemma. These problems are not insurmountable, but they require extensive legal analysis, the capacity for which is lacking in many jurisdictions. The problem is exacerbated in providing treatment to people with mental or other health problems and a substance abuse disorder because federal regulations enacted in 1987 create strict provisions for protecting the confidentiality of substance use and alcohol treatment information, which are inconsistent with HIPAA and with most state health laws. As a result, a health provider that operates a treatment program for substance use within a larger health system may have to contend with and apply at least three different sets of legal rules, including HIPAA, state confidentiality law, and separate rules for substance use. If any patients are HIV positive then a fourth section of law becomes relevant, as most states have separate legal rules governing the privacy and confidentiality of information regarding HIV status.

These are not just complications of clinical care, of course. Data generated by health care transactions are critically important for developing, implementing, and assessing health policy, and the myriad laws on the circumstances under which such information can be disclosed will shape the use of such data. In addition, the hodgepodge of rules can create gaps in privacy protection, exacerbating public distrust of the use of data (Hodge 2012).

Interpretation of the law

In its 2016 white paper, the OMB noted that the "ambiguity, or lack of explicit authority [to use data], can lead to a variety of interpretations about permitted uses, ranging from conservative conclusions that a particular use is not allowable to the establishment of conflicting requirements" (p.1). Federal and state agencies wish to avoid liability and public embarrassment. This risk averseness is often understandable, is not restricted to public agencies, and is as much a function of organizational culture as it is a function of articulated strategies for identifying and minimizing risks (Bozeman and Kingsley 1998). If law is ambiguous, or subject to multiple interpretations, it is not surprising that agency counsel (and their clients) may retreat to the most conservative stance possible. In an environment lately dominated by stories about the hacking of secure databases, and given the imperative to protect privacy, it is easy to understand why some jurisdictions may ask, "Why run the risk?" even if the severity of the risk has not been assessed.

The law simply prohibits certain uses

While most applicable laws permit at least some disclosure of administrative data, some laws simply do not permit the creation or use of databases that would provide good administrative data for more than the most limited purposes. For example, the impact of investments in workforce development is a major economic issue. Data exist to study the issue, particularly at a state level (Hollenbeck and Huang 2017). However, the federal Workforce Investment Act (WIA) cannot be used to create a "national database of personally identifiable information unless it is for program management activities."[4] Whether a national database for purposes beyond program management activities would be valuable is a separate question, but once a federal or state law imposes strict prohibitions on the use of data, it is difficult to reverse or modify those prohibitions.

Many jurisdictions lack the legal and related capacity to fully analyze and address critical issues in the use of administrative data

There are multiple issues that must be addressed to responsibly use administrative data, from creating a governance structure to ensuring that data in fact can be integrated into legal analyses necessary to ensure that the law is being applied appropriately. This requires a set of technical skills and capacity that government sometimes simply lacks.

A 2011 analysis (Johnson, Oliff, and Williams 2011) found that beginning in 2008, when the impact of the Great Recession was being sharply felt, forty-six states and the District of Columbia made sharp cuts to state services. While not all states cut every service, the majority of states made cuts to health care, to education, and to services for the elderly and disabled. These reductions resulted in the elimination of more than 400,000 state government jobs during the same period, and not all those jobs have been restored. The sectors in which cuts occurred (social services, education, health) are sectors that generate an enormous amount of administrative data. However, if the workforce that administers these programs is under pressure because of layoffs, pay freezes, or other factors, it is unlikely that responding to requests for administrative data will be a high priority. Nor is it likely that as workforces are being reduced, states will invest heavily in the technical capacity required to make the use of administrative data possible.

Legal expertise is essential as agencies interpret requests for administrative data. However, attorneys are not immune from state or federal workforce reductions; nor are they immune from other economic realities. It is often difficult for government to compete for the type of highly specialized expertise (attorneys, data scientists) necessary to make the use of integrated administrative data a reality. While it is difficult for a variety of reasons to precisely measure the differences in salary between public and private sector attorneys, a 2014 study estimated that on average lawyers for public agencies make 50 percent less than those in private practice, with the differential being much greater for lawyers considered the most qualified (Winston, Karpilow, and Burk 2014).

Pay of course is not the only issue, nor necessarily the most important one. There are many highly qualified attorneys in federal, state, and local government who are motivated by public service. Another issue is a lack of focus on these issues in law school curricula; most law students learn little about the issues involved in handling the complex analyses and related work (creation of a governance structure, creation of data use agreements, and so on) that are required for administrative data integration. Yet another issue may be how "government" utilizes its attorneys on a matter as complicated as integrating data across government agencies. Attorneys may be brought into discussions simply as technicians late in the process and, as a result, may lack understanding of the political, technological, and governance dimensions of a data integration project. A recent description of Illinois' success in creating data sharing agreements across multiple state agencies suggests that the state's chief information officer was able to successfully accomplish an important objective of the governor in part by making the various state agency attorneys a part of the process from the beginning (Goldsmith 2017). Occasionally, of course, key lawyers may simply lack expertise, or be temperamentally averse to virtually any risk, and so may become a hindrance to the type of granular legal analysis necessary to create the legal framework for sharing and using administrative data for policy purposes.

Thinking Systemically about Law as a Tool Rather than a Barrier

The discussion above identifies several issues affecting the use of law, including cultural and political factors, ambiguity in law, and insufficient technical expertise. The remainder of the article reflects on strategies, some practical, some perhaps quixotic, for addressing each issue.

Cultural issues and the need to reconcile competing versions of the "truth" about administrative data

Some of the issues characterized as cultural above can be resolved. For example, leadership can change organizational culture. Other issues, however, such as the distrust of government and other institutions appear to be part of the landscape for the foreseeable future.

Is there a path forward? One issue that can be addressed is the dichotomous, all-or-nothing way in which concerns regarding the use of data are sometimes articulated: data can/cannot, should/should not be used because privacy will/will not be respected, data will/will not be used appropriately, and law does/does not permit such use to occur. Whichever side of these conflicting views is dominant in a jurisdiction (and the dominating view may be a function of organizational culture) may drive legal analysis down a particular path.

It should be obvious, however, that thinking about these issues in dichotomous, either/or terms can have a detrimental impact on application of the law; as noted earlier, ambiguities and conflicting legal rules create a strong foundation for retreating to the most conservative legal posture possible. Conversely, a jurisdiction eager to use administrative data as expansively as possible may give short shrift to legitimate fears about abuses of privacy and other social goods.

It may be useful, then, to use a framework for the legal issues in data sharing that can explicitly identify, address, and attempt to accommodate these different world views. One potential framework that might be considered as a systemic improvement to considering application of the law is "privacy by design" (Cavoukian 2011).[5] Such an approach ensures that privacy issues are identified and considered as part of the process of designing the administrative data use effort, rather than being treated as barriers to those efforts or issues to be nodded at rhetorically but not considered systematically. For example, Cavoukian (2011) asserts that privacy concerns must be considered proactively rather than reactively and that privacy is embedded in the structure and processes by which information about individuals may be used by others. As Professor Stranburg has noted, such an approach "attempts the *joint* maximization of the social benefits of all relevant values. Taking privacy-related concerns into account during the design of a data use program prevents zero-sum thinking and minimizes the need for after-the-fact patches for privacy problems associated with a data use program."[6]

A policy-maker or politician with interest in the use of administrative data can shape legal interpretation of ambiguous laws

Explicit interest in data sharing from a politically important person or entity can help to shape the way in which legal issues are resolved. Political will focused on sharing data can cause a lawyer tasked with working on these issues to look for opportunities presented by the applicable laws rather than exercising undue caution at every point where discretion can be used. For example, the OMB directives were an important political statement about the need for federal agencies to use data to achieve evidence-based policy.

Political champions also exist at the state and county levels. For example, the National Governors Association (NGA) is a bipartisan organization for the nation's governors. In 2016, the NGA published a paper titled "Improving Human Services Programs and Outcomes through Shared Data" (NGA 2016). This is an excellent paper that summarizes the case for data sharing, discusses the importance of balancing data sharing with privacy, and notes the practical difficulties in doing this. The NGA acknowledges that internal opposition may exist but asserts that governors can serve as an important corrective:

> Program staff may be trained that laws such as HIPAA and FERPA prohibit any data sharing. General counsel, which may not know the ins and outs of those and other privacy laws, may adopt a risk adverse stance and advise against data sharing. As with the public, governors can overcome some of that opposition by emphasizing the value of data sharing, with the measures taken to protect privacy. (NGA 2016, 10)

Similarly, the National Association of Counties (NACo, n.d) maintains websites on data sharing, with specific examples from counties across the United States that have moved forward with data sharing arrangements. Given that the economic burden on counties administering government programs for people in poverty and other conditions is so significant, one can assume NACo, like the NGA, will increasingly focus on data integration and analysis as a fundamental policy tool. Funding that would strategically link the NGA, NACo, and like-minded organizations to individuals and entities with technological, legal and related expertise could help to move the political conversation about administrative data use to practical solutions.

Developing needed legal expertise and resources

One of the legal barriers to the use of administrative data is the lack of sufficient legal expertise to address these issues. Few law students learn more than the rudiments of confidentiality and privacy, and even fewer learn about the technological advances that undergird the revolution in big data. As a result, very few lawyers have been formally trained in or have experience with the legal, cultural, and technological issues flowing from confidentiality and privacy law and those who have will have well paid opportunities in the private sector. But this is beginning to change as law schools develop curricula and programs to create legal expertise that tech firms and others need. Examples of such schools include but are not limited to the Center for Internet and Society at Stanford Law School,[7] the Information Law Institute at New York University Law School,[8] and the High Tech Law Institute at Santa Clara.[9] A list of schools including law schools with privacy curricula is maintained at the website of the International Association of Privacy Professionals.[10]

There are other efforts to fill the gap in legal expertise beyond the development of law school programs. For example, the Laura and John Arnold Foundation is funding an effort through the AISP initiative led by Dennis Culhane at the University of Pennsylvania to create toolkits (model data sharing agreements, for example) to provide lawyers with resources that can be used so that a lawyer new to the field does not have to do everything on his or her own. These toolkits are publicly available at the AISP website.[11] Expansion of these efforts, perhaps leveraging the interest of NGA and NACo, to create additional toolkits and rosters of attorneys with expertise in this area could fill in the gaps in legal expertise that exist in the public sector currently. If legal expertise does not increase, efforts to integrate data will continue to flounder on well-meaning but often misplaced (and sometimes incorrect) interpretations of law.

Enabling comprehensive analyses of existing laws in a holistic manner

While it is possible for skilled lawyers to work through the network of sometimes-conflicting laws that have to be negotiated to create a legally sound framework for sharing data, the legal landscape is far more complex than it needs to be. This is primarily because laws designed to protect privacy and create ground rules for disclosure of data were written for specific purposes and (in most cases) were written long before the explosion of technology that has made the mining of large datasets possible. As noted earlier, there are federal and state laws that affect health information, but there are also separate laws for information on people who are homeless, on workforce incentives, on welfare programs, on education, on justice-related issues, and on nearly every other service that government provides.

There have been efforts to amend existing laws to make data more available,[12] but those efforts, like most of the law in this area, focus on specific types of data in specific types of situations. There is no national strategy, or many examples of state strategies, to review and analyze laws affecting data sharing comprehensively and systematically.[13] Such an analysis undoubtedly would reveal a number of barriers in statutory law that could be addressed comparatively easily; more importantly, such an analysis could lead to the creation of a rational, overarching statutory and regulatory framework that permits enough sharing and integration of data to accomplish important governmental objectives while ensuring the protection of individual privacy.

Some important granular issues

In addition to the systemic approaches just laid out, a jurisdiction may find it easier to get to the legal outcome it wants by approaching data sharing as an enterprise that requires planning, developing structure, and analyzing legal issues within this larger structural approach. The resources developed by AISP provide a guide to such an approach, as do theoretical frameworks such as Privacy by Design.

First, it is essential that those interested in using data do adequate developmental work. A number of questions should be addressed before considering whether there are legal issues that are relevant. Examples of important issues to address at least in a preliminary manner include the following:

- Who are the individuals/organizations that have an interest in the use of data? This is an important threshold question that is more difficult to resolve than might appear at first blush: Is there a single agency that wishes to be more opportunistic about the use of its own data, or are there multiple agencies that wish to integrate data? And which agencies or organizations might find this objectionable?
- What specific questions or types of questions does the group wish to address? Is there a question, for example, that the state legislature or county commission wants answered? That creates a very different scenario than a desire to integrate data to assess the outcome of a major policy initiative such as reducing admissions to the tax supported hospital emergency department.
- How quickly would the group like to address these questions? The integration of administrative data involves politics, law, technology, and the marshaling of often-scarce resources. Whatever the goal of the initiative, it will take longer than anticipated, and so time necessary for expert legal analysis must be realistically allocated as well.
- What types of data sources would or might provide a resource to address the question(s)? Are these data available? Are there administrative barriers to access? Technological barriers to access?
- If the data are available, does the group have the knowledge to know what types of capacity (human and otherwise) might be necessary to integrate and analyze the data?
- What would success look like?
- Are there actual or perceived legal barriers to doing any of this?

These questions, developed more clearly elsewhere (AISP 2017; Ostrom 2011),[14] are simply a framework to provide initial clarity on goals, outcomes, resources, and potential barriers before filtering the results through the law. If an inexperienced or overly cautious lawyer is involved in discussions about data sharing without a framework established by the potential users and sources of such data, the discussions are likely to end with resignation over how the law has yet again defeated efforts at making good policy.

In addition, while lawyers need to be involved early in the process (though what that means will vary depending on the lawyer) and need to understand what their clients are attempting to do, legal objections should not be permitted to end discussions unless a section of law specifically prohibits a proposed action. The role of lawyers in this context (as in most settings) is to find ways to maximize the use of administrative data consistent with available legal exceptions and tools, not to use exaggerated concerns regarding legal risk to derail discussions before they get off the ground. Frameworks such as privacy by design may help to ensure the parties that all important issues are being addressed as part of the process; this is why lawyers should be aware of the advances in technology and analytic methods highlighted in other articles in this volume that can help to ensure the security of data and individual privacy interests even as millions of individual records are analyzed.

Summary

"The law" is too often viewed as an impenetrable barrier to information sharing. This reflects misunderstanding of various laws, a lack of legal expertise, and a failure to leverage possible political support that inevitably would affect the manner in which lawyers approach these issues. The emerging political consensus on the importance of the use of administrative data, the growing interest among funders, and the early efforts to create resources for lawyers working in this field together provide a foundation for a fundamental shift in attitude about and use of the law so that it becomes an essential tool rather than a barrier to information sharing and data integration.

Notes

1. The use of administrative data to inform research germane to policy development is not a new issue. For a very good discussion, see Hotz et al. (1998).

2. The explicit goal of the Evidence-Based Policymaking Commission Act of 2016 (HR 1831), which passed with bipartisan support and was signed by President Obama, is to "focus on the most basic pre-requisite for evidence-based policy: good data." See http://www.urban.org/urban-wire/everything-you-need-know-about-commission-evidence-based-policymaking. The bill creates a fifteen-person commission to review federal data sources and make recommendations on the optimal structures for data integration, data security, and use of integrated data for "program evaluation, continuous improvement, policy-relevant research, and cost-benefit analyses." At the state level, the National Conference of State Legislatures has made opening government data for public use, including in combined (that is, integrated) fashion, a priority. The conference maintains a website devoted specifically to this topic, which among other things provides links to state legislation addressing the issue. See http://www.ncsl.org/research/telecommunications-and-information-technology/open-data-legislation .aspx.

3. These data breaches and the hundreds of millions of people potentially affected are by now almost too numerous to count. One recent summary can be found here: https://www.identityforce.com/blog/2017-data-breaches (accessed 31 May 2017).

4. Workforce Investment Act, sec. 504(b).

5. I am grateful to Professor Katherine Jo Strandburg, Alfred B. Engelberg Professor of Law, NYU Law School, for her suggestion in reviewing earlier drafts of this article that "privacy by design" has a significant role to play in setting the stage for more granular analysis of legal issues that must be done for the successful use of administrative data.

6. Personal communication, Professor Katherine Strandburg, January 3, 2017.

7. See http://cyberlaw.stanford.edu.

8. See http://www.law.nyu.edu/centers/ili.

9. See http://law.scu.edu/hightech/.

10. See https://iapp.org/resources/article/colleges-with-privacy-curricula/.

11. See https://www.aisp.upenn.edu.

12. A notable recent example was the 2012 amendments to the regulations that implement the Family Educational Rights and Privacy Act (FERPA). The regulations were amended to facilitate expanded use of student information to evaluate the effectiveness of publicly funded educational programs. The new regulations are at 34 Code of Federal Regulations (CFR) Part 99. For an overview, see Fuller and Walker (2013). In addition, the U.S. Department of Health and Human Services in January 2017 announced a new rule designed to make alcohol and substance abuse treatment records more available to researchers, among other changes. A summary of the provisions and a link to the full regulation can be found at https://www.samhsa.gov/newsroom/press-announcements/201701131200.

13. There are recent examples of efforts to comprehensively analyze the interplay between federal and state law, in the preemption analyses conducted after enactment of HIPAA. Because HIPAA set a minimum standard for the confidentiality of protected health information, with more protective state laws applying to particular situations, analyses were conducted in at least some jurisdictions to determine whether state or federal law applied to particular types of transactions. For one of many discussions, see Guthrie (2003).

14. Elinor Ostrom's work on institutional analysis and framework development is often cited. While her work is more conceptual than policy-makers often like, she poses a set of practical questions that can be applied to the creation of a governance structure for sharing administrative data. For example, she suggests thinking about questions like these before proceeding with analysis of a policy question: Who are the actors? What positions exist on a question? What actions are available to the group and individual decision-makers? What are the potential outcomes of those actions? What level of control exists over the choices to be made? What information is available to make decisions? And what are the costs and benefits of the actions and outcomes that are taken? (Ostrom 2011, 12).

References

Actionable Intelligence for Social Policy. March 2017. IDS governance: Setting up for ethical and effective use. Actionable Intelligence for Social Policy expert panel report. Available from https://www.aisp.upenn.edu/wp-content/uploads/2016/07/Governance.pdf (accessed 3 June 2017).

Banisar, David. 2006. Freedom of information around the world 2006: A global survey of access to government information laws. *Privacy International*, Article 19. Available from https://papers.ssrn.com/sol3/papers.cfm?abstract_id=1707336.

Bernard, Tara Siegel, Tiffany Hsu, Nicole Perlroth, and Ron Lieber. 7 September 2017. Equifax says cyberattack may have affected 143 million in the U.S. *New York Times*.

Bozeman, Barry, and Gordon Kingsley. 1998. Risk culture in public and private organizations. *Public Administration Review* 58 (2): 109–18.

Cavoukian, Ann. 2011. *Privacy by design. The 7 foundational principles*. Available from https://iab.org/wp-content/IAB-uploads/2011/03/fred_carter.pdf (accessed on 3 June 2017).

Commission on Evidence-Based Policymaking. 2017. *The promise of evidence-based policymaking: Report of the Commission on Evidence-Based Policymaking*. Washington DC: Commission on Evidence-Based Policymaking.

Connelly, Roxanne, Christopher J. Playford, Vernon Gayle, and Chris Dibben. 2016. The role of administrative data in the big data revolution in social science research. *Social Science Research* 59:1–12.

Culhane, Dennis, John Fantuzzo, Matthew Hill, and T.C. Burnett. 2018. Maximizing the use of integrated data systems: Understanding the challenges and advancing solutions. *The ANNALS of the American Academy of Political and Social Science* (this volume).

Fuller, Mathew, and Daniel Walker. 2013. Acts influencing how higher education handles information. *Journal of Higher Education Management* 28:26–40.

Garfinkel, Simson L. 2018. Privacy and security concerns when social scientists work with administrative and operational data. *The ANNALS of the American Academy of Political and Social Science* (this volume).

Goerge, Robert M. 2018. Barriers to accessing state data and approaches to addressing them. *The ANNALS of the American Academy of Political and Social Science* (this volume).

Goldsmith, Stephen. 23 February 2017. How Illinois' CIO got buy-in for the state's data sharing agreement. *Government Technology*. Available from http://www.govtech.com.

Guthrie, Jennifer. 2003. Time is running out—The burdens and challenges of HIPAA compliance: A look at preemption analysis, the "minimum necessary" standard, and the notice of privacy practices. *Annals of Health Law* 12:143–77.

Hodge, James. 2012. National health information privacy and the new federalism. *Notre Dame Journal of Law, Ethics & Public Policy* 14:791–820.

Hollenbeck, Kevin, and Wei-Jang Huang. 2017. Net impact and benefit-cost estimates of the workforce development system in Washington State. *Employment Research* 24 (1): 1–4.

Hotz, V. Joseph, Robert Goerge, Julie Balzekas, and Francis Margolin, eds. 1998. Administrative data for policy-relevant research: Assessment of current utility and recommendations for development. A report of the panel on research uses of administrative data of the Northwestern University/University of Chicago Joint Center for Poverty Research. Available from http://public.econ.duke.edu/~vjh3/working_papers/adm_data.pdf.

Johnson, Nicholas, Phil Oliff, and Erica Williams. 2011. *An update on state budget cuts*. Washington, DC: Center on Budget and Policy Priorities. Available from http://www.cbpp.org/sites/default/files/atoms/files/3-13-08sfp.pdf (accessed on 3 June 2017).

Liebman, Jeffrey B. 2018. Using data to more rapidly address difficult U.S. social problems. *The ANNALS of the American Academy of Political and Social Science* (this volume).

McNabb, Jennifer, David Timmons, Jae Song, and Carolyn Puckett. 2009. Use of administrative data at the Social Security Administration. *Social Security Bulletin* 69 (1): 75–84.

Murray, Charles. 1984/2015. *Losing ground: American social policy, 1950–1980*. New York, NY: Basic Books.

Nakashima, Ellen. 9 July 2015. Hacks of OPM databases compromised 22.1 million people, federal authorities say. *Washington Post*.

National Association of Counties. n.d. *Using and sharing data*. Available from http://www.naco.org/resources/index/using-and-sharing-data (accessed on 3 June 2017).

National Governors Association. 2016. *Improving human services programs and outcomes through shared data*. Available from https://www.nga.org/files/live/sites/NGA/files/pdf/2016/1609ImprovingHumanServicesSharedData.pdf (accessed on 2 June 2017).

Office of Management and Budget. 26 July 2013. *Memorandum to the heads of departments and agencies: Next steps in the evidence and innovation agenda*. Available from https://obamawhitehouse.archives.gov/sites/default/files/omb/memoranda/2013/m-13-17.pdf (accessed 2 June 2017).

Office of Management and Budget. 15 July 2016. *Barriers to using administrative data for evidence building*. Available from https://obamawhitehouse.archives.gov/sites/default/files/omb/mgmt-gpra/barriers_to_using_administrative_data_for_evidence_building.pdf.

O'Hara, Amy, and Carla Medalia. 2018. Data sharing the federal statistical system: Impediments and possibilities. *The ANNALS of the American Academy of Political and Social Science* (this volume).

Ostrom, Elinor. 2011. Background on the institutional analysis and development framework. *Policies Studies Journal* 39:7–27.

Pew Research Center. 2015. *Beyond distrust: How Americans view their government*. Washington, DC: Pew Research Center. Available from http://www.people-press.org/2015/11/23/beyond-distrust-how-americans-view-their-government/ (accessed 17 October 2017).

Phelps, Joseph, Glen Nowak, and Elizabeth Ferrell. 2000. Privacy concerns and consumer willingness to provide personal information. *Journal of Public Policy & Marketing* 19:27–41.

Rubenfeld, Jed. 1989. The right of privacy. *Harvard Law Review* 102:737–807.

Siegel, Reva B. 2015. How conflict entrenched the right to privacy. *Yale Law Journal Forum* 124:316–23.

Szalay, Alexander S. 2018. From SkyServer to SciServer. *The ANNALS of the American Academy of Political and Social Science* (this volume).

U.S. Department of Health and Human Services. 1999. *Mental health: A report of the surgeon general.* Rockville, MD: U.S. Department of Health and Human Services, Substance Abuse and Mental Health Services Administration, Center for Mental Health Services, National Institutes of Health, National Institute of Mental Health.

Winston, Clifford, Quentin Karpilow, and David Burk. 2014. Lawyers' self-selection to work in the public or private sector: Is government performance affected? University of Chicago Department of Economics Research Paper. Available from http://repository.law.umich.edu/alumni_survey_scholarship/27 (accessed 2 June 2017).

Privacy and Security Concerns When Social Scientists Work with Administrative and Operational Data

Social science research is transitioning from working with "designated data," collected through experiments and surveys, to working with "organic data," including administrative data not collected for research purposes, and other data such as those collected from online social networks and large-scale sensor networks. The shift to organic data requires significant innovations in research methodologies. This article reviews the complexities and diversity of organic data and the special efforts that must be undertaken to make those data findable and usable by researchers. In some cases, advanced formal privacy techniques such as differential privacy and secure multiparty computation are needed to work with organic data in a manner that is ethically and logistically permissible, and effort is also required to make studies involving organic data transparent and replicable. These considerations make clear that moving forward, social scientists and information and communications technology (ICT) professionals must work closely to develop appropriate technical controls and ethical frameworks that minimize the risks of research to participants and to society at large.

Keywords: privacy; cryptography; multiparty computation; provenance

L arge-scale information and communications technology (ICT) systems have created voluminous new data on human behavior and interactions, creating heretofore untold opportunities for social science research. Realizing the research potential of these data requires new and stronger partnerships between social scientists and computer scientists. In some cases, social scientists can take advantage of off-the-self technology that has been developed over the past decade and is

Simson L. Garfinkel holds seven U.S. patents and has published research articles and books in computer security and digital forensics, including Database Nation: The Death of Privacy in the 21st Century *(O'Reilly Media 2001). He is an ACM fellow, an IEEE senior member, and a member of the National Association of Science Writers.*

Correspondence: simsong@acm.org

By
SIMSON L. GARFINKEL

DOI: 10.1177/0002716217737267

ready to be deployed. In others, social scientists can work with computer scientists to deploy approaches that have been demonstrated in the lab but still require significant engineering and customization before they can be used more broadly.

The Potential of Organic Data

For nearly a century, social scientists have worked with data from surveys and government statistical agencies. These data were typically collected under a promise of confidentiality—sometimes mandated by law and subject to disclosure limitation (for information on statistical disclosure limitation within the U.S. government, see Federal Committee on Statistical Methodology 2005).

Today, social scientists are supplementing these traditional "designated data" (also called "made data") with "organic data" (also called "found data"), such as administrative records and operational data that are generated in our increasingly digitized society (Groves 2011). Organic data are plentiful and create exciting new research possibilities, but they may also pose challenges in the fairness and accuracy of research that uses them. That's because organic data may contain unknown biases not present in designated data, and may fail to represent various vulnerable populations. And while organic data opens up a potential for important new research projects and evidence-based policymaking the use of such data pose privacy and security challenges as well (Lane et al. 2014; Groves and Harris-Kojetin 2017).

One of the premiere examples of organic data used for statistical purposes is the Longitudinal Employer-Household Dynamics (LEHD) Program, operated by the U.S. Census Bureau. LEHD combines traditional census data products and surveys with administrative records about workers and employers to create high-resolution data products that were previously impossible to conceive.[1] The LEHD online tool OnTheMap,[2] for example, contains detailed information regarding commuting patterns of workers throughout the fifty states and the District of Columbia, allowing transportation planners to understand the source of traffic and congestion and to make accurate predictions about the impact of new transit options. Another online tool, OnTheMap for Emergency Management,[3] "shows potential impact on jobs/workers and population for hurricanes, tropical storms, fires, floods, snow and freezing rain probability and disaster declaration areas. Real-time geographic data of disaster events are automatically updated" (U.S. Census Bureau 2015).

There are also growing opportunities to use "operational data"—another kind of organic data. Operational data are the highly granular data that are used to operate systems. For example, whereas OnTheMap considers payroll tax data to infer where people work, commuting patterns could also be inferred with real-time trip data collected from electronic toll payment systems (e.g., E-ZPass; see Hill 2013) or Internet-enabled smart phones (see Yoon, Noble, and Liu 2007; Lv et al. 2014). Indeed, today operational data from E-ZPass and smart phones are collected and used on a large-scale basis to detect surface traffic flow patterns and display traffic on apps like Google Maps, but not (as far as we know) to create statistical products.

For policy-makers and those in the social sciences, there are several key differences between research with designated data and organic data:

- Organic data tend to be larger and more complex than designated data (Taylor, Schroeder, and Meyer 2014).
- Organic data have the appearance of better coverage, because the data are collected as part of program administration and people cannot opt out (Einav and Levin 2013). However, organic data may systematically miss certain populations, or may be edited by unknown processes before it reaches researchers. For this reason, the data accuracy may be illusionary.
- Because organic data might be collected covertly as part of a person's ordinary activities, such as performing Internet searches or driving around the city, handling and using organic data may require more attention to privacy issues than using designated data.
- Because of these privacy issues, there may be a greater need to remove identifiers in organic data. The process of removing identifiers and other identifying information is called "de-identification." De-identified data are not necessarily safe to publicly release, however, as de-identified data can be reidentified.
- Whereas designated data are created for statistical analysis, organic data are created for other purposes. Unlike designated data, "researchers generally have no input into the design, structure and content of administrative social science data" (R. Connelly et al. 2016, 4). As a result, organic data need to be carefully evaluated to see if they are suitable for the intended research and statistical purposes.
- Because they were not created for research, organic data may have errors and uncertainty that might be known to the primary users of the data, but are frequently not known to the secondary researchers. These "unknown unknowns" (Coakley 1992, 136; Oettinger 2001) can be different from traditional sources of error and uncertainty.

Because they are collected at large scale and for purposes other than scientific research, administrative and operational data can take researchers to places where they do not belong, giving them access to secrets that are outside the scope of legitimate scientific inquiry, crossing into the realm of the private or even the prurient. Administrative controls such as two-person review of queries and unforgeable audit logs can act as a deterrent against abuse by researchers.

Tools like OnTheMap show that important policy questions can be answered with carefully designed tools that use a combination of designated data (surveys) and organic data (tax records). OnTheMap demonstrates that these data products can be generated in a way that preserve confidentiality. (In the case of OnTheMap, personal privacy is protected through the infusion of dynamically consistent noise so that the individual contributions of a specific person or company to data cannot be discerned [Machanavajjhala et al. 2008].)

OnTheMap also shows that efforts to use organic data by social scientists need to address several key issues:

1. Administrative and operational datasets will frequently contain some kind of identifiers. As a result, there frequently needs to be some way to de-identify the data before they are released to researchers.
2. Data confidentiality must be protected, even as the data are made more widely available.
3. Data provenance must be tracked.
4. Researchers should consider advanced techniques for privacy-preserving data processing, such as secure multiparty computation.
5. Because it is a short walk from collecting data on a large number of people to collecting data after minor interventions, social science researchers should acquaint themselves with existing ethical frameworks for working with human subjects and emerging norms for experimentation that involves people using computing systems.

The Challenge of De-Identification

Ethical and logistical complications can arise when working with organic data. For example, there may be more privacy concerns, because people tend to edit themselves when filling out a survey—facts that might be included in the data dump of an operational system. Unlike designated data, data subjects generally have not been given notice that their data will be used for research, and they have not given their consent to be involved in research studies.

The lack of informed consent poses a problem for researchers in the United States, who are operating with federal funding. Such researchers are covered under the Common Rule,[4] which requires that research involving human subjects (or identifiable private data about humans) be approved by an accredited Institutional Review Board (IRB), and that they give informed consent. Although IRBs can waive the informed consent provisions,[5] many researchers find it easier to de-identify organic data—that is, to remove the identifiers, so that the Common Rule does not apply.

Today many agencies practice de-identification. For example, the U.S. Department of Health and Human Services (HHS) Health Insurance Portability and Accountability Act (HIPAA) Privacy Rule[6] states that de-identified health information is not considered protected health information (PHI) and, as such, is not legally protected.[7] As a result, de-identified health information is widely used for both medical research and marketing. Likewise, the Family Educational Rights and Privacy Act (FERPA) specifically allows de-identified data to be "shared without the consent required by FERPA (34 Code of Federal Regulations [C.F.R.] §99.30) with any party for any purpose, including parents, general public, and researchers (34 C.F.R. §99.31(b)(1))" (Privacy Technology Assistance Center, U.S. Department of Education n.d.).

Most de-identification protocols require classifying the variables in a dataset as *direct identifiers* (such as names and phone numbers) that can directly identify a data subject; *indirect identifiers* or *quasi-identifiers* (such as a person's age or height) that can be used to narrow down a data subject from a set of possible subjects; and *nonidentifying sensitive values* (such as a person's diagnosis). Once the variables are classified, direct identifiers are removed and quasi-identifiers are manipulated so that individuals can no longer be reliably identified. This kind of de-identification protocol relies on assumptions about the background information available to a person attempting to reidentify records in a dataset.

In recent years, de-identification techniques have come under attack by computer science researchers, who have shown that many datasets that had been de-identified can be reidentified—that is, individual data records can be matched back up with the true identities (for a discussion of several high-profile attacks on de-identified datasets, see Garfinkel 2015).

As an alternative to releasing de-identified data, social scientists can create interactive query systems that allow limited access to data without risk of compromising the privacy of individuals within the dataset (McSherry 2009). Alternatively, data can be used to create synthetic datasets that preserve some relationships between variables while preventing the reidentification of specific individuals.

As social science researchers transition from working with "designated data" to "organic data," they need to partner with computer scientists to deploy new approaches for working with data in ways that provide protection appropriate to the sensitivity of these datasets. Fortunately, computer science is up to the task, with a wide range of techniques that have been developed over the past decade that can protect the confidentiality of data while unlocking its potential for use by researchers.

Key points

- De-identification protocols typically remove direct-identifiers and may manipulate quasi-identifiers.
- De-identified data can be reidentified.
- The risk of reidentification can be minimized through the use of formal privacy methods, such as interactive query systems for data access, or through the creation of synthetic datasets.

Keeping Data Confidential

In 1986, John Diebold, one of the pioneers of the computer age, explained how transactional data containing place and time information could become far more sensitive than first apparent. The case involved a bank that, in 1979, "had recently installed an automatic teller machine network and noticed that an unusual number of withdrawals were being made every night between midnight and 2:00

a.m.," Diebold wrote. "Suspecting foul play, the bank hired detectives to look into the matter. It turns out that many of the late-night customers were withdrawing cash on their way to a local red light district!" (Diebold 1986, 111). An article about the incident that appeared in the Knight News Service observed, "There's a bank someplace in America that knows which of its customers paid a hooker last night" (Diebold 1986, 111).

Diebold's story vividly demonstrated that administrative and operational data can pose challenges resulting from both sensitivity and scale when compared with traditional social science data. With traditional surveys and laboratory experiments, respondents who do not want to take part in a research project have many means for opting out—for example, by not filling out a survey, or by not answering specific questions. But when it comes to administrative and operational data, opting out is harder. It is unlikely that a person would opt out of using an automated teller in 1979 or a cell phone today to avoid participating in an economist's research project. This inability of opting out is one of the things that make these datasets so particularly attractive: they hold the appearance of both accuracy and completeness, something missing from traditional surveys. But the inability of opting out also means that researchers who have access to such data need to adopt strong controls for preserving data confidentiality, lest the researchers provoke a public backlash. (Researchers also need to realize that this appearance of accuracy and completeness is frequently an illusion, just as it was unlikely that every person withdrawing cash from that ATM in 1979 between midnight and 2:00 a.m. was visiting a prostitute.)

Countless news reports over the past two decades have shown that operational and administrative data are powerful magnets for computer hackers, criminals, and even espionage. As such, researchers have an obligation to protect the data using mechanisms that are appropriate to their sensitivity. Researchers who have been trained and become accustomed to working with publicly available datasets may require significant retraining and retooling before working with datasets containing sensitive information.

At a minimum, sensitive data should be stored on devices featuring full disk encryption to minimize the chance of data compromise when equipment is decommissioned and to protect against the risk of compromise in the event of equipment theft (Garfinkel and Shelat 2003). There should also be written, audited procedures to control devices that store data, including computers, hard drives, and portable storage media, to ensure that these devices are appropriately sanitized or physically destroyed when they are retired from service.

But encryption alone is insufficient to ensure the confidentiality of sensitive data. Sensitive data may become the target of organized hacking efforts by criminals, hacktivists, and even foreign governments. Motives for attack may include financial gain, the desire to embarrass the organization that provided the data, and obtaining information for attacking the data subjects themselves (see El Emam et al. 2011).[8]

To protect against these threats, researchers should use computers that run up-to-date operating systems, with up-to-date antivirus/antimalware systems installed, and researchers should have mandatory and ongoing cybersecurity training. Systems should be professionally managed, and should have network connections that are monitored by a competent entity, such as a security provider. Systems holding confidential data should be accessible only with two-factor authentication: that is, a system that requires both a password and a physical token or a biometric.

Some data may be so sensitive that they should only reside on systems that are physically disconnected from the Internet—for example, a standalone desktop or an "air-gapped" network. An air-gapped network might consist of a storage server and five or ten workstations connected to a gigabit switch. To copy software or data from the Internet to the private network, the data are burned onto a DVD. The DVD is then taken to a standalone computer where it is virus-scanned. If the scan is successful, the DVD is then taken to the air-gapped network and copied to the server. Removing information follows the same procedure in reverse. Clearly, building and maintaining an air-gapped network is complicated—and easy to get wrong (Byres 2013). Sadly, there are few resources available with step-by-step instructions for creating and maintaining such networks (Schneier 2013).[9]

A workable middle ground between networks that are full-connected to the Internet and air-gapped networks is to build a so-called secure enclave, in which the data reside on secure servers that can only be reached through audited, controlled mechanisms. A *physical secure enclave* might be a physical facility with locks, a guard, and computers that can reach the research data but not connect to the Internet. This is the approach that the Federal Statistical Research Data Centers and the NORC Data Enclave take. A *virtual secure enclave* might be a computer system that can only be reached by secure low-bandwidth interconnections. In either case, users can enter the secure enclave and run queries and see the results, but they cannot export the data until they have undergone some kind of review process, ideally one that is formally vetted by a disclosure review board. Untrusted users may even be prohibited from seeing the results of their queries until a formal review is completed.

Security techniques are also needed to protect data from the researchers themselves. Strong internal security measures can protect data subjects from inappropriate accesses to their data, and serve as a deterrent to help keep researchers on the correct side of proper ethical conduct. For example, column-level encryption locks some fields of the database to some users, preventing unrestricted access (e.g., Ge and Zdonik 2007).[10]

Properly implemented, encryption blocks inadvertent or unauthorized access to sensitive information, while not eliminating the possibility of having authorized individuals access the encrypted data using appropriate mechanisms. In general, access control technologies such as encryption force designers to think out and plan for what kind of access is needed in advance. Pilot studies, end-to-end tests, and "dress rehearsals" can help to identify unanticipated usability challenges that might impact data quality, such as the use of encrypted fields that makes it difficult to evaluate the quality of a database linkage.

Because of its richness and broad coverage, operational and administrative data can tempt individuals in ways that data collected for traditional statistical projects do not. For example, in 2013, *The Wall Street Journal* featured an article detailing how analysts at the National Security Agency used intelligence collection systems to spy on their own love interests (Gorman 2013; see also Peterson 2013). Similar abuses of official information systems occur at the state and local level: in 2012 Anne Marie Rasmusson, a former police officer, was awarded $1 million in her federal invasion-of-privacy lawsuit against the cities of Minneapolis and St. Paul, after 104 police offers illegally accessed her photo and other driver's license data (Zetter 2012; see also Lussenhop 2012).

Secure audit logs to detect inappropriate data searches and browsing (see, for example, Hartung 2016; Ma and Tsudik 2009). But care must be taken so that reasonable security measures do not inadvertently deter quality research. As Diebold's story demonstrates, sometimes the very artifacts that make data interesting also make data sensitive. Minor inconsistencies and variations can attract the attention of an inquisitive mind; drilling down reveals secrets: there needs to be a way for researchers to explore data, conduct spot checks, and look for potentially interesting artifacts, without setting off alarms and trashing careers.

Key points

- Administrative and operational data can contain information that is sensitive; unlike traditional social science data collected by surveys, there is no obvious way for members of the public to "opt out." As a result, there is a higher ethical obligation on researchers to keep such data confidential.
- Encryption can protect data from unauthorized access by individuals or organizations, and can be applied to a device (such as a laptop), a file (such as a database), or a specific column of a database.
- Data can also be compromised by malware and hostile outsiders. One way to prevent compromise is to confine data to computers that are never connected to the Internet, such as standalone computers or computers connected to an "air-gapped" network.
- Another way to protect data confidentiality is by placing a "data enclave" that has a limited connection to the Internet. There are many kinds of data enclaves. One kind has a limited connection that allows information such as queries and query results to move back-and-forth, but the connection does not allow entire datasets to be transferred.
- Sensitive data are subject to abuse. Administrative controls such as two-person checks and unforgeable query logs can act as a deterrent against insider abuse.

Data Curation and Data Provenance

To use organic data in ways that are both fair and accurate requires more than good security: it requires a principled approach to data management and data processing. Administrative and operational data can be messy. Data from production systems frequently contain format inconsistencies—errors that look like typos, for example. Depending on the data source, the inconsistencies may be actual typos, transmission errors, format changes over time, or even real data. Failure to handle such errors can result in systematic bias being introduced into the dataset, which may prime the unwary experimenter for false discovery.

The term *data curation* has emerged to describe the process of managing data through the data lifecycle. Data curation is widely seen as an important task in any organization that relies on data for operations, research, or policymaking.

For example, avoiding, detecting, and correcting errors requires careful attention to data specifications, formats, and changes in software versions. Thus, capturing information about processing software and runtime environments is an important aspect of data curation. (There are cases of commercial software behaving differently on different operating systems—and even behaving differently if the software is run in the summer, when daylight saving time is in effect, or in the winter, when it is not.)

An added complication is that the data curator might be mistaken and edit data that is thought to be erroneous, but which, in fact, is not. For these reasons, it is important to record both old and new values when editing.

By its very nature, operational data have the tendency to grow without limit. Researchers must decide what data to keep and what to discard. Uncomfortable when placed in the position of having to decide about data retention, some researchers punt and keep it all. Thus, data tend to increase over time. And because researchers need multiple copies of data to protect against operator error (Brown and Patterson n.d.) and silent data corruption, storage requirements tend to grow geometrically (for silent data corruption, see Narayan et al. 2009; Fiala et al. 2012; Gomez and Cappello 2014).

Data provenance is a term used to describe information about how data are collected, processed, stored, and distributed. Provenance can (and should) also document the individuals, systems, and software that collect, process, store, and distribute data. Provenance thus includes what is commonly thought of as "metadata"—but it also includes information that is not typically captured, such as the name of the person who performed the data analysis, the specific version of the software that was used to perform the analysis, and the steps that were taken to clean the data. Systematically capturing and maintaining provenance is an important part of data curation.

Researchers purchasing or developing large-scale storage systems should investigate approaches for automatically capturing provenance and storing it as part of their metadata. Collecting and analyzing provenance can have unexpected benefits, such as helping to understand and improve database performance (Macko, Margo, and Seltzer 2013).

Users of commercial statistics packages tend to underestimate the amount of provenance that is required to reconstruct a finding. For example, it may be necessary to capture both the user's scripts (e.g., a Stata "do-file"), the version of the statistics package, the version of the host operating system, the model number of the computer's microprocessor (CPU), the time and date that the software was run, the time zone, the amount of random access memory (RAM) installed in the computer, and other seemingly benign information. Having all this information captured, stored, and permanently recorded can be vital years later, when future researchers are trying to understand why today's results cannot be replicated. Even in the short term, this information can be vital to other scientists seeking to reproduce findings.

It is critical to automatically collect and index provenance to make data findable in a large-scale data research environment. With multiple researchers at multiple institutions, provenance can feed a search engine and respond to queries such as *find data collected between 2010 and 2014 that was processed with R to produce a table of household income vs. immunization rates*. Of course, to be findable, the search interface must be accessible to would-be downstream users. One way to ensure this is through a technique called *federated search*, in which multiple search engines are tied together so that a single search request can be answered by dozens or hundreds of independent but federated search engines (Nguyen et al. 2012). Federated search can produce results that are both more relevant and more diverse than queries to a single search engine, and approaches to address privacy issues have been developed (see Hong and Si 2013; Jiang, Si, and Li 2007).

Key points

- Provenance documents what happens to data, including collection, processing, dissemination, and storage.
- Provenance documents how data are transformed, including the names of the people who perform the transformations, the software that they use, and the process.
- Provenance can be stored with data or separately.
- Provenance can be collected and stored automatically, or manually.
- Carefully collected and indexed, provenance can make data more findable and usable.

Privacy Preserving Data Collection, Processing, and Publishing

So far, this article has been concerned with techniques developed by computer scientists for securely storing sensitive information and making the results of data processing findable. But computer scientists have also developed techniques over the past three decades that can be used for collecting, processing, and publishing sensitive information in a manner that preserves privacy.

Many of these techniques find their intellectual heritage in the work of Andrew Yao, a cryptographer who in 1982 introduced the concept of *secure two-party computation*, also called *secure function evaluation*. Yao developed a solution to the Millionaires' Problem, in which two millionaires, Alice and Bob, engage in a two-person mathematical protocol that lets them determine who is the richer of the two without revealing their wealth to each other or to a third party (Yao 1982). For an example of how such a multiparty computation might take place, see the Multiparty Computation Example in Box 1.

BOX 1
A Multiparty Computation Example

Although the solution for two-party protocols is too complicated to present here, there is a simple three-party protocol for a similar problem that is presented below.

Consider the problem *Average Salary Problem*, in which a group of people wish to compute their average salary without revealing their specific salary to each other or to a third party. In this case, we will consider Alice, Bob, and Carol, whose salaries are A, B, and C, respectively. The three wish to compute value of $(A + B + C)/3$ without revealing A, B, or C to each other.

The solution to this problem is straightforward. Alice, Bob and Carol each chose a random number—R_A, R_B, and R_C, respectively. Alice sends to Bob the number $A - R_A$ and to Carol the number R_A. Neither Bob nor Carol has enough information to reconstruct Alice's number A. Bob, meanwhile, sends to Alice the number $B - R_B$ and Carol the number R_B. Carol sends the number $C - R_C$ to Alice and R_C to Bob. Next, each of the players add together the numbers that they have received from the other two: Alice adds the numbers $(B - R_B)$ and $(C - R_C)$ to get $(B + C - R_B - R_C)$; Bob adds the numbers $(A - R_A)$ and R_C to get $(A - R_A + R_C)$; and Carol adds R_A and R_B to get $(R_A + R_B)$. Alice, Bob, and Carol now each write their sum on a whiteboard at the front of the room:

Alice writes the single number AA that is $(B + C - R_B - R_C)$.

Bob writes the single number BB that is $(A - R_A + R_C)$.

Carol writes the single number CC that is $(R_A + R_B)$.

The three numbers are now added and divided by three. This number, $(AA + BB + CC)/3$, is equal to $((B + C - R_B - R_C) + (A - R_A + R_C) + (R_A + R_B)) / 3 = (A + B + C) / 3$, which is the value that was to be computed! Thus, Alice, Bob and Carol have computed their average salary without revealing their individual salaries to each other.

Since Yao's discovery, many protocols and procedures for various kinds of security and privacy preserving computations have been discovered.

Private information retrieval describes a family of protocols that allows for a user to retrieve encrypted data from a server without revealing to the server which item is retrieved. The first scheme was introduced by Kushilevitz and Ostrovsky (1997); recently Yi, Paulet, and Bertino (2013) published a survey of many techniques.

Search on encrypted data are techniques that allow for a client to conduct searches on an encrypted database, without revealing the contents of the encrypted documents or the search terms. Early work was done by Song, Wagner, and Perrig (2000); follow-up work by others has discovered approaches for searches that are tolerant of minor misspellings (Li et al. 2010), rank keywords (Wang et al. 2010), and can even find medical imagery (Yuan, Yu, and Guo 2015).

Oblivious RAM (ORAM) is a mechanism in which information is stored on and retrieved from a remote server, but the server is unable to determine what is stored, what is retrieved, or the update patterns (Goldreich 1987).

In *cryptographic voting protocols* (Karlof, Sastry, and Wagner 2005), participants vote and votes are tallied, but it is impossible to determine the vote of any specific voter. Many voting protocols have additional properties, such as the ability of voters to verify that their votes were counted, or the ability to mathematically prove that the votes were properly counted.

In *differentially private algorithms* (Dwork et al. 2006; Dwork and Roth 2014) queries executed over a dataset are reported in a way that any specific individual's contribution cannot be inferred with a degree of certainty. Many differentially private algorithms are based on the addition of Laplace noise to the results of queries: by carefully controlling the amount of noise added, these algorithms can produce results that are both reasonably accurate and reasonably privacy preserving.

Collectively, these approaches can be called *formal privacy techniques*, because the privacy assumptions and guarantees are formally stated and privacy loss or protection is mathematically provable. When using a formal privacy technique, it is important to understand how words like *privacy* and *security* are formally defined, since the defined meanings may be subtly different than the colloquial ones.

Formal privacy techniques can be combined with the other privacy protecting techniques. For example, an organization that has sensitive data within a data enclave could use an algorithm like Ullman's Private Multiplicative Weights (Ullman 2015) to produce a differentially private synthetic dataset that is publicly distributed. Researchers could use this dataset to develop queries and to perform their initial data analysis. Once the code is working, the researchers could then provide their code to operators of the secure data enclave, who would then run the code on the actual data and review the results for inappropriate disclosures prior to making the results available to the researchers.

Key points

- Cryptographic techniques exist that can compute functions over private data such as sums and averages without releasing the actual data to anyone, including a trusted third party.
- A rich tool chest of algorithms exists, but they have not seen wide adoption yet.

Found Experimental Opportunities

Just as organic data create the possibility for social scientists to perform statistical analyses at a scale never before possible, *found experimental opportunities* make it possible for social scientists to intervene and conduct experiments on people and societies at a new, grand scale as well—experiments involving thousands, millions, or even billions of people. These capabilities have the potential to cause significant disruption to the way that many people do science.

Only a few short years ago, recruiting 500 or 1,000 people for a survey or study could be a painstaking task. Today there are numerous services such as Mechanical Turk,[11] CrowdFlower,[12] and Prolific Academic[13] that let a solitary researcher create a web-based experiment, ship it out to "workers," and get a response within hours. Prices for tasks can be so low—perhaps 20 cents per subject—that a student or even an enthusiastic amateur can fund an experiment on hundreds or thousands of people without having to rely on institutional funds.

Experimenting with ones' own funds can place a faculty researcher in an ethically ambiguous area. The primary mechanism by which human subjects research is regulated in the United States, the IRB system as defined by the National Research Act[14] and the Common Rule,[15] apply only to research that is federally funded. Although many universities require that all research involving human subjects performed under the auspices of a university be approved by the university's IRB, there is no general requirement that experiments on human subjects, even medical experiments, be approved by a disinterested, objective body. Some academics might think that using their own funds, on their own time, with their own computers, might somehow absolve them of the need to get IRB approval.

Individuals who carry out social science research without oversight have the potential to "poison the well" of good will—and even societal tolerance—for social science research in general, just as so-called push polls (M. Connelly 2014), also known as advocacy polls, have damaged the credibility, effectiveness, and even the legitimacy of traditional, rigorous public opinion polls. But whereas sending out a push poll to several thousands of homes might cost thousands of dollars, sending out a survey by Mechanical Turk to thousands of respondents might cost less than $100.

Another way to experiment on thousands of people is to package the experiment into an app and upload it to Apple's App Store or Google Play. An ethical experimenter might clearly disclose its purpose, protocol, and obtain the user's permission to proceed—a kind of informed consent. Alternatively, the app might simply offer some sort of compelling feature to its users and perform the experiment covertly.

Yet another way to experiment on people—perhaps millions—is to embed the experiment in a web service that is already being widely used, or package the experiment into a web-based advertisement. A growing number of researchers have made headlines with such covert experiments:

- In 2005, researchers at Indiana University sent targeted email messages to 921 members of the university community who became experimental subjects who did not know that they were part of an experiment. The email, which used email addresses that were spoofed from another 810 community members, directed the recipients to a website where their Indiana University username and password was requested. After the password was verified, the community members were told that they had been successfully "phished" and were directed to another website where they were provided with security training. Even though the study had been approved by the university's IRB and its computer security team, the timing of the experiment at the end of the semester and the fact that subjects were involved without their permission resulted in substantial negative publicity (see Jagatic et al. 2007; see also Finn and Jakobsson 2007).

- In 2010, Facebook conducted a study on an astounding 61 million of its users to see if it could influence the outcome of an election by selectively mobilizing different segments of its user population to vote. Facebook's researchers theorized that by showing clickable buttons in a user's newsfeed saying "I Voted," a user's friends would be incentivized to vote because they knew that their friends had voted. After it conducted the research, Facebook concluded that it could influence the outcome of an election (Bond et al. 2012).

- In 2012, researchers at Facebook manipulated the "news feed" feature of 689,003 Facebook users to see if such manipulations could alter the users' affective outlook. The researchers wanted to see if they could facilitate the transference of an emotional state from one user to another. In fact, Facebook could. There was significant negative publicity after the study was published (Kramer, Guillory, and Hancock 2014; a comprehensive analysis can be found in Jouhki et al. 2016).

- Between May 2014 and January 2015, researchers at Georgia Tech and Princeton University purchased online advertisements that delivered an experimental payload 141,626 times to 88,260 distinct IP addresses in 170 countries, resulting in more than 1,000 measurements each in China, India, the United Kingdom, and Brazil, and more than 100 measurements each in Egypt, South Korea, Iran, Pakistan, Turkey, and Saudi Arabia. The purpose of the experiments was to measure the pervasiveness of web censorship on a country-by-country basis, and this measurement was performed by instructing the unwitting users' web browsers to attempt to visit sensitive or controversial web content that was known to be blocked for moral or political reasons in some of these countries (Burnett and Feamster 2015). The research received considerable notoriety, as some of the researchers' colleagues believed that initiating such requests from web browsers in some countries might expose the users to undue risk from their governments. This was even more problematic because the users did not know that they were participating in a U.S.-sponsored research experiment. This study was so controversial that the editors of the conference proceedings in which the article appeared felt compelled to include a boxed disclaimer statement on the first page of the article (see Box 2).

BOX 2
Statement from the SIGCOMM 2015 Program Committee

The SIGCOMM 2015 PC appreciated the technical contributions made in this paper, but found the paper controversial because some of the experiments the authors conducted raise ethical concerns. The controversy arose in large part because the networking research community does not yet have widely accepted guidelines or rules for the ethics of experiments that measure online censorship. In accordance with the published submission guidelines for SIGCOMM 2015, had the authors not engaged with their Institutional Review Boards (IRBs) or had their IRBs determined that their research was unethical, the PC would have rejected the paper without review. But the authors did engage with their IRBs, which did not flag the research as unethical. The PC hopes that discussion of the ethical concerns these experiments raise will advance the development of ethical guidelines in this area. It is the PC's view that future guidelines should include as a core principle that researchers should not engage in experiments that subject users to an appreciable risk of substantial harm absent informed consent. The PC endorses neither the use of the experimental techniques this paper describes nor the experiments the authors conducted.

SOURCE: Burnett and Feamster (2015).

In 1979, the National Commission for the Protection of Human Subjects of Biomedical and Behavioral Research published the Belmont Report (U.S. Department of Health, Education and Welfare 1978), named after the Belmont Conference Center in Elkridge, Maryland, where the report was drafted. Written largely in reaction to the public disclosure of the Tuskegee Syphilis Study,[16] the Belmont Report laid the ethical groundwork for what became the National Research Act[17] and the Common Rule.[18] Today many federally funded researchers in the United States who perform human subjects research are required under the Common Rule to be trained and tested on the report's three fundamental ethical principles: respect for persons, beneficence, and justice.

In recognition that ICT research might require additional ethical principles, between 2010 and 2012 the U.S. Department of Homeland Security convened a series of workshops with leading experts in the computing field to create a new report regarding the ethical conduct of research in the cyber age. Called the Menlo Report (Dittrich and Kenneally 2012), the new guide expanded the Belmont Report's original three ethical principles to include a fourth principle, "respect for law and public interest." This principle was added because experimentation on modern computer systems could result in significant damage to both those systems and the greater society.[19]

Key points

- The same technology trends that make it easy to work with organic data make it easy to experiment on a large number of people without their permission.

- Such experiments can have significant impact on real-world events, such as influencing the outcome of elections and changing the emotional state of millions of people.
- Few mechanisms exist for regulating large-scale experiments outside of the IRB system, and there are many concerns regarding the ability of the IRB system to handle these kinds of experiments.

Conclusion

In the past, social scientists largely confined their work to datasets that they either made themselves or that they acquired from official statistics agencies. Today there is a growing interest in using organic data that result from administrative or operational systems. These datasets promise a look into parts of the economy and society that were never before available to social scientists, and offer resolution that was unimaginable until now. But these datasets also come with the risk of significant privacy violations and unknown data quality.

Computer scientists have developed techniques over the past four decades that offer the promise of being able to work with these new datasets in a way that is ethically appropriate and scientifically defensible. But these techniques, although they have been mathematically demonstrated and published in the peer-reviewed literature, have not matured to the point that they can be readily incorporated into production systems with manageable costs. Social scientists need to work with computer scientists to move these techniques from the laboratory into practice. The benefits of doing so are clear.

Notes

1. See https://www.census.gov/ces/dataproducts/lehddata.html.

2. See http://onthemap.ces.census.gov/.

3. See https://onthemap.ces.census.gov/em/.

4. See 45 C.F.R. §46.

5. See 45 C.F.R. §46.116(d) for the criteria for waiving informed consent. Note that the Food and Drug Administration's (FDA's) version of the Common Rule (21 C.F.R. §50 and §56) and the Department of Health and Human Services (DHSS) regulations (21 C.F.R. §46) are more restrictive regarding such waivers.

6. 45 C.F.R. §160 and 45 C.F.R. §164 subparts A and E; see also https://www.hhs.gov/hipaa/for-professionals/privacy/.

7. See also https://privacyruleandresearch.nih.gov/pr_08.asp.

8. El Emam et al. (2011) reference the federal court case: *Mike Gordon v. the Minister of Health and the Privacy Commissioner of Canada: Memorandum of Fact and Law of the Privacy Commissioner of Canada* (Can. 2007).

9. One of the main challenges in operating an air-gapped network is installing updates to software packages. See also http://www.ibm.com/support/knowledgecenter/SS63NW_ 9.2.0/com.ibm.tem.life.doc_9.2/Lifecycle_Man/OSD_Users_Guide/c_osd_setup_airgap.html.

10. A general overview for less technical readers can be found in Kamaraju (2012).

11. See https://www.mturk.com/mturk/.

12. See https://www.crowdflower.com/.

13. See https://www.prolific.ac/.

14. The National Research Service Award Act of 1974, Public Law 93-348.

15. 45 C.F.R. 46.

16. See https://www.cdc.gov/tuskegee/timeline.htm.

17. The National Research Service Award Act of 1974, Public Law 93-348.

18. 45 C.F.R. 46.

19. For example, in 1988 Robert Tappan Morris created a computer worm that was designed to assess the size of the Internet, but resulted instead in disabling more than 6,000 Internet-connected computers, roughly 10 percent of the computers that were connected to the Internet at the time. See Hafner and Markoff (1995).

References

Bond, Robert M., Christopher J. Fariss, Jason J. Jones, Adam D. I. Kramer, Cameron Marlow, Jaime E. Settle, and James H. Fowler. 2012. A 61-million-person experiment in social influence and political mobilization. *Nature* 489:295–98. Available from http://fowler.ucsd.edu/massive_turnout.pdf.

Brown, Aaron B., and David A. Patterson. n.d. To err is human. Available from http://roc.cs.berkeley.edu/papers/easy01.pdf.

Burnett, Sam, and Nick Feamster. 2015. Encore: Lightweight measurement of web censorship with cross-origin requests. In *Proceedings of the 2015 ACM conference on special interest group on data communication*, 653–67. New York, NY: ACM.

Byres, Eric. 2013. The air gap: SCADA's enduring security myth. *Communications of the ACM* 56 (8): 29–31.

Coakley, Thomas P. 1992. *Command and control for war and peace.* Washington, DC: National Defense University Press.

Connelly, Marjorie. 18 June 2014. Push polls, defined. *New York Times.*

Connelly, Roxanne, Christopher J. Playford, Vernon Gayle, and Chris Dibben. 2016. The role of administrative data in the big data revolution in social science research. *Social Science Research* 59:1–12.

Diebold, John. 1986. Computerization and the modern society. In *Today's American: How free?* eds. James Finn and Leonard R. Sussman, 107–14. New York, NY: Freedom House.

Dittrich, D., and E. Kenneally. 2012. *The Menlo report: Ethical principles guiding information and communication technology research.* Washington, DC: U.S. Department of Homeland Security. Available from https://www.caida.org/publications/papers/2012/menlo_report_actual_formatted/.

Dwork, Cynthia, Frank McSherry, Kobbi Nissim, and Adam Smith. 2006. Calibrating noise to sensitivity in private data analysis. In *Theory of Cryptography Conference (TCC)*, 265–84. New York, NY: Springer.

Dwork, Cynthia, and Aaron Roth. 2014. The algorithmic foundations of differential privacy. *Foundations and Trends in Theoretical Computer Science* 9 (3–4): 211–407.

Einav, Liran, and Jonathan D. Levin. 2013. The data revolution and economic analysis. National Bureau of Economic Research Working Paper 19035, Cambridge, MA

El Emam, Khaled, Elizabeth Jonker, Luk Arbuckle, and Bradley Malin. 2011. A systematic review of re-identification attacks on health data. *PLoS ONE* 6 (12): e28071.

Federal Committee on Statistical Methodology. 2005. Report on statistical disclosure limitation methodology. Statistical Policy Working Paper 22, Washington, DC.

Fiala, David, Frank Mueller, Christian Engelmann, Rolf Riesen, Kurt Ferreira, and Ron Brightwell. 2012. Detection and correction of silent data corruption for large-scale high-performance computing. In *Proceedings of the international conference on high performance computing, networking, storage and analysis.* Los Alamitos, CA: IEEE Computer Society Press.

Finn, P., and M. Jakobsson. 2007. Designing ethical phishing experiments. *IEEE Technology and Society Magazine* 26 (1): 46–58.

Garfinkel, Simson L. 2015. *NISTIR 8053: De-identification of personal information.* Washington, DC: National Institute of Standards and Technology Interagency. Available from 8053http://nvlpubs.nist.gov/nistpubs/ir/2015/NIST.IR.8053.pdf.

Garfinkel, Simson L., and A. Shelat. 2003. Remembrance of data passed: A study of disk sanitization practices. *IEEE Security & Privacy* 1 (1): 17–27.

Ge, Tingjian, and Stan Zdonik. 2007. Fast, secure encryption for indexing in a column-oriented DBMS. Presented at the 2007 IEEE 23rd International Conference on Data Engineering. doi:10.1109/ICDE.2007.367913.

Goldreich, Oded. 1987. Towards a theory of software protection and simulation by oblivious RAMs. In *Proceedings of the nineteenth annual ACM symposium on theory of computing (STOC '87)*, ed. Alfred V. Aho, 182–94. New York, NY: ACM.

Gomez, Leonardo Bautista, and Franck Cappello. 2014. Detecting silent data corruption through data dynamic monitoring for scientific applications. In *Proceedings of the 19th ACM SIGPLAN symposium on principles and practice of parallel programming (PPoPP '14)*, 381–82. New York, NY: ACM.

Gorman, Siobhan. 23 August 2013. NSA officers spy on love interests. *The Wall Street Journal*. Available from http://blogs.wsj.com.

Groves, Robert M. 31 May 2011. "Designated data" and "organic data." Director's blog. U.S. Census Bureau. Available from https://www.census.gov/newsroom/blogs/director/2011/05/designed-data-and-organic-data.html.

Groves, Robert M., and Brian A. Harris-Kojetin, eds. 2017. *Innovations in federal statistics: Combining data sources while protecting privacy*. Washington, DC: National Academies Press.

Hafner, Katie, and John Markoff. 1995. *Cyberpunk: Outlaws and hackers on the computer frontier*. New York, NY: Simon and Schuster.

Hartung, Gunnar. 2016. Secure audit logs with verifiable excerpts. In *Proceedings of the RSA conference on topics in cryptology - CT-RSA 2016*, ed. Kazue Sako, 183–99. New York, NY: Springer-Verlag.

Hill, Kashmir. 12 September 2013. E-ZPasses get read all over New York (not just at toll booths). *Forbes*. Available from http://www.forbes.com.

Hong, Dzung, and Luo Si. 2013. Search result diversification in resource selection for federated search. In *Proceedings of the 36th international ACM SIGIR conference on research and development in information retrieval (SIGIR '13)*, 613–22. New York, NY: ACM.

Jagatic, Tom N., Nathaniel A. Johnson, Markus Jakobsson, and Filippo Menczer. 2007. Social phishing. *Communication of the ACM* 50 (10): 94–100.

Jiang, Wei, Luo Si, and Jing Li. 2007. Protecting source privacy in federated search. In *Proceedings of the 30th annual international ACM SIGIR conference on research and development in information retrieval (SIGIR '07)*, 761–62. New York, NY: ACM.

Jouhki, Jukka, Epp Lauk, Maija Penttinen, Niina Sormanen, and Turo Uskali. 2016. Facebook's emotional contagion experiment as a challenge to research ethics. *Media and Communication* 4 (4): 75–85.

Kamaraju, Ashvin. 9 February 2012. Database encryption demystified: Four common misconceptions. *ZDNet*. Available from http://www.zdnet.com.

Karlof, Chris, Naveen Sastry, and David Wagner. 2005. Cryptographic voting protocols: A systems perspective. *SSYM'05 Proceedings of the 14th Conference on USENIX Security Symposium* 14:3–3.

Kramer, Adam D. I., Jamie E. Guillory, and Jeffrey T. Hancock. 2014. Experimental evidence of massive-scale emotional contagion through social networks. *Proceedings of the National Academy of Sciences of the United States of America* 111 (24): 8788–90.

Kushilevitz, Eyal, and Rafail Ostrovsky. 1997. Replication is not needed: Single database, computationally-private information retrieval. In *Proceedings of the 38th annual symposium on foundations of computer science*, 364–73. Miami Beach, FL: IEEE Computer Society.

Lane, Julia, Victoria Stodden, Stefan Bender, and Helen Nissenbaum. 2014. *Privacy, big data, and the public good: Frameworks for engagement*. New York, NY: Cambridge University Press.

Li, Jin, Qian Wang, Cong Wang, Ning Cao, Kui Ren, and Wenjing Lou. 2010. Fuzzy keyword search over encrypted data in cloud computing. In *2010 proceedings IEEE INFOCOM*. doi:10.1109/INFCOM.2010.5462196.

Lussenhop, Jessica. 22 February 2012. Is Anne Marie Rasmusson too hot to have a driver's license? *City Pages*. Available from http://www.citypages.com.

Lv, Mingqi, Ling Chen, Gencai Chen, and Daqiang Zhang. 2014. Detecting traffic congestions using cell phone accelerometers. In *Proceedings of the 2014 ACM international joint conference on pervasive and ubiquitous computing: adjunct publication*, 107–10. New York, NY: ACM.

Ma, Di, and Gene Tsudik. 2009. A new approach to secure logging. *ACM Transactions on Storage* 5 (1): Article 2. doi:http://dx.doi.org/10.1145/1502777.1502779.

Machanavajjhala, A., D. Kifer, J. Abowd, J. Gehrke, and L. Vilhuber. 2008. Privacy: Theory meets practice on the map. In *Proceedings of the 2008 IEEE 24th international conference on data engineering*. Red Hook, NY: Curran Associates.

Macko, Peter, Daniel Margo, and Margo Seltzer. 2013. Performance introspection of graph databases. In *Proceedings of the 6th international systems and storage conference (SYSTOR '13)*. New York, NY: ACM.

McSherry, Frank. 2009. Privacy integrated queries. In *Proceedings of the 2009 ACM SIGMOD international conference on management of data*. New York, NY: ACM. Available from https://www.microsoft.com/en-us/research/publication/privacy-integrated-queries/.

Narayan, Sumit, John A. Chandy, Samuel Lang, Philip Carns, and Robert Ross. 2009. Uncovering errors: The cost of detecting silent data corruption. In *Proceedings of the 4th annual workshop on petascale data storage (PDSW '09)*, 37–41. New York, NY: ACM.

Nguyen, Dong, Thomas Demeester, Dolf Trieschnigg, and Djoerd Hiemstra. 2012. Federated search in the wild: The combined power of over a hundred search engines. In *Proceedings of the 21st ACM international conference on information and knowledge management* (CIKM '12), 1874–78. New York, NY: ACM.

Oettinger, Anthony G. 2001. Future innovations: The endless adventure. *Bulletin of the Association for Information Science and Technology* 27 (2): 10–15.

Peterson, Andrea. 24 August 2013. LOVEINT: When NSA officers use their spying power on love interests. *The Washington Post*. Available from https://www.washingtonpost.com.

Privacy Technology Assistance Center, U.S. Department of Education. n.d. *Data de-identification: An overview of basic terms*. Available from http://ptac.ed.gov/sites/default/files/data_deidentification_terms.pdf.

Schneier, Bruce. 2013. Air gaps. Schneier on Security Blog. Available from https://www.schneier.com/blog/archives/2013/10/air_gaps.html.

Song, Dawn Xiaoding, David Wagner, and Adrian Perrig. 2000. Practical techniques for searches on encrypted data. In *Proceeding 2000 IEEE symposium on security and privacy. S&P 2000*. Available from https://people.eecs.berkeley.edu/~dawnsong/papers/se.pdf.

Taylor, L., R. Schroeder, and E. Meyer. 2014. Emerging practices and perspectives on big data analysis in economics: Bigger and better or more of the same? *Big Data and Society*. doi:10.1177/2053951714536877.

Ullman, Jonathan. 2015. Private multiplicative weights beyond linear queries. In *Proceedings of the 34th ACM SIGMOD-SIGACT-SIGAI symposium on principles of database systems (PODS '15)*, 303–12. New York, NY: ACM.

U.S. Census Bureau. 2015. *LED (Local Employment Dynamics): New data from the states and the U.S. Census Bureau*. Available from https://lehd.ces.census.gov/doc/LEDonepager_2015.pdf.

U.S. Department of Health, Education and Welfare. 1978. *The Belmont report*. Washington, DC: U.S. Government Printing Office.

Wang, Cong, Ning Cao, Jin Li, Kui Ren, and Wenjing Lou. 2010. Secure ranked keyword search over encrypted cloud data. In *2010 IEEE 30th international conference on distributed computing systems*, 253–62. Washington, DC: IEEE.

Yao, Andrew C. 1982. Protocols for secure computations. In *FOCS. 23rd annual symposium on foundations of computer science (FOCS 1982)*, 160–64. Washington, DC: IEEE.

Yi, Xun, Russell Paulet, and Elisa Bertino. 2013. Private information retrieval. In *Synthesis lectures on information security, privacy, and trust*, eds. Elisa Bertino and Ravi Sandhu. San Rafael, CA: Morgan and Claypool Publishers.

Yoon, Jungkeun, Brian Noble, and Mingyan Liu. 2007. Surface street traffic estimation. In *Proceedings of the 5th international conference on mobile systems, applications and services*, 2201–32. New York, NY: ACM.

Yuan, Jiawei, Shucheng Yu, and Linke Guo. 2015. SEISA: Secure and efficient encrypted image search with access control. In *2015 IEEE Conference on Computer Communications (INFOCOM)*, 2083–91. Washington, DC: IEEE.

Zetter, Kim. 5 November 2012. Female cop gets $1 million after colleagues trolled database to peek at her pic. *Wired*. Available from https://www.wired.com.

Research Infrastructure for the Safe Analysis of Sensitive Data

By
IAN FOSTER

To use administrative and other new data sources for the scientific study of human beings and human behavior, analysts need to be able both to connect to these new data and to deploy new methods for linking and analyzing the data. These efforts are often hindered by legal, technical, and operational difficulties. In this article, I examine how new digital research infrastructures can be used to reduce such barriers. Experiences with data stewardship in other scientific domains shows that appropriate infrastructure can enable the efficient, secure, and collaborative integration of domain expertise, data, and analysis capabilities. I review the state of the art in these areas and argue for the use of cloud-hosted enclaves as a safe interaction point for analysts, data, and software, and as a means of automating and thus professionalizing data stewardship processes.

Keywords: safe data; enclaves; cloud computing; data stewardship

Access to new types of data has revolutionized much of science (Hey, Tansley, and Tolle 2009). That revolution, though, has yet to fully make its way to the scientific study of human beings and their interactions in such areas as program management, policy development, and scholarly research (Lane, Heus, and Mulcahy 2008; Metzler 2016). Progress has

Ian Foster is a professor of computer science at the University of Chicago and a senior scientist and distinguished fellow at Argonne National Laboratory. His research contributions span high-performance computing, distributed systems, and data-driven discovery. He has published hundreds of research articles and seven books on these and other topics.

NOTE: I thank Kyle Chard, Simson Garfinkel, and Todd Harbor for insightful comments on a draft of this article; and Rachana Ananthakrishnan, Dan Black, Charlie Catlett, Ron Jarmin, Frauke Kreuter, Julia Lane, and Steven Tuecke for many helpful conversations. This research was supported in part by the U.S. Department of Energy under contract DE-AC02-06CH11357.

Correspondence: foster@uchicago.edu

DOI: 10.1177/0002716217742610

been hindered by the legal, technical, and operational difficulties inherent in connecting *analysts* (domain experts with questions) to the multiple sources of sensitive *data* from which answers are to be extracted and the analysis *methods* required to link and analyze those data. Indeed, the high cost of assembling these three essential elements of data-driven scholarship on human systems has often prevented its large-scale application, at least outside the narrow realms of commercial data mining and national security.

This article examines how digital *research infrastructure* can be used to reduce barriers to connecting analysts, data, and methods, thus accelerating data-driven investigations of human systems. A research infrastructure encompasses both technology and process. As *technology*, it is a collection of computer hardware, software, and networks designed and operated to support research activities. As *process*, it implements and enforces policies, conventions, and rules to ensure that the technology is applied in ways that meet user needs in such areas as security and trust. Experience in other scientific domains (Atkins et al. 2003; Finholt 2002; Foster 2002) shows that appropriate research infrastructure can enable the efficient, secure, and collaborative integration of domain expertise, data, and analysis capabilities. For example, the LHC Computing Grid (Lamanna 2004) enables thousands of physicists worldwide to access data produced at the Large Hadron Collider (LHC), a physics experiment in Geneva, Switzerland, and to collaborate on the analysis of those data. While LHC data do not pertain to human subjects, great care is taken to ensure their integrity. In astronomy, the SkyServer online database (Szalay et al. 2002) has enabled tens of thousands of astronomers and students to conduct research on data collected from digital sky surveys, performing queries to retrieve data of interest and then creating private data spaces for intermediate results.

I focus here on the technological aspects of research infrastructure. I am not ignorant of the profound legal and ethical challenges associated with the analysis of sensitive human data that no technology or process, however sophisticated, can ever fully address. However, I believe that well-designed technologies, when subject to appropriately controlled processes, can reduce barriers to secure data access, use, and reuse. They can, for example, provide safe environments for data cleaning; ensure secure auditing of data accesses; and protect against attack vectors that individual research labs, statistical agencies, and other institutions are hard pressed to counter. And they can package these solutions in ways that can be replicated rapidly and easily in different jurisdictions.

In the next section, I elucidate technology and process requirements for a research infrastructure for sensitive human data. I then review approaches taken and lessons learned from previous work in other domains. In the section that follows, I explore how cloud computing can enable new approaches to research infrastructure that may transform how data on human subjects are handled, and end with a concluding section.

Problem Statement

My overarching goal is to accelerate data-driven research and policy around human beings and their interactions by giving analysts the ability to link highly sensitive data from multiple sources. To this end, I want to enable efficient, effective, and secure access to sensitive data about societal systems. To give just one example of how this approach could be beneficial, consider the ways in which analysis of detailed data about the life histories of ex-offenders and on factors such as educational and employment opportunities, housing programs, and health services in the locales to which ex-offenders are released could suggest new approaches to reducing recidivism.

My approach to the data access and linking problem distinguishes among the interests of three classes of actors: data providers, analysts, and method developers.

Data providers are those who collect data, such as federal agencies, state agencies, municipalities, companies, and universities. A data provider may be prepared to make their data available to external analysts, but typically only if they see the benefits as outweighing the costs and risks. *Benefits* can include new information or insights that result from their data being analyzed from fresh perspectives or combined with data from other data providers; *costs* are the effort required to organize data for external access; and *risks* are the legal, reputational, or other negative consequences if legal, regulatory, or other constraints on data access and use are not followed. We need research infrastructures that maximize benefits for data providers while minimizing associated costs and risks.

Analysts are those who work with data for such purposes as program management, policy development, or scholarly research. It is analysts who ultimately (we hope) will deliver benefits to data producers. Thus, a second set of requirements for a research infrastructure relates to analyst productivity, which may be compromised by difficulties in data discovery, access, linkage, and analysis. While analysts may have deep knowledge about specific domains of social science (e.g., criminal justice, employment, education), they will not necessarily be conversant with datasets from sources with which they were previously unfamiliar, making both discovery and use difficult. Steps taken by data providers to reduce risk, such as de-identification, can hinder subsequent analysis. As the volume and variety of data grow, analysts may find themselves requiring new methods and tools: for example, new linkage methods and high-performance computing tools to process large datasets. Increasingly, also, they may find themselves under pressure to document the steps that were followed to reach their conclusions.

Method developers are social scientists, statisticians, computer scientists, and others who develop new methods for linkage, analysis, and visualization of large datasets. These individuals can have much to offer analysts working with large datasets, but historically they have had limited or no access to realistic test data (Metzler 2016), reducing their ability to tackle problems that really matter to data providers and analysts. By treating them as stakeholders in research infrastructure, we recognize that data providers and analysts alike may have an interest in facilitating their work.

Inevitably, the interests of these different parties can conflict, and thus a research infrastructure that is intended to support the interests of all three groups needs to be able to manage trade-offs.

Research Data Integration and Analysis Infrastructures

Social scientists are not the first to grapple with the challenges of "big data." Indeed, people have been building infrastructures for storing and sharing large quantities of information in support of research since at least the Library of Alexandria in the third century BCE. Computers have transformed how we work with information by enabling automated management and analysis, and it is now routine for researchers in the physical and biological sciences to create and use research infrastructures that store and enable the analysis of trillions of data elements. Developers of such systems have negotiated trade-offs among scale, cost, the types of questions that can be asked and answered, security, reliability, and other factors. Here I review some important approaches.

Repositories and services

Community data repositories. Physical and biological scientists have encountered and addressed a variety of big data challenges as improved instrumentation and computational capabilities have produced ever more data. One important innovation was the online data repository that aggregated data from many producers. Such systems have proven highly successful, particularly when backed by policies that require data deposit. For example, the Protein Data Bank (PDB) (Berman et al. 2000), established in 1971 with seven protein structures, has grown to more than 120,000 protein structures; GenBank (Benson et al. 2014), established in 1982, now holds close to 2 trillion bases of genetic sequence data; the Genomic Data Commons (GDC), established in 2016, holds more than 2 quadrillion (2×10^{15}) bytes (Grossman et al. 2016). However, these systems are primarily data repositories, not data analysis systems (although PDB provides some comparison functions): once researchers identify data of interest, they must download them to perform analysis locally. Such download and local analysis can become impractical as data grow in complexity and size, particularly when analysts want to compute over *all* data rather than simply examining individual data elements.

Federated data repositories. The cost and governance issues associated with a centralized repository can lead communities to develop federated repositories, in which many data providers implement common protocols and standards so that researchers can query to determine what data are available at any site and then download those data for analysis. For example, the Earth System Grid Federation (Williams et al. 2016), an evolution of the centralized Earth System Grid (ESG) (Bernholdt et al. 2005) established to store and distribute climate simulation results associated with Intergovernmental Panel on Climate Change assessments, links climate data providers at dozens of sites worldwide. Federated repositories avoid the cost and governance challenges of a centralized site, but they can introduce significant challenges of consistency in protocols. And they still require that researchers download data for analysis.

High-energy physics provides an example of an inverse approach. Data are produced in extremely large volumes at a small number of locations, such as the LHC. The data volumes are too large for the computational capacity that could be acquired at CERN, and thus the LHC Computing Grid (Lamanna 2004) distributes data from the central LHC site to many computing centers for analysis.

Data services. When data are large, it can be impractical for analysts to download them to their local computers for analysis. Thus, some data providers implement data service interfaces that perform computations on data in response to user requests. This *server-side computation* (so-called because it is performed on the data server, not the client) may be restricted to predefined operations (e.g., subsetting, certain statistical analyses) or may allow for the execution of arbitrary user-supplied code. The ability to run arbitrary user-supplied code is powerful, but can raise challenging security concerns. One partial solution is to restrict user-supplied code to specific programming dialects of execution types, as is done for example in the SkyServer astronomical database: only Structured Query Language (SQL) queries are supported (Szalay et al. 2002).

Systems that allow for user-initiated server-side computation may also need to manage potentially large computational demands, particularly if remote analysts are allowed to request computations over large quantities of data. This problem can be dealt with by restricting the amount of computation that can be performed, implementing queues, leveraging grid computing (Foster 2002), and running on a cloud that provides for elastic computing capacity, perhaps with accounting to enable recouping of costs.

Server-side data analysis can also be attractive as a means of accessing complex software that may require considerable expertise to install and operate. In the biological sciences, systems like Galaxy (Goecks et al. 2010) that allow analysts to upload data for processing with standard software have become popular, particularly for those with limited local infrastructure and expertise. By incentivizing data upload, such systems can also encourage the accumulation of large datasets. SEED (Overbeek, Disz, and Stevens 2004) and MG-RAST (Meyer et al. 2008) exemplify this approach: they retain microbial genomes and metagenomic data, respectively, that researchers upload for analysis, increasing their coverage of species and environments.

Federated data services. Data services, like databases, can be federated via the definition and implementation of appropriate protocol and data standards (Foster and Grossman 2003). For example, in astronomy, different groups have created databases of the sky at different wavelengths. To enable cross-database queries, the virtual observatory community has defined standards that allow a researcher to query a digital sky survey database for objects with certain characteristics (Szalay and Gray 2001). A user interested in finding, for example, stars that are visible in the infrared but not the optical spectra (possible brown dwarves) would perform queries against both infrared and optical databases.

The systems described so far deal with data that may be completely open (e.g., PDB or GenBank data) or available to anyone who registers their scientific interest (e.g., ESGF). In other cases, access is granted only to researchers who agree to abide by specified policies. This is the case, for example, for the GDC and for the Cancer Genome Atlas (TCGA), which holds genetic sequence data from more than five hundred cancer tissue samples. The TCGA's Data Use Certification Agreement[1] requires that researchers agree to maintain the privacy of the patients who provided tissue samples, access the data securely, and follow publication guidelines. However, such agreements are typically enforced by social norms rather than by automated processes.

Marts, lakes, and spaces

Another important dimension along which research data infrastructures vary is the extent to which their contents are harmonized to simplify discovery, access, and analysis. For example, if a data infrastructure contains scientific articles, are those documents in a common format (e.g., structured XML) or in multiple formats (e.g., XML, PDF)? Are the documents annotated with metadata about their source journal and field, using a common vocabulary? If a data infrastructure contains data about human subjects from different sources, are those data in a common format? Many scientific data repositories are organized as highly structured *data marts*, with all data and metadata being converted to standardized formats and schema before being uploaded. Access then occurs via standardized protocols and APIs. This is the case with systems such as PDB, GenBank, and ESGF, for example: each defines file format and metadata conventions that must be followed by data providers. In essence, such systems impose costs on data providers to simplify life for data consumers. The question of where costs should be incurred in a data publication pipeline is often a hot topic of debate when federating data. Changing business processes "upstream" can simplify life for data aggregators and also improve data quality. But the associated costs may be unacceptable.

An alternative approach to data repository design focuses on minimizing costs for data providers. In so-called *data lakes* (Terrizzano et al. 2015) data of potentially many types and from potentially many sources can be deposited without concern for conventions. Thus, for example, raw data from an experiment may be found alongside more processed data that have undergone further processing, for example to transform them into common formats. Some data will be highly documented and standardized, while other data may have no associated descriptive metadata. Data lakes work well when analysts who work with important or popular data to improve the quality of associated metadata over time. Franklin, Halevy, and Maier (2005) coined the term *data space* for systems that encourage such pay-as-you-go improvements, by, for example, cataloging all datasets and recording provenance relationships between initial and derived datasets. Google's GOODS system (Halevy et al. 2016) uses such methods to manage a data lake of more than 20 billion datasets; however, these datasets are not subject to the access controls required for the human subjects considered here.

Todd Harbour proposes the term *brickyard* to denote a place where people go to obtain materials that they can expect to be regularized, with predictable dimensions and formats: for example, bricks and patio slabs.[2] An effective data sharing system must incorporate methods or incentives for such regularization. A brickyard is also like a research data enclave in another respect: people cannot take whatever they want. Business processes, documentation, and permissions must accompany any removal of materials.

Collaboration, provenance, data and code reuse, and reproducibility

Data space concepts illustrate one of the many ways in which collaboration can facilitate productive data analysis. All too often in science, individual researchers work independently to understand, correct, and analyze source data. In the process, they may duplicate work that has already been performed by others. The result can be not only wasted effort but also poor science, if, for example, subtly different, but undocumented, assumptions made by different analysts lead to different results.

These concerns can be addressed by mechanisms that allow work performed by one analyst (e.g., documenting a dataset, creating a derived data product, or developing code for a specific analysis) to be shared with others. Various methods have been developed and applied for this purpose in science. Collaborative tagging mechanisms (Cattuto, Loreto, and Pietronero 2007) enable researchers to share structured or unstructured annotations on documents, data, and code. Notebook technologies such as Jupyter (Kluyver et al. 2016) are used to share code in understandable ways. Conventions and tools have been developed for recording provenance relationships between datasets and code (Moreau et al. 2011). The ability to assign persistent identifiers to datasets, data subsets, and code is important for provenance, reuse, and citation (Paskin 2005; Chard et al. 2016).

Data Infrastructure and Sensitive Data

Sensitive data are sufficiently confidential that data providers cannot rely on researcher declarations to maintain confidentiality: data providers instead need to maintain positive control over data access and use, to reduce the risk of unwanted disclosure. We consider two classes of such control mechanisms: the *curator model* and *secure enclaves*. The first approach limits the data that analysts can access, the operations that they can perform on data, and the results that can be obtained from analyses, to prevent them from ever seeing sensitive data. Secure enclaves, in contrast, allow full access to data but then restrict who is allowed that access and what data can be exported.

Statistical disclosure control and the curator model

Statistical disclosure control approaches seek to allow analysts to operate on data without ever obtaining access to information about individuals (Willenborg and De Waal 2012). Dwork and Smith (2010) formalize the problem by defining a curator model in which a trusted and trustworthy curator (e.g., the U.S. Census Bureau) gathers sensitive information from many respondents (the sample) and then works to release to the public statistical facts about the underlying population, in a way that does not compromise the privacy of the individual respondents. They distinguish between noninteractive access, in which the set of statistics to be computed is predefined, and interactive access, in which the curator responds to requests from individual analysts. (The latter approach can introduce scalability challenges.)

Various techniques have been developed to enable access to data statistics without revealing information about individuals. Curators may aggregate data, suppress certain information data, or perturb the values of variables before publication (Domingo-Ferrer and Mateo-Sanz 2002; Seastrom 2010; Skinner 2009). The concept of *differential privacy* provides a formal framework for thinking about such issues, stating that the results of a query against a dataset with data on a specific individual removed should not be distinguishable from the results when data on that individual are present (Dwork 2014; Dwork et al. 2006). Related models allow for reasoning about the probability that personal information will be revealed by a series of information releases, such as responses by a curator to multiple interactive requests.

One form of information suppression is de-identification (Uzuner, Luo, and Szolovits 2007), which may involve removing personal identifiers completely (anonymization) or replacing each identifier in the dataset with a unique key (pseudonymization or coding; Phillips and Knoppers 2016). The effectiveness of such approaches is vigorously debated, with some arguing that essentially any data can be reidentified via linkage with other datasets or knowledge (Barocas and Nissenbaum 2014; Ohm 2010), and others arguing that such steps are often noisy and thus may not be revealing for more than a few individuals.

Secure enclaves

Another approach to preventing disclosure of sensitive information is to place physical constraints on data access and export. Desai, Ritchie, and Welpton (2016) argue for a portfolio approach to data security, with processes defined to ensure *safe people* (i.e., restrictions on who is allowed to access the enclave), *safe projects* (i.e., audits of the purposes for which the data are to be used), *safe settings* (i.e., secure environments), and *safe outputs* (e.g., via manual review of data outputs before they are released). Variants of this approach make different trade-offs between security and convenience.

Air-gapped enclaves. In this first approach, all analysis must be performed in a secure enclave with no Internet connection. This approach is frequently employed by national security organizations and stewards of public datasets such as the U.S. Census Bureau's Federal Statistical Research Data Centers, which create "air-gapped" data infrastructures comprising computers that are not connected to the Internet and that users have to visit and use in person, with tight control over what data, if any, they can take with them when they leave. The unfettered access to data provided by these enclaves is invaluable, allowing data to be exploited to its fullest potential. However, we do not view air-gapped enclaves as an adequate solution for the data sharing and analysis use cases considered in this volume due to their inconvenience, cost, and lack of support for importing data from other sources for purposes of data integration. The analyses that we aim to support require that many people be able to access, integrate, and analyze multiple sensitive datasets.

Secure remote access

The inconvenience inherent in air-gapped enclaves has led various groups to develop systems in which the analyst connects remotely, for example over a virtual private network, to the data enclave (Lane, Heus, and Mulcahy 2008). The identity of the analyst is established via secure authentication, and the analyst can then interact with software running at the enclave to perform analyses, review results, and ultimately download outputs (perhaps after review by data enclave staff). This approach is far more convenient for the remote analyst but introduces risk because the data enclave has little control over the remote analyst's computing environment. To counter that risk, some enclaves require that remote access be allowed only from dedicated secure sites, under the supervision of qualified staff (Bender and Heining 2011). In another related approach, analysts construct data capsules—virtual machine images with analyst-provided and -configured code—that can then be deployed and run on data in an enclave, with controls applied on what data can be released while the capsule runs (Borders et al. 2009; Zeng et al. 2014).

Note that secure enclaves, whether or not they support remote access, do not directly address the need for analysts to integrate data from multiple sources, which may require that data from one source be transported to another for linkage and analysis.

Cloud computing

Internet search and social networking companies such as Amazon, Facebook, Google, and Microsoft represent another approach to large-scale data aggregation and analysis. Each of these companies has created an enormous computational infrastructure—a cloud—that they use to store and analyze large quantities of data, both public (e.g., public websites and social media postings) and sensitive (e.g., searches performed, private messages between individuals, books purchased). It is important to note that these systems are structured to permit rapid analyses of large fractions of those data, reliably and cost-effectively. Professional systems management, supported by the massive revenues of these companies and their large economies of scale, make them highly reliable and, it seems, also secure, although large disclosures of cloud-hosted information are reported periodically.

FIGURE 1
Cloud Security Responsibilities

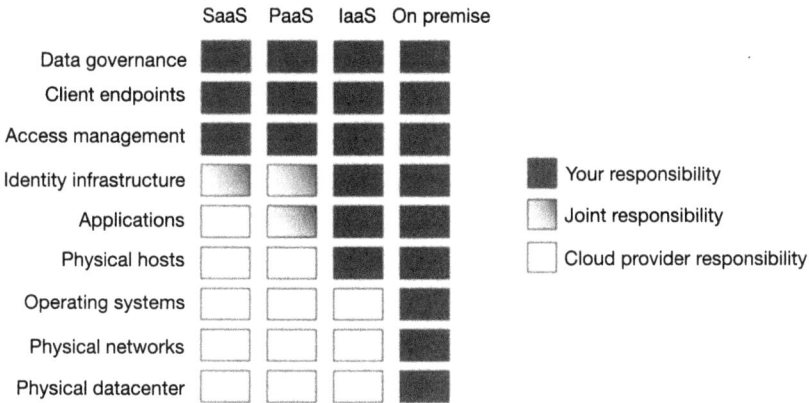

	SaaS	PaaS	IaaS	On premise	
Data governance	■	■	■	■	
Client endpoints	■	■	■	■	
Access management	■	■	■	■	
Identity infrastructure	□	□	■	■	■ Your responsibility
Applications	□	□	■	■	□ Joint responsibility
Physical hosts	□	□	■	■	□ Cloud provider responsibility
Operating systems	□	□	□	■	
Physical networks	□	□	□	■	
Physical datacenter	□	□	□	■	

NOTE: Adapted from Simorjay (2016).

Few external researchers and analysts can access the data that these infra-structures contain. However, several companies also operate public clouds that anyone with a credit card can access: for example, Amazon Web Services, Google Cloud, and Microsoft Azure. Each of these systems allows interested parties to acquire storage, computing, and other resources and services in an on-demand, pay-as-you go manner. It thus becomes straightforward to instantiate a private data enclave by allocating cloud storage, loading data into that storage, and allo-cating cloud computers to run analyses on that storage.

Can one reasonably use such a private data enclave to store, share, and analyze sensitive data? The answer to this question varies with geographical location and the data in question, but in the United States, the federal government has defined policies and procedures that can be followed to satisfy government regu-lations. To understand the nature of these policies, it is helpful to study the nature of the software components that go into creating a cloud-based service. Figure 1 shows how responsibilities may be divided according to whether one relies on the cloud provider just for infrastructure (IaaS) or also for platform services (PaaS). (The case in which the cloud provider operates application soft-ware, software-as-service or SaaS, is also shown, but is not relevant here.) The cloud provider is responsible for securing the low-level infrastructure that one would have to secure if he or she established a secure data enclave at his or her own institution ("on premise"), but that still leaves him or her responsible for the security of at least some higher level components.

Security in a cloud-hosted secure data enclave is thus the joint responsibility of the cloud provider and the user, which in the case of human subjects data, might be an individual institution or agency—or a *cloud data enclave operator* who provides services for many users and purposes.

In the United States, the federal government has defined an assessment and authorization process, the Federal Risk and Authorization Management Program (FedRAMP) (Office of Management and Budget 2013), for determining whether a particular combination of cloud provider and user software and procedures can be used for sensitive data from federal agencies. Becoming FedRAMP certified is an onerous process that involves not only substantial engineering but also documentation, assessment by a FedRAMP-accredited third-party assessment organization, and finally review by the FedRAMP joint assessment board. Thus, it is not a process to be taken lightly. However, once completed, the associated documentation can be relied upon by many potential consumers of the cloud service in question: another example of the economies of scale provided by cloud computing (Barnard 2016).

The Cloud Data Enclave: A Transformative New Approach?

I have reviewed a variety of approaches to large-scale data sharing and analysis. Each has distinct advantages and disadvantages for data providers, analysts, and method providers, and each has a place in the data universe. However, I believe that the emergence of secure, scalable, reliable, and inexpensive public clouds represents an opportunity for transformative change in how data about human subjects are organized, shared, and analyzed. In this section, I explain why this is so and outline steps that can be taken to realize its potential.

The basic idea is to leverage a commercial cloud as a secure, scalable *cloud data enclave* for data sharing, access, and analysis, implementing within that cloud a *safe data platform* that provides automated implementations of the various processes associated with data usage. In so doing, sensitive data from many providers can be discovered, linked, and analyzed in a controlled manner; and can permit analysts and method developers to share data, analysis methods, results, and expertise in ways not easily possible today. The approach thus combines elements of the data enclave, cloud, data lake, and data space approaches described above to meet the stakeholder requirements I identified.

Use public cloud to implement a secure and scalable virtual data enclave

The emergence of high-quality public clouds over the past decade has transformed how people, companies, and institutions work with information technology. Anyone with a credit card can now obtain cost-effective access not only to essentially unlimited storage and computing but also to many higher-level services that would be prohibitively expensive to implement within a single institution. A growing number of startups, research institutions, and research projects now take advantage of these capabilities.

The requirements that I identified for working with data about human subjects are distinctive but no less amenable to cloud hosting and automation.

Appropriately configured cloud services can be used to provide a secure location for datasets and software; enable packaging of software in reusable forms via virtual machines and containers; permit secure, controlled sharing of data and code; scale computation elastically as required; and enable monitoring and auditing of activity for reliability and security. In each case, users can leverage the enormous investment made by cloud providers in these areas.

The use of a public cloud to host a data enclave also enables other economies of scale. We can implement standardized, reusable implementations of data stewardship processes, such as those used to enforce data access policies. For example, if policy requires that a designated data steward approve all access requests, then cloud-hosted software can be used to route each request to the proper person, log the response for auditing purposes, and enable access if granted. Another policy might permit fully automated approvals, based for example on textual analysis of the proposed research project and prior approvals granted to the applicant. And, as noted, FedRAMP standards provide a framework for security reviews of the entire system and permit the sharing of review results and authority to operate packages across different data providers (Barnard 2016). A single location also facilitates collaboration, as data, code, results, and best practices can be shared more easily (subject of course to stewardship) when implemented in a uniform manner.

Provide automated safe stewardship mechanisms

As noted, a research infrastructure comprises not only technology but also process. I assert that the public cloud's uniform environment and economies of scale can make it feasible to replace current ad hoc, manual, incomplete implementations of data protection approaches with automated, and thus fully auditable and replicable, implementations, as I now discuss.

Safe people. We can use secure authentication to validate the identity of people seeking access to the enclave. Modern identity federation methods can enable reuse of existing credentials such as those associated with a researcher's home institution, thus leveraging existing investments in identity management (Barnett et al. 2011; Tuecke et al. 2016). Where policy demands, the enclave can impose additional authentication requirements, such as the use of multifactor authentication, whereby a user must demonstrate not only knowledge (something they know, such as a password) but also possession (something they hold, such as a mobile phone) and/or something about themselves (e.g., a fingerprint).

To ensure that users of the enclave operate from a common understanding of roles, responsibilities, and authorities, we can also require that potential users participate in an educational program. Certification by an approved program can be made a prerequisite for access.

Safe settings. The detailed security specifications and reviews defined by FedRAMP are one part of the technical security procedures required to provide safe settings. A key point is that the resources and expertise that cloud providers can bring to managing and monitoring access, testing for vulnerabilities, applying security patches, and the like will always be greater than can be brought to bear in an underresourced data provider. If data are to be accessible via the Internet, they will invariably be more secure in an appropriately configured cloud enclave than in a computer system within your own institution.

We can in addition provide supporting mechanisms such as *safe collections*; sets of data and associated metadata; plus policies governing, for example, where data within a collection must be stored, the approval process that must be followed to request access, and the monitoring required for access and use. Other platform capabilities can include secure logging of all user actions for audit and forensic purposes. Thus, we can ensure that, for example, whenever personally identifiable data from a particular state agency are loaded into the enclave, they are located on FedRAMP-compliant storage, enable access only via a particular remote desktop client and only after multifactor authentication, and do not permit data export except after review by a data steward.

Safe projects. We can implement structured and traceable project review and audits to ensure safe projects. We can provide supporting mechanisms for users such as *safe search*, to allow analysts to discover datasets that meet research goals and that they are allowed to access; and *safe workspaces*, sets of data plus code that can be used to analyze the data. Other mechanisms can allow a user to discover sensitive datasets, request access to those datasets, copy them into a workspace once access is granted, run analyses on the data within the workspace, and then export both data and code subject to approval processes.

Safe outputs. We can implement data export controls, such as processes that require review of a data export request by an authorized data steward, using suitably secure mechanisms to validate the identity of both the requesting user and the steward and to log the authorization decision.

Data providers will need to be able to specify which processes and policies should apply to each dataset that they make available in the enclave. Alternatively, it may be possible to reach agreement across data providers as to data classifications, in a manner analogous to the information security marking metadata defined within the national security context to enable "interagency access control, automated exchanges, and appropriate protection of shared intelligence."[3] Given such marking metadata, data stewardship tools can then determine without further user input where data are to be placed, what access policies apply, and what policies apply to derived data products.

We note that a system that streamlines the processes by which derived datasets are first created and then described, discovered, and reused does not necessarily ensure that data reuse will become commonplace. If users typically stop at the creation step, then the data enclave is likely to accumulate large quantities of "dark data" (Heidorn 2008): data that are meaningful only to their creator and thus are never reused by others. Potential solutions include incentives (e.g., for producing high-quality datasets that are reused), visibility (e.g., by notifying users

of datasets that have been produced with a particular set of inputs), and automation (e.g., to detect unused and duplicate data).

Build on a safe data platform to encourage contributions

The various mechanisms introduced above can be viewed as constituting a
cloud-hosted safe data platform that automates important elements of the sensitive data stewardship process. I use the word *platform* here deliberately. As
explained by van Alstyne, Parker, and Choudary (2016), a platform provides
infrastructure and rules that together realize a marketplace where producers and
consumers can meet.[4] A successful platform, like the iPhone, Android, Python,
or R, substantially eliminates the friction associated with developing, sharing,
finding, and consuming solutions. Similarly, a successful safe data platform will
enable many researchers and communities to prepare and analyze sensitive data,
share data and code, and collaborate. By enabling a rich ecosystem of methods
and tools, a safe data platform will allow research communities to continuously
contribute and test new approaches to research and policy questions as the nature
of data on human subjects changes. To this end, it will need to incorporate an
exchange where communities can deposit and discover reusable code and recipes
that they can use to build their own solutions and solution environments—thus enabling the dissemination of ideas and methods.

Figure 2 depicts how a safe data platform might work in practice. In this figure, (1) an analyst searches across multiple collections (e.g., data from different
federal or state agencies) to find data that meet specified criteria. This search is
performed based on metadata that the analyst is authorized by the appropriate
data steward(s) to see. (2) The analyst requests access to a dataset identified via
search, which triggers an approval workflow as specified by the associated policy.
(The figure shows an example policy: "Any workspaces to which data are loaded
must be located in FedRAMP-certified storage; researchers must present two-
factor credentials; and all approvals are manual.") In this case, the policy requires
(3) manual sign off by the associated data steward.

If approval is granted, then (4) the dataset can be loaded into a workspace with
the analyst's desired analytics environment. The analyst may also (5) import additional open or restricted data and code into the workspace. The analyst can then
use the data by working in the workspace, eventually creating new data that (6)
she or he can request permission to export for (7) external use (e.g., to create a
table in a research article) or for (8) publication to an existing or new collection
for sharing with other platform users for reuse. The latter *release process* involves
assigning a persistent identifier, assembling metadata for discovery, and organizing the data for easy loading into workspaces. The definition of standardized
release processes that can be adopted by different data providers is another area
that could facilitate the smooth operation of a cloud data enclave.

A steward can also use platform capabilities to facilitate use. For example, she
or he can create a workspace for data ingest, (5) import a restricted access dataset
to that workspace for preparatory clean-up and de-identification, and then (7)
publish the processed dataset to a collection for access. A specialized workspace

FIGURE 2
A Cloud-Hosted Safe Data Platform, Showing the Various Actors and Actions

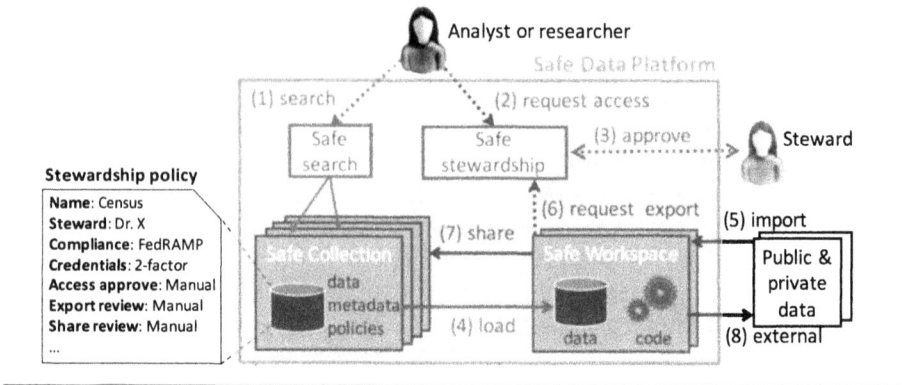

can be provided to support data stewards in this work. Note that a workspace itself can become data: a user can publish an entire computing environment, including data, tools, and so on, as she or he would any other dataset, to support reuse. The platform can also incorporate mechanisms designed to simplify or even enforce the implementation of the data management plans that federal institutions are increasingly requiring the researchers that they fund to follow.

Analysis of stakeholder needs

I suggest that the approach that I have just described can address stakeholder needs as follows. For data providers, it can

- *minimize data contribution costs* by implementing simple data upload protocols and APIs, supported by standardized data ingest methods where feasible;
- *improve releasability of data and publications*, by providing automated, secure, validated pipelines for extracting releasable data and associated metadata, and thus simplify adherence to data publication policies;
- *minimize risks* by enforcing data provider–specified policies for data access, analysis, and output—ideally supported by standardized data classifications; and
- *maximize benefits* by integrating their data into a rich ecosystem of other data providers, analysis, and method providers, in which controlled sharing of data, analysis methods, and expertise is encouraged.

For analysts, it can

- *simplify access to data* by providing standardized methods for discovering, requesting access to, and accessing sensitive data;
- *enable integration* of datasets from different sources;

- *educate them in best-of-breed methods*, by providing access to common analysis procedures/techniques and examples of how tools are used by other researchers;
- *encourage collaboration* by providing standardized methods for creating and sharing annotations on datasets and code;
- *facilitate reproducible research* by automating the capture of the steps followed to obtain a particular result; and
- *enable big data analysis* by allowing analysts to scale computational resources to meet computational needs—as long as they (or someone else) can pay for the cloud computing time.

For method providers, it can

- *provide access to data* required to design, test, and evaluate new methods; and
- *provide access to communities* of individuals who share interests and experience in problems and methods.

Conclusion

New data sources present fascinating opportunities for new understandings of human beings and their interactions and, thus, better policies, programs, and science. For example, analysts might combine detailed hospital admissions and outcomes records with fine-grained data from networks of environmental sensors to study the impact of pollution on health and well-being in ways not possible today, or integrate data from multiple state and federal agencies with high-resolution map data to examine geographical factors effecting recidivism. But seizing such opportunities requires new research infrastructures that will enable *analysts* to easily access, integrate, and analyze datasets from multiple sources, while also maximizing benefits and minimizing costs and risks for *data providers*. The fact that new data sources are often larger, noisier, and less structured than data conventionally studied in social science leads to a third set of requirements for research infrastructures, relating to scale and access by *method providers*.

I have reviewed approaches for large-scale sharing and analysis of both general science data and sensitive data about human subjects. I argue that developments in cloud computing present opportunities for transformative new approaches to working with sensitive data, in which public clouds are used to create secure data enclaves in which currently manual and ad hoc data stewardship processes are standardized and automated. Such systems can enable sensitive data from different sources to be discovered, integrated, and analyzed in appropriately controlled manners. The use of such cloud enclaves may appear scary. But with appropriate care and controls, data can be more secure and better managed when located in the cloud than in a local machine room, much as money is safer in a bank than in your home or office. Cloud data enclaves can, furthermore, allow researchers to share analysis methods, results, and expertise in ways not easily possible today. The development of such systems, thus, has the potential to both accelerate research and enable a flowering of new methods for studying human subjects.

The analysis of sensitive human data raises profound legal and ethical challenges that no technology, however sophisticated, can ever fully address. However, I believe that well-designed technologies, when operated in appropriately controlled cloud environments, can reduce both opportunities for improper use and barriers to secure data access, use, and reuse. They can, for example, provide safe environments for data cleaning; ensure secure auditing of data access; and protect against attack vectors that individual research labs, statistical agencies, and other institutions would be hard pressed to counter.

The proposed approach can also serve to broaden the community of researchers working to improve the state of the art in safe data management and analysis. New statistical inference methods are needed to deal with dramatically larger, noisier, and more diverse datasets. Both social scientists and computer scientists will gain from being able to access real data about social problems, without having to create and certify their own trusted data service. The platform should spur the development of many new methods and tools as computer scientists work with different research communities to customize environments; an extensible code exchange can facilitate the transfer and adoption of new methods in many research communities.

Notes

1. The Cancer Genome Atlas (TCGA) Data Use Certification Agreement. 20 August 2014. Available from cancergenome.nih.gov (accessed 1 June 2017).
2. Personal communication.
3. Information security marking metadata. Office of the Director of National Intelligence. Available from www.dni.gov (accessed 1 June 2017).
4. See https://hbr.org/search?term=sangeet+paul+choudary.

References

Atkins, Daniel E., Kelvin K. Droegemeier, Stuart I. Feldman, Hector Garcia-Molina, Michael L. Klein, David G. Messerschmitt, Paul Messina, Jeremiah P. Ostriker, and Margaret H. Wright. 2003. *Revolutionizing science and engineering through cyberinfrastructure: Report of the National Science Foundation blue-ribbon panel on cyberinfrastructure*. Washington, DC: NSF. Available from www.nsf.gov.
Barnard, Rick. 26 October 2016. Think FedRAMP is a bottleneck? Think again. *Federal Computing Week*.
Barnett, William, Von Welch, Alan Walsh, and Craig A. Stewart. 2011. *A roadmap for using NSF cyberinfrastructure with InCommon*. Available from http://hdl.handle.net/2022/13024.
Barocas, Solon, and Helen Nissenbaum. 2014. Big data's end run around anonymity and consent. In *Privacy, big data, and the public good: Frameworks for engagement*, eds. Julia Lane, Victoria Stodden, Stefan Bender, and Helen Nissenbaum, 44–75. New York, NY: Cambridge University Press.
Bender, Stefan, and Jörg Heining. 2011. The research-data-centre in research-data-centre approach: A first step towards decentralised international data sharing. Paper presented at the IASSIST Conference, 2 June 2011, Vancouver, BC.

Benson, Dennis A., Karen Clark, Ilene Karsch-Mizrachi, David J. Lipman, James Ostell, and Eric W. Sayers. 2014. GenBank. *Nucleic Acids Research* 42 (D1): D32–D37.

Berman, Helen M., John Westbrook, Zukang Feng, Gary Gilliland, Talapady N. Bhat, Helge Weissig, Ilya N. Shindyalov, and Philip E. Bourne. 2000. The protein data bank. *Nucleic Acids Research* 28 (1): 235–42.

Bernholdt, David, Shishir Bharathi, David Brown, Kasidit Chanchio, Meili Chen, Ann Chervenak, Luca Cinquini, Bob Drach, Ian Foster, Peter Fox, et al. 2005. The Earth System Grid: Supporting the next generation of climate modeling research. *Proceedings of the IEEE* 93 (3): 485–95.

Borders, Kevin, Eric Vander Weele, Billy Lau, and Atul Prakash. 2009. Protecting confidential data on personal computers with storage capsules. Paper presented at the 18th USENIX Security Symposium, Ann Arbor, MI.

Cattuto, Ciro, Vittorio Loreto, and Luciano Pietronero. 2007. Semiotic dynamics and collaborative tagging. *Proceedings of the National Academy of Sciences* 104 (5): 1461–64.

Chard, Kyle, Mike D'Arcy, Ben Heavner, Ian Foster, Carl Kesselman, Ravi Madduri, Alexis Rodriguez, Stian Soiland-Reyes, Carole Goble, Kristi Clark, et al. 2016. I'll take that to go: Big data bags and minimal identifiers for exchange of large, complex datasets. In *Proceedings of the IEEE International Conference on Big Data*. Washington, DC: IEEE.

Desai, Tanvi, Felix Ritchie, and Richard Welpton. 2016. Five safes: Designing data access for research. University of the West of England Economics Working Paper Series 1601, Bristol.

Domingo-Ferrer, Josep, and Josep Maria Mateo-Sanz. 2002. Practical data-oriented microaggregation for statistical disclosure control. *IEEE Transactions on Knowledge and Data Engineering* 14 (1): 189–201.

Dwork, Cynthia. 2014. Differential privacy: A cryptographic approach to private data analysis. In *Privacy, big data, and the public good: Frameworks for engagement*, eds. Julia Lane, Victoria Stodden, Stefan Bender, and Helen Nissenbaum, 296–322. New York, NY: Cambridge University Press.

Dwork, Cynthia, Frank McSherry, Kobbi Nissim, and Adam Smith. 2006. Calibrating noise to sensitivity in private data analysis. In *Proceedings of the Theory of Cryptography Conference*, 265–84. Berlin: Springer.

Dwork, Cynthia, and Adam Smith. 2010. Differential privacy for statistics: What we know and what we want to learn. *Journal of Privacy and Confidentiality* 1 (2): 135–54.

Finholt, Thomas A. 2002. Collaboratories. *Annual Review of Information Science and Technology* 36 (1): 73–107.

Foster, Ian. 2002. The grid: A new infrastructure for 21st century science. *Physics Today* 55 (2): 42–47.

Foster, Ian, and Robert Grossman. 2003. Data integration in a bandwidth-rich world. *Communications of the ACM* 46 (11): 51–57.

Franklin, Michael, Alon Halevy, and David Maier. 2005. From databases to dataspaces: A new abstraction for information management. *ACM SIGMOD Record* 34 (4): 27–33.

Goecks, Jeremy, Anton Nekrutenko, James Taylor, and the Galaxy Team. 2010. Galaxy: A comprehensive approach for supporting accessible, reproducible, and transparent computational research in the life sciences. *Genome Biology* 11 (8): R86.

Grossman, Robert L., Allison P. Heath, Vincent Ferretti, Harold E. Varmus, Douglas R. Lowy, Warren A. Kibbe, and Louis M. Staudt. 2016. Toward a shared vision for cancer genomic data. *New England Journal of Medicine* 375 (12): 1109–12.

Halevy, Alon, Flip Korn, Natalya F. Noy, Christopher Olston, Neoklis Polyzotis, Sudip Roy, and Steven Euijong Whang. 2016. Goods: Organizing Google's datasets. In *Proceedings of the 2016 International Conference on Management of Data*, 795–806. Washington, DC: ACM.

Heidorn, P. Bryan. 2008. Shedding light on the dark data in the long tail of science. *Library Trends* 57 (2): 280–99.

Hey, Tony, Stewart Tansley, and Kristin M. Tolle. 2009. *The fourth paradigm: Data-intensive scientific discovery*. Redmond, WA: Microsoft Research.

Kluyver, Thomas, Benjamin Ragan-Kelley, Fernando Pérez, Brian Granger, Matthias Bussonnier, Jonathan Frederic, Kyle Kelley, Jessica Hamrick, Jason Grout, Sylvain Corlay, et al. 2016. Jupyter Notebooks—A publishing format for reproducible computational workflows. In *Positioning and power in academic publishing: Players, agents and agendas*, eds. Fernando Loizides and Birgit Schmidt, 87–90. Amsterdam: IOS Press.

Lamanna, Massimo. 2004. The LHC computing grid project at CERN. *Nuclear Instruments and Methods in Physics Research Section A: Accelerators, Spectrometers, Detectors and Associated Equipment* 534 (1): 1–6.

Lane, Julia, Pascal Heus, and Tim Mulcahy. 2008. Data access in a cyber world: Making use of cyberinfrastructure. *Transactions on Data Privacy* 1 (1): 2–16.

Metzler, Kate. 22 November 2016. The big data rich and the big data poor: The new digital divide raises questions about future academic research. LSE Impact Blog. Available from blogs.lse.ac.uk/impactof socialsciences.

Meyer, Folker, Daniel Paarmann, Mark D'Souza, Robert Olson, Elizabeth M. Glass, Michael Kubal, Tobias Paczian, Alex Rodriguez, Rick Stevens, Andreas Wilke, et al. 2008. The metagenomics RAST server—A public resource for the automatic phylogenetic and functional analysis of metagenomes. *BMC Bioinformatics* 9 (1). doi:10.1186/1471- 2105-9-386.

Moreau, Luc, Ben Clifford, Juliana Freire, Joe Futrelle, Yolanda Gil, Paul Groth, Natalia Kwasnikowska, Simon Miles, Paolo Missier, Jim Myers, et al. 2011. The open provenance model core specification (v1. 1). *Future Generation Computer Systems* 27 (6): 743–56.

Office of Management and Budget. 2013. *Enhancing the security of federal information and information systems*. Washington, DC: OMB. Available from obamawhitehouse.archives.gov.

Ohm, Paul. 2010. Broken promises of privacy: Responding to the surprising failure of anonymization. *UCLA Law Review* 57:1701–77.

Overbeek, Ross A., Terence Disz, and Rick Stevens. 2004. The SEED: A peer-to-peer environment for genome annotation. *Communications of the ACM* 47 (11): 46–51.

Paskin, Norman. 2005. Digital object identifiers for scientific data. *Data Science Journal* 4:12–20.

Phillips, Mark, and Bartha M. Knoppers. 2016. The discombobulation of de-identification. *Nature Biotechnology* 34 (11): 1102–3.

Seastrom, Marilyn M. 2010. *Statistical methods for protecting personally identifiable information in aggregate reporting*. National Center for Education Statistics Report 2011-603. Washington, DC: National Center for Education Statistics.

Simorjay, F. 2016. *Shared responsibilities for cloud computing*. Redmond WA: Microsoft. Available from gallery.technet.microsoft.com.

Skinner, Chris J. 2009. Statistical disclosure control for survey data. *Handbook of Statistics* 29:381–96.

Szalay, Alexander, and Jim Gray. 2001. The world-wide telescope. *Science* 293 (5537): 2037– 40.

Szalay, Alexander S., Jim Gray, Ani R. Thakar, Peter Z. Kunszt, Tanu Malik, Jordan Raddick, Christopher Stoughton, and Jan vandenBerg. 2002. The SDSS Skyserver: Public access to the Sloan Digital Sky Server data. In *Proceedings of the 2002 ACM SIGMOD International Conference on Management of Data*, 570–81. Washington, DC: ACM.

Terrizzano, Ignacio, Peter M. Schwarz, Mary Roth, and John E. Colino. 2015. Data wrangling: The challenging journey from the wild to the lake. Paper presented at the 7th Biennial Conference on Innovative Data Systems Research, 4–7 January 2015, Asilomar, CA.

Tuecke, Steven, Rachana Ananthakrishnan, Kyle Chard, Mattias Lidman, Brendan McCollam, and Ian Foster. 2016. Globus Auth: A research identity and access management platform. In *Proceedings of the 12th IEEE International Conference on e-Science*, 203–12. Washington, DC: IEEE.

Uzuner, Özlem, Yuan Luo, and Peter Szolovits. 2007. Evaluating the state-of-the-art in automatic de-identification. *Journal of the American Medical Informatics Association* 14 (5): 550–63.

van Alstyne, Marshall W., Geoffrey G. Parker, and Sangeet Paul Choudary. 2016. Pipelines, platforms, and the new rules of strategy. *Harvard Business Review* 94 (4): 54–62.

Willenborg, Leon, and Ton De Waal. 2012. *Elements of statistical disclosure control*, vol. 155. New York, NY: Springer.

Williams, Dean N., V. Balaji, Luca Cinquini, Sébastien Denvil, Daniel Duffy, Ben Evans, Robert Ferraro, Rose Hansen, Michael Lautenschlager, and Claire Trenham. 2016. A global repository for planet-sized experiments and observations. *Bulletin of the American Meteorological Society* 97 (5): 803–16.

Zeng, Jiaan, Guangchen Ruan, Alexander Crowell, Atul Prakash, and Beth Plale. 2014. Cloud computing data capsules for non-consumptive use of texts. In *Proceedings of the 5th ACM workshop on scientific cloud computing*, 9–16. Washington, DC: ACM.

Section II: Data Producers

Barriers to Accessing State Data and Approaches to Addressing Them

By
ROBERT M. GOERGE

The technical challenges of accessing large administrative datasets are easily addressed with the advances in data security, computational resources, and the Internet. The most vexing barriers are legal and ethical issues, and control of the data by the agencies that generate it. This article describes those issues and promotes the notion that partnerships with the data providers are necessary to facilitate access to researchers, both inside and outside government, but also to provide benefits, in the form of evidence, research, and information to the data providers themselves. Ultimately, training of all stakeholders around the secure and responsible use of data and appropriate data stewardship is necessary to facilitate the increased use of administrative data that is required to develop evidence that will have an impact on government services and programs for individuals and families.

Keywords: administrative data; state government; intergovernmental relationships; public private partnerships; data security; barriers

While it was not always so, it is now generally accepted that administrative data are a valuable resource for rigorous research and evaluation (Card et al. 2010; NSF 2007).[1] Administrative datasets can contain data on the outcomes of program participation and the characteristics of all program participants. It can contain identifying information for both individuals and organizations and data that are sensitive and confidential because

Robert M. Goerge is a Chapin Hall senior research fellow with more than 25 years of research focused on improving the available data and information on children and families, particularly those who require specialized services related to maltreatment, disability, poverty, or violence. He is also a senior fellow at the Harris School of Public Policy and Computation Institute at the University of Chicago and a senior fellow and lecturer at the Harris School for Public Policy Studies.

Correspondence: rgoerge@chapinhall.org

DOI: 10.1177/0002716217741257

characteristics of specific individuals can be known. Because the outcomes and program data are not always in the same dataset, multiple administrative datasets need to be combined or administrative data need to be linked to survey data for administrative data to be a powerful tool for doing rigorous research at a large scale in a cost-effective manner. The federal government has recognized the potential value of administrative data by asking the Commission on Evidence-Based Policymaking to

> determine the optimal arrangement for which administrative data on federal programs and tax expenditures, survey data, and related statistical data series may be integrated and made available to facilitate program evaluation, continuous improvement, policy-relevant research, and cost-benefit analyses by qualified researchers and institutions.[2]

The creation of the commission recognizes that the current state of affairs is not optimal. Administrative data are not often easily available to researchers either inside or outside of government as there are few arrangements whereby the data easily flow to researchers and research organizations. Much has been written and said about the barriers to accessing such data from states for research, policy, and program purposes (Goerge 1997; Hotz, Goerge, et al. 1998; U.S. General Accounting Office 1992). However, even as the federal government states that "the increased use of administrative data for statistical purposes can generate a range of benefits," little has been done to ensure that a primary collector of such data—state agencies—has the incentives or resources to improve data use for research and evaluation.[3] The premise of this article is that to address the barriers, states need to be more closely engaged in the analysis of their data for their benefit.

State agencies are not required to provide access to any researcher. These data are collected primarily for operational purposes, be it determining eligibility for programs, tracking benefits paid to program participants, paying providers of services, and as frontline case management—the management of prisoners, patients, foster children, students, and others for whom the state has responsibility. These systems track data on human resources employed by the state and services provided by non-governmental organizations (NGOs). These systems compile information on taxes paid by individuals and businesses. They collect data on births, deaths, disabilities, and diseases for public health and other purposes. Using administrative data for research, be it done by analysts inside or outside of government, is low on the list of primary uses. Until 30 years ago, researchers in the domains of employment, criminal and juvenile justice, human services, higher education, early childhood education, and health care used either survey methods or paper record extraction to compile data to conduct their work. Using administrative data for research is still not routine, but it is becoming more commonplace as states are increasingly expected to become data-driven by elected officials and the public. Even those government staff trained in research in universities may not be familiar with the notion of using administrative data for research.

There are multiple stakeholders concerned with improving access to administrative data from state agencies. Each of the stakeholders can impact access either as providers, users, or facilitators of data use. As the controller of the data, state agencies are the primary stakeholder. Researchers and research organizations increasingly value administrative data to conduct research. This article focuses on the interests of state agency leaders as the primary decision-makers around access and researchers as the primary user of state administrative data. Aligning the interests of these two stakeholder groups would benefit both. Closer collaboration and greater communication would help to address the barriers and modify what is often an adversarial process between the holders and users of the data.

There are clearly others who have a special interest and can be instrumental in improving the use of a specific set of administrative data in a secure and effective manner. As the funder of many programs and the collection of much of the data, the federal government has an interest in the quality of federal program management and the implementation of policy, including the protection of human subjects. Governors and state agencies other than that of the state agency holding the data also have a stake in that they may need administrative data to evaluate and improve other state programs. Advocates can be both interested in the analysis of the data as they can point to where classes of individuals may require protection under the law. They, in addition to the agencies that collect the data, are also protectors of the privacy of individuals. Class action lawsuits have been both a positive and negative force around the use of administrative data.[4] Finally, the public has an interest in such data—individuals can be served by better use of data, but can also harmed by breaches or other improper uses, which is why data security and responsible use is of the utmost importance.

This article describes the barriers and risks, but primarily focuses on how state agencies may benefit when researchers and research organizations have increased access to state administrative data to improve the effectiveness of state programs. A less appealing and likely politically unfeasible alternative, which would benefit the federal government, is to require state and local agencies to provide data to researchers to evaluate federally funded programs. Listing the multiple strands of public and political pushback on such a requirement is beyond the scope of this article. The focus is on the better option of moving toward optimizing the benefits of increased access for all stakeholders.

While this article focuses on researcher access to data, both inside and outside of government, other stakeholders seeking access to an agency's data face similar issues. The barriers are similar, and the potential approaches to addressing them are as well.

This article argues for the creation and use of curated longitudinal administrative data that can be linked at the individual level with programmatic and outcome data in a secure, legal, and efficient manner. Access to these data should be governed by data sharing agreements (DSA) or memoranda of understanding (MOU) that describe the conditions under which researchers could access the administrative data. Other data, such as survey data, could be linked to longitudinal administrative data to enhance both datasets. Ideally, data across states could be linked.

The approach I advocate centers on state agency leadership as a driving force for the increased analysis of their data to improve federal, state, and local policy and programs. I discuss the current circumstances around accessing state administrative data in terms of barriers to access, then present approaches that would facilitate the goal of accessing the data necessary to improve the well-being of U.S. residents.

Barriers to Access

This section discusses the barriers to accessing administrative data. Both the need for such data and concerns about how these data are protected are increasing. The final report of the Commission on Evidence-Based Policymaking (2017) states that "the American public will be concerned about exactly how those data are being used and whether the privacy and confidentiality of individuals and organizations are being protected" (p. 8). And as the report calls for additional evidence to support policymaking, it also states that "these administrative data, collected in the first instance to serve routine program operation purposes, also can be used to assess how well programs are achieving their intended goals" (p. 9).

The concerns that key stakeholders have around privacy and confidentiality as they protect the public can act as barriers to access and to the increased use of administrative data. Organizations providing administrative data to third parties must be confident that the data will be kept secure and not disclosed for purposes beyond the explicit purposes of evidence-building.

It is important to point out that getting permission to access the data and actually accessing the data are two different activities and should likely be the job of two different units of an organization. The capacity of state agencies to produce a dataset varies tremendously. Some can produce one in days if they regularly curate their own data and the data fit the need of the researchers. At the other extreme, there may be no one whose role includes the creation of appropriate datasets, and doing so could mean months of delay.

Risk aversion

Although access to state agency data for external research and other purposes happens, the controllers of the data—state agency leaders—are often either reluctant to provide data to researchers or simply have not made their use a priority. It is reasonable for them to be reluctant because the results can potentially be harmful to the agency or to a particular leader. Although good data sharing agreements can ensure that a state agency has the ability to review interpretations of results and to provide input, even in these cases, a report may negatively impact the funding for a program and, more importantly, vulnerable individuals and families who rely on the program. Often, the reaction to a critical evaluation may not be to improve the program, but to defend it through political or anecdotal arguments.

Inadequacy of federal datasets compiled from state data

State agencies do provide data to other agencies, particularly federal agencies, when there are requirements to do so. This compliance, though, requires significant state resources. In theory, these data, held by federal agencies could be used for research and evaluation, just as federally collected data, such as tax data, has been shown to be an excellent resource for research. However, although federal agencies receive these data from states, the data often have significant prohibitions around re-use, such as using the data for another purpose (e.g., research). They either cannot be used for general research or evaluation purposes due to federal law (National Database on New Hires at the U.S. Department of Health and Human Services [HHS]) or require permission from states to be used for research or evaluation purposes (unemployment insurance wage data at the U.S. Census Bureau, for example). Addressing these restrictions, particularly when the federal government has an interest in knowing what programs are working for whom, would be a step forward especially if states benefit from the increased ability to reuse data. However, legislative change, which would be required in many cases to use such data, is slow to come, and in some cases, there have been steps backward. Recently, the Child Care Development Fund program (HHS) removed the requirement of providing PII (Social Security Numbers) to HHS for parents and children participating in this program.[5] Another example is the unemployment insurance wage data that the U.S. Census Bureau receives under the Longitudinal Employer-Household Dynamics program. In most cases, the U.S. Census Bureau cannot use the state data for other purposes without permission from the state.

Is it legal?

Some state agency leaders believe that it is not legal for them to share data with researchers, because, in several programs, administrative data have to be used to improve or benefit the administration of the program. This includes research that is conducted with administrative data from Temporary Assistance for Needy Families (TANF), Medicaid, and Supplemental Nutrition Assistance Program (SNAP), and education programs. For example, Medicaid data can be used to improve the administration of the Medicaid program. Education data with PII can be used for "conducting studies for, or on behalf of, schools, school districts, or postsecondary institutions."[6,7] Internal Revenue Service (IRS) data can be used for research if it contributes to tax administration. Clearly, whether research supports the administration of the program is open to interpretation. The onus is on either party to justify that the use of administrative data does inform the administration of the program. An evaluation of a program should improve the administration of the program in some way.

The most straightforward way for a research organization to access administrative data is to have a contract between the state agency and the research organization. States may also participate in national evaluation efforts where the intention is to provide evidence for the effectiveness of a new program or policy. External researchers are often part of these efforts, as national evaluators or as evaluators for specific states. That being said, this access, as well as contracts, are restrictive in that the product is controlled by the state or federal agency, and the administrative data can only be used for the specific evaluation purpose.

What is the benefit?

States do provide data to researchers when they see that there is a benefit to a state agency. That these data should improve program administration can be the basis for overcoming all other barriers—it changes the premise under which state agencies and researchers are discussing the reasons to provide access to researchers. The requests for data should always include how states would benefit from the research. If researchers cannot describe the benefit for a state providing the data, they should perhaps not get access.

Defining the legal relationship

As mentioned above, state administrative data sharing requires a data sharing agreement (or DSA or MOU). Once a researcher gets to the stage of creating a DSA with a state agency, some of the barriers will have been addressed. Although templates have been developed, they are seldom used, and these DSAs are often created from whole cloth. Good DSAs clearly outline the duties and interests of each party and the ability for the data providers to review draft reports and comment on them, clearly provide permission for specific research activities or how permission for each activity happens, have a duration beyond a single project and official contacts for all parties, and specify requirements for data security. Other features may include authorizing rules, regulations, or legislation; detailed descriptions of the data to be shared; and lists of individuals who will access the data. All the components of data sharing agreements can be considered to be barriers to accessing data and using it. There may be contention on any of these particular issues.

Once a DSA is in place, the path to data access may be clearer, even if the process does not move quickly. Even with a DSA, state agencies can decide that addressing a particular research question is not in their interest and can employ language in the DSA to reject a particular project.

It comes down to trust

Currently, the core of successful state administrative data sharing is trust between the agency and the individual researcher or research organizations. State agency leaders and staff must trust researchers (and other external entities) to protect data from breaches, to not disclose data or preliminary findings to other organizations (researchers, media, advocacy groups) without explicit permission, and to pursue research that is unknown to the agency. They must also trust researchers to protect human subjects and follow institutional review board

(IRB) regulations where applicable, to understand their programs, to understand the data, to facilitate the review of the methods and findings by the state, to employ that most rigorous methods possible, to work with the state to understand the implications of the research, and to work in good faith to improve the programs of the state agency. Ultimately, a lack of trust between state leaders and researchers acts as a primary barrier to using administrative data, because state agency leaders have so much control.

The need for multiagency or program data

Because addressing a research question often requires the combination or linking of data across agencies, accessing data from multiple sources may be a barrier simply because of the need to convince multiple state decision-makers to share their data. It increases the number of "yes" answers needed to accomplish a goal. Many projects stumble because key datasets cannot be accessed.

Furthermore, state leadership may be concerned about researchers having data from multiple agencies. When data are combined from multiple sources, new data can be created that increase the potential costs of a breach in data security—for example, if combining school and health data results in a current street address of an individual with a disability. However, since such breaches are rare, perhaps a more pertinent concern for government leaders is what will be said about their program participants on topics for which they do not have data.

State agencies tend to be reluctant to share data with each other. Some of their concerns about sharing with other government agencies are similar to those that they have in sharing data with external researchers. In addition, there are sometimes concerns about other agencies "knowing their business." The reality is that state agencies are often in competition for scarce resources, that their programs are at risk of being cut, that their staff may be reassigned, or that their authority over their operations is diminished as a result of information that is externally compiled. These factors sometimes actually benefit researchers since state agencies would rather share data with a third party than with each other when the benefit is clear or the risk is low. Again, however, it is difficult to disentangle the complex relationships between stakeholders.

Can the data be produced?

The capacity of states to provide access to external organizations is another potential barrier to using administrative data. Even if state leaders are supportive and a DSA can be finalized, the ability of a state agency to physically provide data may be limited. Both the technical and time capacity of state agency staff may be limited. Many states do not create datasets that can be easily shared. If any file that contains the data that a researcher needs does exist, if it is possible for a researcher to receive and work with that file, accepting existing formats is often the most expedient route to an external organization receiving the data. Any special extracts or reformatting of data may either ultimately prevent access or delay it significantly.

Documentation

Similarly, the capacity of researchers to both assist states in providing them with what is needed or to use the data provided is a potential barrier. Numerous proposed projects end because researchers simply do not know what is available. This lack of capacity is brought about in part by a lack of documentation about what is available. States have sparse, if any, metadata to inform researchers about the contents or quality of the data. Because the raw data are typically only used by a few agency staff who work near each other, all the knowledge about a particular dataset may be "in their heads" or kept in documentation that is impossible for an outsider to understand. Combinations of numbers and letters describing fields (variables), such as "H05AB," may be obvious to those who work with the data all the time, but are foreign to a researcher who acquires a dataset without documentation. The lack documentation or metadata usually results in back-and-forth between agency staff and researchers about what is available and what is needed. Such conversations often lead to additional delays while the staff pull together information. Often, the first dataset does not meet the specific needs of the researcher—either because of its contents or the researcher's inability to use the data.

Skills of the researcher

States today often use relational databases to store their data, and the structure of these databases is optimized to support the administration of relevant programs. This means that the database is likely highly normalized to promote speedier processing of individual transactions. However, this also means that the data that a researcher is asking for may exist in dozens, if not hundreds, of individual database tables. For example, one table may only contain the race of individuals in a program, while another only contains the gender. This requires either the state programmers to de-normalize the data or the researcher to do this. Again, this creates a delay for the researcher's analysis. The existence of any type of file that the agency is using to calculate statistics is, as mentioned above, often the quickest way to get most of the data that a researcher might need.

Cost

Obtaining the financial resources to process administrative data into research-ready datasets is another significant barrier. While it is often said that using administrative data is a less expensive way to obtain data than primary data collection, the extraction, transformation, and curation of administrative data is an expense that is not easily funded through traditional funding mechanisms. Several foundations have made a commitment to funding such efforts, particularly in university settings, but as standards and best practices are developed, it is clear that sustainability is a challenge.[8]

It is often impossible for an external party to understand the internal decision-making process of an agency that is deciding whether to provide access to a researcher. The reason given for denying access may not be the actual reason access was denied. This lack of transparency makes it difficult to address barriers one by one. Most state agencies do not have clear policies regarding access to their publicly available data; this creates further barriers.

The next sections address promising approaches to overcoming these barriers, approaches that have worked in some places and have features that could be generalized to other contexts. I begin with a set of requirements that is necessary for both the state and the researcher to go forward.

Addressing Data Security

First and foremost, administrative data must be kept secure and protected from unauthorized access. Without the peace of mind that identified data will not be released or "hacked," state leaders would not take the first step in providing external access. The good news is that the technology exists to keep the data secure and restrict access to only those who are fully vetted to view and process the data. State agencies are increasingly able to assess a researcher's ability to keep the data secure. Technical and procedural safeguards must be implemented, maintained, updated, and then communicated to the owners of the data so that data security is no longer a barrier.

A few states and private research organizations have curated data for use by researchers. Best practices—policies and procedures that organizations must implement—are forming as federal law such as the Health Insurance Portability and Accountability Act (HIPAA), the Family Educational Rights and Privacy Act (FERPA), and Code of Federal Regulations (CFR) 42 Part 2 require specific procedures and policies to be in place.[9] This is the topic of another article in this volume, but it is important for state administrators, who increasingly employ chief information security officers, to have confidence in the research organizations' data security.

Opportunities

The leadership of state agencies clearly have important programmatic and policy challenges that could be addressed by increased analysis of their own data and likely data from other local, state, or federal agencies. In a recent needs assessment, state agency leaders expressed the need to link to data outside of their agencies to better understand the characteristics of their program participants and the outcomes that they experience (Weigensberg et al. 2015).

It is difficult for them to pursue this when they cannot attract the workforce or financial resources to both acquire and curate high quality data and to analyze the databases once built. With a few exceptions, state agencies in the health, human services, education, and public safety areas are understaffed.

To improve researcher access to state and local agency data, the research and academic communities should fill the gaps of both the leadership's need for more analysis and their lack of the human resources to do it. Researchers must show that their work can address the needs of state agencies and is not meant only for their peers. The academic community can train the current and future federal, state, and local agency workforce so that, at a minimum, these agencies can partner with researchers to make their data work for them. Ideally, government analysts could do more to meet their leadership's needs for analysis and help them to realize the benefit of more analysis.

Working to address state agency need is typically not rewarded in the university setting, because it often does not impact whether research is published. Most researchers do not have incentives to maintain relationships in which they provide benefits to state agencies over a long period of time, because a couple of well-placed peer-reviewed journal articles can be sufficient for promotion. Perhaps the process of securing data from government agencies needs to be given the same credit in academic departments as designing primary data collection efforts.

Research organizations, which have a mission to produce high-quality research that impacts public policy, depend on the cooperation of operating state agencies and rely on "soft" money, have a greater incentive to maintain relationships with state agencies, and provide technical or research assistance over a sustained period. The quid pro quo is for these research organizations to receive administrative data from state agencies, often on a regular basis, so that the data can be maintained and the quality can be ensured.

A common complaint among state agency leaders is that they cannot get information from researchers quickly when they need it. University faculty are not often able to provide information quickly—they often rely on student research assistance and cannot drop everything to address the need of a state agency leader. Also, again, this activity provides few benefits for the university faculty member. However, research centers, like the Institute for Research on Poverty at the University of Wisconsin, which curates Wisconsin state agency data, does have the ability to provide a quick response. Often, a state leader is extremely appreciative of whatever he or she can get when the agency's staff cannot provide needed information. This is a capacity issue that could be addressed to improve access to organizations that can provide a quick response.

The fluency of all stakeholders in the use of administrative data should be continually enhanced. Federal statistical agencies require yearly training on how to handle sensitive data, how to address data security, and the legal requirements and penalties associated with their positions. This, while very important, is only the first step. As the Big Data meme is upon us, the expectations of government leaders to address the use of their own data have increased. While being data-driven has been a goal for years, the informed general public, including advocates and the media, is asking why government is not using its data better.

However, even when a state leader may provide his or her agency's data for study, data from other state agencies may be necessary for the research. There are multiple efforts that clarify and facilitate the linkage of datasets across programs.

Perhaps the best example of this is the use of unemployment insurance (UI) wage data to measure the impact of job training or other programs that have increased earnings as a primary outcome, such as the TANF leaver studies at the time of welfare reform (Cancian et al. 2002). Another example is a study including multiple states that looked at the impact of the Great Recession on the use of UI and SNAP (Finifter and Prell 2013). Accessing data from multiple programs or agencies to build comprehensive datasets (Integrated Data Systems, or IDS) is at the very least on a few agencies' agendas in most states. The State Longitudinal Data Systems program of the Department of Education exists in multiple states and is an example of a database-building initiative that can benefit researchers inside and outside of government.

Strategies for Creating Infrastructures for Increased Data Sharing

There have been several efforts to share state administrative data with external researchers over the past three decades, although no one effort has been replicated to the extent that it has become a model for access. What can we learn from these efforts to build more generalized best practices around securing external state administrative data access?

State government examples

State governments have been traditionally inhospitable to researchers, although there are notable exceptions. The Washington State Department of Social and Health Services, since welfare reform; the Illinois Department of Children and Family Services; the New York State Office of Temporary and Disability Assistance; and the Florida Department of Education have (or have had) research units that operate very successfully within the bureaucratic structure. Does this internal success have implications for external data sharing? In these particular cases, the answer is that it has facilitated data sharing to external research organizations in limited ways. Trusted researchers and research organizations have received data regularly to conduct multiple research projects. The Actionable Intelligence for Social Policy (AISP) project has, in recent years, brought together states that have built integrated data systems internally along with research organizations that have done the same. Within the AISP group, there is variation in how welcoming government agencies are to sharing data with external research organizations.

A state government–based model is the South Carolina Budget Control and Review Board (now the Revenue and Fiscal Affairs Office). After nearly 30 years of building data capacity across state agencies and programs, South Carolina has the capacity to provide datasets to researchers. South Carolina state agencies and qualified researchers can purchase data, at cost, from this agency. Many researchers have benefitted from this model.

Illinois recently began the State Data Practice, housed in the Illinois Department of Innovation and Technology, the intention of which is to produce analytics to improve services provided to state program participants across the human services, health, public safety, and employment sectors. It has employed a data scientist and data architect and will have access to an unprecedented set of data within Illinois. Its mandate is to work with state agencies to produce actionable results that improve the well-being of its residents.

In the past year, a few states have implemented "enterprise memorandum of understanding" or E-MOUs.[10] Currently, these E-MOUs do not include sharing data with external parties, although the state intends to do so eventually. These E-MOUs are intended to facilitate data sharing among state agencies. Given that these E-MOUs are new, it is yet to be seen whether they will be well implemented and work to improve access to data within state government. The additional hope is that these E-MOUs can be used as a model to improve access to data for external organizations and researchers.

Federal agency examples

A different model has been implemented by the U.S. Census Bureau over the past two decades (Johnson, Massey, and O'Hara 2014). Initially, the Census Bureau began collecting administrative data from federal agencies to improve its ability to address coverage issues in the census count of the U.S. population. Currently, the Center for Administrative Records and Research Applications (CARRA) collects state administrative data to improve its coverage and data quality but also to support program evaluation. In most cases, state agencies still have some level of control over the administrative data as specified in agreements between the state agency and the U.S. Census Bureau. CARRA researchers and external researchers can access this administrative data for research purposes (Goerge et al. 2009; Meyer and Goerge 2011).

The U.S. Census Bureau, CARRA, and the IRS allow for federal data across multiple states to be accessed in certain instances (Chetty, Friedman, and Rockoff 2014). For example, research with IRS data should contribute to tax administration. Building good evidence, in part, may require outcomes to be measured across states. If employment, earnings, incarceration, college attendance, or welfare program utilization, among others, are the intended outcomes to be measured for a particular intervention, looking only within a particular state's data holdings may be insufficient to adequately measure these outcomes. The National Student Clearinghouse collects postsecondary data from nearly all such institutions in the United States, but there are few such examples that are readily available to researchers.

Especially for states where there are high population densities at the borders, state agency leaders might be particularly interested in data from multiple states. Likewise, given inexpensive travel, higher mobility even among poor individuals may result in the need to measure certain outcomes across states. Therefore, having a data infrastructure that brings together datasets across domains for all states is not only an important tool for evidence-building, but would inform state leaders about the true outcomes for their populations without the bias of looking within only the state's own outcome data.

University examples

Chapin Hall at the University of Chicago and the Center for Urban Poverty at Case Western Reserve are two examples of university-based research organizations that are compiling, curating, linking, and analyzing state data for the purposes of research and evaluation. Their data holdings cut across multiple decades and multiple state agencies. The value in this model is showing how an external party can effectively facilitate the production of evidence and knowledge through innovations that are valued by state agencies and the research community alike.

Embedded researchers

One potential approach for improving the communication between researchers and state agency leaders is for researchers to work inside state government as either temporary or permanent staff. The federal government uses the Intergovernmental Personnel Act to employ researchers in federal agencies to conduct research that is of mutual benefit to the agency and researcher.[11] State agencies have employed embedded researchers to assist leadership in the management and implementation of research. For example, Washington State's Department of Social and Health Services has a Research and Data Analysis unit that "develops, initiates and supervises activities designed to meet the needs of agency decision-makers."[12] This can be a relatively low cost and quick method to address the barriers described above because the researcher is brought to the data instead of the data having to leave the agency.

Clearinghouse

Finally, the U.S. Census Bureau has funded a university consortium, including New York University and the University of Chicago, to create a prototype administrative data research facility (ADRF) to pilot the notion of an administrative data clearinghouse. The ADRF is being built with state of the art technical resources and including tools that would facilitate the creation of high-quality metadata and build a learning community around specific datasets. Such an ADRF could provide services to state agencies, as well as researchers, to reduce costs and provide state-of-the-art tools to facilitate access.

Concluding Thoughts

In this article, I have posited that a closer partnership between state agencies and researchers is necessary to increase access to state agency data by researchers for rigorous evaluation and analysis. The collaboration between the two is not a natural one because the interests of each have not typically overlapped. Other stakeholders, particularly the federal government, will need to facilitate such a collaboration.

Collaboration between government and researchers may seem to blur what should be a clear line between program operators and researchers that ensures objective, independent research. Researchers or research organizations closely affiliated with specific programs may have their objectivity or integrity questioned. Vigilance to ensure objectivity will be needed on both sides.

A data security standard to certify organizations to perform the functions listed above for research purposes is needed. Currently, the federal government employs the Fedramp standard, which is required for an entity to have the "authority to operate" a data facility that provides access to researchers. Many states employ the HIPAA standards for covered entities (i.e., health care providers, insurers, government agencies) that do not necessarily apply to research organizations. The E-MOU is one piece of this, but states require full solutions that have not yet been specified. Is the Fedramp specification the right one for the states to employ? Or should states buy in to a service that is built to address the specific requirements and produce the ideal conditions for the production of evidence that states so desperately need?

To transform their raw administrative data into high-quality data, states require funding. Funding is provided to states to collect data and transmit it to the federal government for compliance purposes, so funding should be available to states for this purpose also. If states would be given the flexibility to use their federal funds earmarked for administration for evaluation, this would also increase the use of administrative data.

Data must be curated and the quality must be known to the extent it can be.[13] Where and how that is done is an open issue. Is that the role of the state agency that perhaps knows the data best? Is it up to the researcher to address issues of data quality and communicating them? Or should this be the purview of a third party—a government or private organization that has the responsibility for ingesting administrative data, developing metadata, managing legal and physical access to the data, facilitating the analysis of data, fostering discovery and learning about the data, and checking for disclosure of the output.

The creation of de-identified datasets—to the extent that it does not restrict analysis—is necessary and must be an area of further research. The creation of hashed identification numbers or ID numbers that are unique to a particular linkage of a number of datasets is a strategy that is being used more. Active management of the risks around the disclosure of PII is a requirement that must be addressed. Researchers should have access only to data that they require to conduct rigorous research.

Recommendations

- Encourage ongoing collaborations among state and local agencies and researchers to jointly address the barriers in using administrative data across programs and agencies.

- Build collections of data in secure facilities with the proper controls to ensure that only those individuals with the proper permission have access to data in a quick, manageable fashion.
- Develop and hire agency leadership that understands the need for evaluation and research.
- Train state and local government staff in the use of administrative data for program management and evaluation.
- Train researchers not only in the techniques necessary to process and analyze administrative data, but also in state information system contents and database technologies that will allow them to facilitate the physical transfer of data from state agencies.

Notes

1. Archives of de-identified or open data exist and can lead to important research, but these are limited in their ability to support program evaluation (e.g., Adoption and Foster Care Report System, National Child Abuse and Neglect Data System, or state or municipal data portals).

2. Evidence-Based Policy Commission Act of 2016, Pub. L. No. 114-140.

3. OMB 14-06, "Guidance for Providing and Using Administrative Data for Statistical Purposes."

4. Administrative records have been used by advocates to document the poor treatment of special populations. Also, legal advocates have sued governments for the illegal use of administrative records. See http://www.childrensrights.org/our-campaigns/class-actions.

5. https://www.acf.hhs.gov/occ/resource/overview-of-proposed-changes-to-acf-800-and-acf-801-ccdf-administrative-data-reports.

6. http://ptac.ed.gov/sites/default/files/Guidance_for_Reasonable_Methods.pdf.

7. http://ptac.ed.gov/sites/default/files/FERPA%20Exceptions_HANDOUT_horizontal_0.pdf.

8. The Annie E. Casey Foundation, the Sloan Foundation, and the Laura and John Arnold Foundation are three that have recently made large investments in the development of state data sources.

9. HIPPA (Health Insurance Portability and Accountability Act of 1996) is U.S. legislation that provides data privacy and security provisions for safeguarding medical information. The Family Educational Rights and Privacy Act (FERPA) is a federal privacy law that gives parents certain protections with regard to their children's education records, such as report cards, transcripts, disciplinary records, contact and family information, and class schedules. 42 CFR Part 2 outlines under what limited circumstances information about the client's treatment may be disclosed with and without the client's consent.

10. Virginia and Illinois are two states that have implemented E-MOUs.

11. https://www.opm.gov/policy-data-oversight/hiring-information/intergovernment-personnel-act.

12. See https://www.dshs.wa.gov/sesa/research-and-data-analysis/rdas-organization.

13. "Digital curation involves maintaining, preserving, and adding value to digital research data throughout its lifecycle. The active management of research data reduces threats to their long-term research value and mitigates the risk of digital obsolescence." See http://www.dcc.ac.uk/digital-curation/what-digital-curation.

References

Cancian, Maria, Robert Haveman, Daniel R. Meyer, and Barbara Wolfe. 2002. Before and after TANF: The economic well-being of women leaving welfare. *Social Service Review* 76 (4): 603–41.

Card, David, Raj Chetty, Martin Feldstein, and Emmanuel Saez. 2010. Expanding access to administrative data for research in the United States. National Science Foundation SBE 2020 White Paper.

Chetty, Raj, John N. Friedman, and Jonah E. Rockoff. 2014. Measuring the impacts of Teachers I: Evaluating bias in teacher value-added estimates. *American Economic Review* 104 (9): 2593–632.

Commission on Evidence-Based Policymaking. 2017. *The promise of evidence-based policymaking.* Washington, DC: Commission on Evidence-Based Policymaking. Available from https://www.cep.gov/content/dam/cep/report/cep-final-report.pdf (accessed 14 October 2017).

Finifter, David H., and Mark A. Prell. 2013. *Participation in the Supplemental Nutrition Assistance Program (SNAP) and Unemployment Insurance: How tight are the strands of the recessionary safety net?* Economic Research Report 157. Washington, DC: U.S. Department of Agriculture, Economic Research Service.

Goerge, Robert. 1997. Potential and problems in developing indicators on child well-being from administrative data. In *Indicators of children's well-being*, eds. Robert M. Hauser, Brett V. Brown, and William R. Prosser, 457–71. New York, NY: Russell Sage Foundation.

Goerge, Robert, Allison Harris, Lucy Mackey Bilaver, Kerry Franzetta, Mairead Reidy, Deanna Schexnayder, Daniel G. Schroeder, Jane Staveley, J. Lee Kreader, Sally Obenski, et al. 2009. *Employment and TANF outcomes for low-income families receiving child care subsidies in Illinois, Maryland and Texas.* Chicago, IL: University of Chicago, Chapin Hall Center for Children.

Hotz, V. Jospeh, Julie D. Balzekas, Norman Bradburn, Henry E. Brady, Gerald Gates, Robert Goerge, Carol Luttrell, Frances Margolin, Bruce Meyer, Deanna Schexnayder, et al. 1998. *Administrative data for policy-relevant research: Assessment of current utility and recommendations for development.* Report of the Advisory Panel on Research Uses of Administrative Data of the Northwestern University/University of Chicago Joint Center for Poverty Research.

Johnson, David S., Catherine Massey, and Amy O'Hara. 2014. The opportunities and challenges of using administrative data linkages to evaluate mobility. *The ANNALS of the American Academy of Political and Social Science* 657 (1): 247–64.

Meyer, Bruce D., and Robert M. Goerge. 2011. Errors in survey reporting and imputation and their effects on estimates of food stamp program participation. U.S. Census Bureau Center for Economic Studies Paper. Washington, DC: U.S. Census Bureau.

National Science Foundation (NSF). 2007. Advancing measures of innovation. Advancing Measures of Innovation June 2006 Workshop Report. Arlington, VA: NSF.

United States General Accounting Office. 1992. *Integrating human services. Linking at-risk families with services more succesful than system reform efforts.* Washington, DC: United States General Accounting Office.

Weigensberg, Elizabeth, Colleen Schlecht, Emily Wiegand, Sherry Farris, Carol Hafford, Robert Goerge, and Scott Allard. 2015. *Family self-sufficiency data center: Needs assessment report.* Chicago, IL. University of Chicago, Chapin Hall Center for Children. Available from https://www.acf.hhs.gov/opre/resource/family-self-sufficiency-data-center-needs-assessment-report.

Data Sharing in the Federal Statistical System: Impediments and Possibilities

AMY O'HARA
and
CARLA MEDALIA

While federal agencies have engaged in data sharing for decades, current systems of exchange must be transformed to meet the growing needs of analysts in public policy, program evaluation, and basic research. Primary barriers to intra-agency data sharing include both perceived legal barriers and actual financial barriers. To address these problems, the potential path forward could include mandating data sharing for key sources, increasing transparency, and improving efficiency by making it easier for agencies to share data (including developing standards, templates, and incentives). We argue that an agency within the federal statistical system should serve as an intermediary for data integration across the federal statistical system and that the U.S. Census Bureau, with its experience and uniquely broad authority to seek data from any public or private entity for statistical purposes, is well positioned to fill this role.

Keywords: administrative data; infrastructure; evidence-building; program evaluation

Policy-makers, researchers, program administrators, and government employees need to access more data to understand program performance and measure outcomes. The most recent federal budget dedicates a chapter to "Building Evidence to Improve Government Effectiveness," defining the need for evidence for an effective and efficient federal government (Office of Management and Budget [OMB] 2017). To use

Amy O'Hara is a senior research scholar at the Stanford Institute for Economic Policy Research. Before coming to Stanford, she led the U.S. Census Bureau's Center for Administrative Records Research and Applications.

Carla Medalia engages with internal and external parties to develop projects that optimize the use of administrative data at the U.S. Census Bureau, including the development of new data infrastructures to support evidence building.

NOTE: The views expressed are those of the authors and not necessarily those of the U.S. Census Bureau.

Correspondence: amyohara@stanford.edu

DOI: 10.1177/0002716217740863

evidence to answer important policy-relevant questions, an evidence-based infrastructure is required. The infrastructure will enable shared and linked administrative data across programs and build longitudinal panels that reveal how programs have affected participants' lives over the long term. The U.S. Census Bureau, situated at the forefront of the federal statistical system (FSS), should coordinate these efforts. To a limited degree, some of this work is already happening. The Census Bureau currently provides data acquisition, integration, and access services for projects that achieve the agency's mission of improving statistics measuring the U.S. population and economy. The Census Bureau should expand this role, acting as a hub for data integration across the FSS; coordinating best practices in data acquisition and agreements; and taking a lead role in data curation, data integration, and secure data access. The Census Bureau should engage with state and local clearinghouses, academic and research warehouses, and private sector data enclaves to support evidence building. To succeed, the Census Bureau would embrace this role with a mandate from Congress. In multiple meetings over the past year, the Commission for Evidence-Based Policymaking has discussed the need for an entity to lead this work with a transparent and service-oriented approach. The Census Bureau would expand and improve its current methods to serve more users in a responsible fashion, maintaining the trust of data providers and continuing to build trust with the public. To achieve this vision, key stakeholders must work together to address the core impediments to sharing administrative data. Specifically, *perceived barriers* and actual *financial constraints* limit administrative data sharing and use. Affirming the findings of Laurie and Stevens (2016) in the UK context, this article describes these problems for the United States and proposes ways to move forward.

Background

Government agencies generate data through their administrative, regulatory, and enforcement activities. Such administrative data on persons, families, businesses, and institutions were not originally collected for statistical purposes, but are valuable for measurement purposes.

Federal agencies use administrative data to monitor programs and produce reports for policy-makers. The FSS[1] uses administrative data to generate statistics, including population estimates, economic indicators, and national benchmarks. Data are produced and used for statistical purposes, never for enforcement, surveillance, or marketing purposes. Statistical purposes are defined as follows: "Statistical purposes *exclude* uses that affect the rights, benefits, or privileges of individuals; indeed, one of the defining characteristics of statistical use is that data about an individual are never made public, and are never used to make decisions about that individual" (Office of Management and Budget 2016, 200–218).

Data sharing is essential for access and use of administrative data to produce federal statistics. Agencies often use a combination of data collection, data acquisition, and procurement. Examples of administrative data uses for a few statistical agencies include the following:

- The Bureau of Economic Analysis (BEA), which uses data from the Census Bureau, Bureau of Labor Statistics (BLS), Internal Revenue Service (IRS), Centers for Medicare and Medicaid Services (CMS), Economic Research Service (ERS), National Agricultural Statistical Service, Institute of Education Sciences, Energy Information Administration, and commercial vendors to measure the economy.[2]
- The Bureau of Justice Statistics (BJS), which releases crime data compiled from the Federal Bureau of Investigation (FBI) from the Uniform Crime Reporting program, prisoner data from state correctional facilities and federal facilities through the Bureau of Prisons (BOP), and data on arrests from U.S. Marshals Service and Drug Enforcement Administration.
- The Census Bureau, which uses data from many sources, including the Social Security Administration (SSA), Department of Housing and Urban Development (HUD), IRS, CMS, and BOP. The Census Bureau uses administrative data as frames and content for many surveys and censuses. For example, data from the U.S. Postal Service and local governments form the master address list that is the backbone of the Decennial Census, and data from the IRS form the basis of the business register and economic census.[3]

Impediments

What is preventing more agencies from sharing data, and how can more analysts access the data? It is not typically an *actual* legal barrier that curtails sharing and access. Rather, there are *perceived* legal barriers and actual financial constraints limiting progress.

Perceived barriers include long-standing practices based on experience instead of law or policy, narrow or irregular interpretations of statute and regulations, and resistance to change. These cognitive limits prevent the establishment of new data access pathways and collaborations, not because of technical obstacles or legal prohibitions but because people think it cannot be done, that laws in general prevent sharing administrative data (Petrila, this volume), or that the administrative data can only be shared to assist in program administration (Goerge, this volume).

When approached about a data-sharing opportunity, agencies often demur or decline because data sharing has not happened before. They rely on long-standing practices, concluding that their data never leave their agency and that they cannot produce an extract. Irregular interpretation of laws and policies can also halt progress. A frustrating example of this limitation involves federal statutes being interpreted differently by counsel in different states. This happened when the Census Bureau approached states to share food stamps and welfare data. Federal agencies at the Department of Agriculture (USDA) and the Department of Health and Human Services (HHS) were interested in linked data analyses using data from these federally sponsored programs. Some states read Title 7 for the

Supplemental Nutrition Assistance Program data (from USDA) and Title 42 for Temporary Assistance for Needy Families data (from HHS) and believed that sharing was permitted, while other states thought sharing was prohibited. A memo from the Office of General Counsel at both the USDA and HHS clarified that data sharing with the Census Bureau for statistical purposes was both legal and encouraged. The attorneys took this position after seeing that data sharing would enable evidence building through statistics that could help the states to administer their programs. Despite this guidance, some states are still resistant to sharing their data, potentially for actual financial reasons.

Agencies lack staff to document, extract, and transmit data even when sharing is advantageous. Programs and agencies have varied or missing metadata. There are few interoperability requirements, and none funded across departments. Another financial impediment is the distinctness of funding streams. Across agencies, dollars appropriated for food security cannot be spent on other programs. Given these silos of funding—on top of the silos of data—the establishment and enforcement of data standards is challenging. The funding of a federal intermediary to serve the needs of the research community and state/local programs and governments would be similarly difficult to fund. It is unclear whether the base infrastructure would be funded through appropriations and user fees could address the variable costs. Coordinated investments in technology to permit secure networks across existing clearinghouses are also lacking. Currently, no agency or organization exists to support the governance around data sharing and access of this magnitude.

Data Sharing: Current Practices and Possible Paths

Data sharing is taking place on a mandatory or voluntary basis, and data requests are managed through a designated staff/process or diffusely through an organization. Below are examples of ways that agencies are currently sharing data despite the impediments listed above, followed by possible paths forward. This is an informal summary of data sharing from a bureaucrat's perspective, as opposed to formal models such as those reviewed by Jeng, He, and Oh (2016) from the information science perspective.

Some data owners want to share data; others have to share data. In the former, a voluntary desire to comply with a request or to generate new measures drives the arrangement. Voluntary agreements often rely on language in a statute that authorizes (but does not compel) data sharing. The Confidential Information Protection and Statistical Efficiency Act of 2002 (CIPSEA) authorizes BLS, BEA, and the Census Bureau to share confidential business data for the purposes of improving the nation's economic statistical system. Many voluntary data sharing or access arrangements are possible only when the parties can achieve mutual benefits. Examples include the IRS Statistics of Income Joint Statistical Research Program, which permits data sharing only to achieve a tax administration benefit; and the SSA Retirement Research and Disability Research Consortia, which allows data sharing only to understand and improve SSA program administration. States are encouraged to share food security program data with the Census Bureau to support a joint research agenda with USDA's ERS and the Census Bureau.

Required data-sharing arrangements are driven by statutes, often ad hoc, preventing reuse beyond the specific purposes mandated. Mandated data sharing is common for government enforcement functions. For example, the Do Not Pay Portal at the Department of the Treasury aggregates data from the Department of Justice, HUD, Veterans Affairs, and SSA for eligibility verification purposes. Required data sharing in the FSS includes the Census-IRS arrangement in which the Internal Revenue Code compels IRS to share data with the Census Bureau.

Data-sharing arrangements are handled through a designated office or process at some agencies, but through extemporaneous processes at many others. Some agencies have professionalized the data exchange process. They post request and access procedures on their websites, and staff offices handle data exchanges. SSA's Office of Data Exchange has documented and streamlined the process of accessing retirement and disability program data. CMS has a clear process and assistance available (Research Data Assistance Center) to support data access requests. The Defense Manpower Data Center also has a transparent process for data requests (DMDC Data Request System). At the same time, many other agencies lack such dedicated resources and struggle to process data-sharing requests. Most agreements rely heavily on interpersonal relationships and informal quid pro quo arrangements, handling data requests in a less centralized fashion. Data-sharing agreements within a department, such as HUD or the Department of Education, are handled within business units, each with different routing channels and legal teams. This can confuse reviewers when multiple data requests between the same parties are routed simultaneously but separately.

Agencies currently support data sharing with mixtures of the characteristics above: with required versus voluntary data sharing and designated resources to handle requests versus informal administrative processes. It is possible to continue with current circumstances, but it is not optimal, and certainly not suitable for expanded uses of administrative data. The following suggestions aim to affect the willingness to share data, and to alter the way such arrangements are managed.

- Congress should mandate data sharing for key sources. Many evaluations seek data on outcomes—tackle the perceived barriers and actual constraints to have broader use of income and earnings data currently housed at HHS, IRS, and/or SSA. Dedicated funding must accompany requirements for data sharing and provide resources to document and arrange secure access.
- Incentivize data sharing when not mandated—make more agencies want to share data. Offer them something they want or need, perhaps production of metadata; data harmonization or standardization; or hosting their analysts in a data facility that has great tools, data structures, and security protocols.
- Make it easy for agencies to share data with an intermediary. Pursue templates that clarify terms for different types of uses and users. Pursue standards

for data transport. Pursue methods to allow data to stay in place (e.g., privacy protecting record linkage, secure multiparty computation).

- Be transparent about costs and benefits—share information on how long data linkage projects take (from idea to manuscript), how much it costs, and how the results addressed a measurement gap. Use this information to market opportunities for similar projects.
- Congress should establish a federal intermediary to centralize these efforts and provide acquisition, linkage, and access services to agencies. Have assistants at the central hub that assist with agreement development, data documentation, data extract and transport, and reporting/monitoring on uses.
- Have agencies improve their existing approaches. Develop and implement more efficient processes, rely on templates that have been cleared through offices of general counsel, have greater clarity on precedents, and institute common descriptions of uses and users. Such actions could be coordinated through the Interagency Council on Statistical Policy (ICSP) or Data Cabinet.

Pursuing the Possibilities

Improving the data-sharing model for federal and federally sponsored state programs requires investment in methods and tools and coordinated implementation. Below are proposed specific investments in standards, templates, and incentives to induce more and better managed data sharing.

Standards

Government agencies use many different information systems, even within departments or agencies. Standards make data sharing and integration more efficient. We can improve data structures, data transport, data security, and access/services through application program interfaces (APIs) by investing in interoperability. Federal agencies, including those that fund state programs, should support the establishment and adoption of standards to unlock data from the large federal and federally sponsored state program silos. Buy-in from the data source (or their agency or department) is critical; it will be simpler to engage with a federal agency, with one information system or set of systems, than with the state-level programs administering federally sponsored human services benefits that have many information systems. One potential solution is the establishment of "integrated data systems," which integrate data on individuals across agencies and programs to improve understanding of how services are used (Culhane et al., this volume).

Data documentation and schema harmonization would greatly improve data sharing. Many agencies lack financial and human capital to improve metadata. Despite that researchers and evaluators benefit from this infrastructure, the costs are often imposed most heavily on the provider (Foster, this volume). A data intermediary can work with data sources, offering tools and technical assistance to improve data documentation. This can also be offered as a service to data sources, shifting the role and burden to the hosting entity. The Census Bureau is striving to improve documentation for data the Census Bureau collects and administrative data that have been acquired by the Census Bureau. In fiscal year 2016, the Census Bureau launched the Data Linkage Infrastructure website.[4] Although a work in progress, this site provides the first public-facing information about the Census Bureau's administrative data holdings, policies, and projects using linked data. The Census Bureau is piloting several methods to improve the documentation of metadata. For example, the Census Bureau is working with the National Science Foundation–Census Bureau Network (NCRN) funded Cornell node to test their Comprehensive Extensible Data Documentation and Access Repository (CED²AR) on administrative data. Recently, an internal team was awarded funds from the Census Bureau's Improving Operational Efficiency program to discover ways to document and share metadata via the University of Michigan's open metadata platform through the Inter-University Consortium for Political and Social Research (ICPSR). The Census Bureau is also working with academic partners from New York University and the University of Chicago on a new approach to enable data curation, including data documentation, provenance, and version control, within a cloud-based data facility that enables data discovery and secure access.

Better metadata will aid schema harmonization, which will improve the accuracy and efficiency of data integration. Again, many data agencies lack the financial and human capital to test and implement schema harmonization tools and methods. The Census Bureau is striving to improve its processes to ingest, link, provision, and analyze administrative data. Partnerships with external organizations allow testing and implementation of innovative approaches, but there are challenges to working within the centralized information technology (IT) environment of a federal agency. Policies and practices limit the use of microdata to test applications and restrict opportunities for researchers to develop new methods, such as data linkage (Foster, this volume). The Census Bureau is working on approaches that enable the agency to modernize while maintaining a strong security posture. These include schema alignment to assess and align the characteristics of multiple datasets, including filenames, titles, layouts, variable and category names, values, and format (e.g., string, numeric, length); models to assess the trustworthiness of a source, a compilation, or a transformation to create provenance and other tags that support data discovery and auditing needs; and testing of algorithms for classification to improve data cleaning and de-duplication.

Standards will improve data sharing and use. But who will decide which standards are needed and how adherence will be enforced? It is possible that Congress could direct an agency or a clearinghouse-type unit to propose, implement, and enforce standards. Or perhaps the OMB could direct such action through budget language or via memoranda providing guidance and direction. Alternatively, the OMB could direct the actions through the ICSP. Chaired by the chief statistician of the United States, the ICSP coordinates activities across the FSS and could determine and pilot standards that could be implemented across agencies.

Standards are essential to deal with the increasing number of administrative data sources, growing data volumes, and the need for high-frequency data. Standards to produce adequate documentation will help with data management, discovery, and analysis. Standards affecting data structures, transport, and encryption will improve the security posture for sending and receiving institutions. Standards address many of the financial problems described above: once understood and implemented, they help data providers to document data, extract data, and transmit data. Dedicated effort and resources to developing standards is the cross-agency step needed for interoperability. To proceed, the system should encourage the ICSP to catalog the interoperability efforts under way across the FSS, and encourage collaboration across industry, academia, and department CTO offices. The FSS should assess which tools and best practices could be shared across the system (e.g., how Census pilots on schema harmonization tools or the secure cloud-based data facility could be tested at other agencies).

Templates

Universal data access templates must be developed to support broad uses by analysts inside and outside of government. Efficient data sharing is not only about getting files "over the transom," but also about facilitating access for qualified users. Data-sharing agreements need to incorporate nimble processes for reviewing requests, approving researchers, monitoring data access and study scope, conducting disclosure avoidance, and reviewing any research output to ensure no confidential information is disclosed. Efficient data exchange is pointless if it is not also accompanied by clearly specified usage guidelines that are understood by all parties. These operational details need to be incorporated into new agreement templates. The standards described in the previous section inform and shape content in data-sharing templates.

Templates address part of the perception problem: they offer a way forward when an agency stands on past practice, providing examples of how other agencies have entered similar arrangements. Templates also help with irregular interpretation of laws by stating the authority under which sharing can occur for departments and programs.

The Census Bureau's administrative infrastructure includes dedicated staff who identify new data sources, negotiate data-sharing arrangements, and coordinate researcher access to data files. These agreement negotiators are versed in the Census Bureau's authority to obtain and use data for statistical purposes. They have a set of templates to facilitate data sharing for Census Bureau needs and sponsored work. They have experience working with lawyers, privacy officers, database experts, and program administrators to identify the most efficient ways to share data between agencies. Parts of this process are more scalable than others: more staff does not necessarily result in more or quicker agreements. Data owners or their attorneys may reject agreement templates. Templates often speed review, but many delays on the data provider's side involve leadership and staffing changes, the data provider's interpretation of their own legal authorities to share data, or a lack of resources to review and approve a template. On the Census Bureau side, a dedicated legal staff and an automated agreement development system could improve efficiency and therefore aspects of the infrastructure.

While the Census Bureau has followed a standardized acquisition path for decades, in fiscal year 2016, the Census Bureau initiated twelve pilot evaluation projects to test and document every aspect of the data-sharing process. The pilot projects span housing, health, welfare, education, and labor market outcomes. Each pilot requires multiple agreements to clarify roles and responsibilities of statistical uses and data sharing. Many of the agreements for the pilot projects are narrowly scoped. A transformed model could have tiered agreement templates, with graduated scope levels. Requests to access the data could have similar graduated uses, permitting users to select the depth and breadth of data needed for their evaluation. The agreement process must be transformed if data sharing and data use/access are to support timely analyses that range from producing performance metrics to scholarly work, from the use of near real-time data to longitudinal studies requiring pooling data over years or decades.

To move forward, the Census Bureau must continue to refine templates, seek more support to obtain legal review of agreements, implement its agreement tracking tools, and document the gaps and shortcomings of our current process. An administrative data unit at the Census Bureau could coordinate such efforts, disseminate templates and best practices, and offer technical assistance.

Incentives

The academic, evaluation, and policymaking communities must incentivize or require data sharing to make data controllers want to share data (or have to share data). Incentives must be appropriate and consistent across agencies, using common and transparent language on uses and retention. Access to high-value datasets (e.g., mortality, employment, earnings) should be expedited or required. When data sharing is voluntary, the data quality, availability, and delivery are fragile and subject to change when executive buy-in or budgets shift. Requiring data sharing of high-value sources should be accompanied by clear requirements and terms on the treatment of identifiable data and approved uses. To support further data sharing, laws and regulations must clarify and encourage data access for statistical use. For example, legislation or budget language could state that data sharing is required to produce statistics evaluating programs or outcomes.

In any document incentivizing data sharing, the terms of use must describe the treatment of identifying information and retention terms. What will be kept, for how long, and why? The Australian public's reaction to their 2016 census planned compulsory collection and retention of names and addresses was instructive. The public was surprised by the planned uses of the data and threatened boycott or fraudulent responses. Transparency is required to gain and maintain the trust of data sources and the public.[5]

TABLE 1
Use of Standards, Templates, and Incentives to Address Barriers to Sharing Data

Impediment Example	Standards	Templates	Incentives
Long-standing practices (e.g., we can't do that)		√	√
Irregular interpretations of laws	√	√	
Resistance to change			√
Inadequate resources to document data/poor or missing metadata	√		√
Inadequate resources to extract data	√		
Inadequate resources to transmit data	√		
Inadequate investment in interoperability	√		√
Distinct funding streams			√

Properly designed incentives could address many of the challenges that we face today. Incentives can help agencies that say "we have never done that" and resistant-to-change agencies to see the need for or advantage of data sharing. Incentives can shift burden away from data controllers who often lack resources to clean or document their data to agencies with more experience and tools. For example, states may lack the resources to produce metadata but could see production of documentation and harmonized data as an incentive to share files. Incentives or mandates to share data could also address the distinct funding-stream problem by directing data sharing to evaluate programs and measure outcomes.

The FSS, or a federal intermediary, should design and pursue a research agenda to create data-sharing incentives. Beyond the basics, including enabling new measurements and confirmation of previously published results, we need to determine how to incentivize researchers and agencies to share data. Best practices should be drawn from the natural, social, and health sciences. The United Kingdom Data Archive has also conducted studies on the topic.[6] The research agenda should assess the parties who can affect behavior such as funders, academic institutions, publishers, and the OMB.

Table 1 summarizes how standards, templates, and incentives can address some of the impediments to greater data sharing across the FSS. Together, these efforts can make more parties want to or have to share data through uniform processes.

Examples of Programs Seeking, Establishing, or Enforcing Standards

The 2014 Farm Bill (Public Law 113–79) included data exchange standards for food security and family self-sufficiency legislation. As stated in Section 4016, states must incorporate a widely accepted, nonproprietary, searchable, computer readable format such as the eXtensible Markup Language, and contain interoperable standards developed and maintained by intergovernmental partnerships such as the National Information Exchange Model. These requirements cover data exchanges across state agencies for federal reporting and data exchanges required by applicable law. USDA was to issue a proposed rule to amend the Food and Nutrition Act (7 U.S. Code [U.S.C.] 2020) regarding data exchanges. This bill had good intentions, but lacked either requirements or resources.

The Administration for Children and Families (ACF) sought investment at the state level.[7] This unfunded proposal would create a statewide human services data system through grants for states to develop data systems to analyze program investments and outcomes across multiple programs and over time, and a systems innovation technical assistance center that would develop standards/architecture and provide reusable technology components and shared services so states and tribes can address common requirements, including eligibility and enrollment. The ACF proposal was developed in the spirit of the grant-based investment in states to develop statewide longitudinal data systems for education. Again, this proposal had good intentions and would have provided technical assistance and resources but lacked sufficient investment.

The Digital Accountability and Transparency Act of 2014 (DATA Act) at the U.S. Treasury makes government-spending data available as open data. The Treasury designed a data platform to enable harmonization and ease of use. In 2015, they released fifty-seven data standards (final standards were available one year later) and established a standard data exchange. They identified thirty key data elements that will be standardized in their system. In summary, this act had success in establishing standards, and had sufficient investment and enforcement.

The National Directory of New Hires (NDNH) at HHS contains data on unemployment insurance wages and benefits, new hires, and the federal parent locator program data. NDNH requires that states submit the same elements in a set format. States had set up state directories of new hires, which roll up to the federal collection that is used for child support enforcement. This initiative had successful implementation, with both sufficient investment and enforcement.

Conclusion

Data sharing is a critical component of our decentralized federal statistical system. While nearly all units in the system participate in data sharing, they face common burdens (real and perceived) in their efforts to acquire and use data from other federal government agencies and states. This article has described paths to more efficient data sharing through implementation of standards, the need for legal templates and protocols, and the need to incentivize data sharing. Improvements in these areas will promote not only the efficient and legal exchange of data but also the credibility of analyses based on the shared data.

This article calls for a centralization of these efforts and the establishment of a federal data-sharing intermediary. A coordinating unit is needed to manage investments in standards and template development. Such a unit should be situated within the FSS to leverage the system's abilities to protect data and support analyses free from political influence and thereby build the trust of data providers, the research community, and the public. Federal statistical agencies are ready partners for other federal agencies, federally funded state program agencies, local governments, research organizations, academics, and policy-makers that form the evidence-producing ecosystem. Our path forward requires modernizing the infrastructure and creating governance processes that support a much broader analytic capacity.

Notes

1. The FSS comprises thirteen principal statistical agencies and approximately 130 statistical programs housed in agencies across the federal government that support program planning and evaluation functions. These agencies or organizational units are in the Executive Branch, overseen by the Office of Management and Budget, with activities involving the collection, compilation, processing, or analysis of information for statistical purposes. See https://www.whitehouse.gov/sites/default/files/omb/assets/information_and_regulatory_affairs/statistical-programs-2015.pdf for more information.

2. See https://bea.gov/about/pdf/acm/2016/improving-regional-pce-estimates-using-credit-card-transactions-data.pdf for example of vendor data testing.

3. The Census Bureau protects the confidentiality of data that it acquires from other agencies just as it protects the information it collects directly from individuals and businesses. Data sharing supports operational uses, evaluation uses, and research uses. However, using data collected for nonstatistical purposes can be challenging. When using data from other agencies, the Census Bureau reviews data quality, assessing dimensions including relevance, accuracy, timeliness, punctuality, accessibility, clarity, coherence, and comparability.

4. See www.census.gov/datalinkage.

5. Another example of the importance of clarifying retention terms involves Unemployment Insurance (UI) data held at HHS. Federal law requires deletion of data in the National Directory of New Hires (NDNH) system 24 months after the date of receipt. However, the Social Security Act allows HHS to keep samples of data as needed to support research on child support topics if personal identifiers are removed. Other data development projects have maintained panels longer than two years (e.g., the Longitudinal Employer Household Dynamics program at the Census Bureau has decades of data for most states). States themselves may also retain the data, depending on their own statues. But the mandated, central repository at HHS has limited use and a rolling window of retention. Such issues need to be transparently addressed.

6. See http://www.data-archive.ac.uk/about/projects/incentive.

7. See www.acf.hhs.gov/blog/2016/03/interoperability-at-acf.

References

Culhane, Dennis, John Fantuzzo, Matthew Hill, and TC Burnett. 2017. Maximizing the use of integrated data systems: Understanding the challenges and advancing solutions. *The ANNALS of the American Academy of Political and Social Science* (this volume).

Foster, Ian. 2017. Research infrastructure for the safe analysis of sensitive data. *The ANNALS of the American Academy of Political and Social Science* (this volume).

Goerge, Robert M. 2017. Barriers to accessing state data and approaches to addressing them. *The ANNALS of the American Academy of Political and Social Science* (this volume).

Jeng, Wei, Daqing He, and Jung Sun Oh. 2016. Toward a conceptual framework for data sharing practices in social sciences: A profile approach. *Proceedings of the Association for Information Science and Technology* 53:1–10.

Laurie, Graeme, and Leslie Stevens. 2016. Developing a public interest mandate for the governance and use of administrative data in the United Kingdom. *Journal of Law and Society* 43:360–92.

Office of Management and Budget. 2016. *Overview of the federal performance framework.* OMB Circular No. A-11. Washington, DC: U.S. Government Printing Office. Available from https://obamawhitehouse.archives.gov/sites/default/files/omb/assets/a11_current_year/s200.pdf.

Office of Management and Budget. 2017. *Analytical perspectives: Budget of the U.S. government, fiscal year 2018.* Washington, DC: U.S. Government Printing Office.

Petrila, John. 2017. Turning the law into a tool rather than a barrier to the use of administrative data for evidence-based policy. *The ANNALS of the American Academy of Political and Social Science* (this volume).

This article examines government's opportunities and challenges as it relates to the use of data as the key strategy to prepare cities for the future. It examines what is possible when twenty-first-century data management practices are effectively implemented in city government. The article offers examples from real-world implementation and service delivery and provides tactics and strategies that will prime cities for the next transformative era in technology.

Keywords: data; city; analytics; government; future; technology

Building the Data City of the Future

By
BETH BLAUER

The twenty-first-century city is a growing and thriving environment where most of the world's population lives, where new generations are choosing to call home, and where government is at the forefront of improving public services and implementing new ideas—everything from bike shares to algorithmic led optimization of service delivery.[1]

With more people choosing to live in cities and with their borders being more defined than the sprawl of prior generations, the needs of the modern city dweller are also evolving. Take, for example, the adoption of the shared economy services such as Uber and AirBnB; these services have blindsided cities and forced rapid adoption of new regulations, revenue collection methods, and laws. City government did not proactively plan for the impact the shared economy has had on its systems or its residents, and as a result, the

Beth Blauer is the executive director and founder of the Center for Government Excellence (GovEx) at Johns Hopkins University. As a dedicated public servant and international expert on government performance programs, Beth has spent her career working to improve people's lives by bringing data into governments' decision-making processes. Prior to leading GovEx, Beth designed and launched Socrata's GovStat platform for federal, state, and local governments.

Correspondence: bblauer1@jhu.edu

DOI: 10.1177/0002716217746359

effects have been uneven and clunky, typically with the biggest loss felt in the pockets of government. If city governments remain in this responsive posture, they will ultimately be left behind, with private sector organizations effectively forcing their hand. How do we avoid this? Government must be agile and responsive to the changing needs of their constituencies.

The starting point of this article finds cities struggling to remain competitive in the age of twenty-first-century innovations such as mobile applications, machine learning, and artificial intelligence—tools that most people, whether or not they know it, are expecting to see in use. This struggle is largely due to a failure of building systems within government that create the capacity for absorbing innovation. To better prepare for the future and to keep cities competitive, their government must undergo a transformation that changes its culture, its perspective on data use, and its value on human capital. These changes must be connected to an organization that is mission-driven and has the potential to deliver outcomes for all people.

As executive director of the Center for Government Excellence (GovEx) at Johns Hopkins University, I have led a team that has provided technical assistance to nearly one hundred cities in the United States and abroad as part of the Bloomberg Philanthropies What Works Cities initiative. At GovEx, I have seen how midsized cities are adapting, and not adapting, to twenty-first-century challenges.

This article describes what is possible when twenty-first-century data management practices are effectively implemented in city government. I break down the components in greater detail, provide examples of real-world implementation, and discuss challenges and questions for practitioners to consider when seeking to improve service delivery and conditions for residents.

Living in the City of the Future

The city of the future is not beyond our grasp—a city where the value of data is high and everyone from the front lines of city programs to the city leadership is using data to drive decision-making, provide better services, and meet the changing needs of city residents. The elements of such a city are already being tested and implemented globally, with some public sector organizations paving the way. These ideas are not being driven by large federal governments hamstrung by bureaucratic rules and antiquated visions of progress. Successful approaches are incubated and hatched in local communities around the globe—in places such as London, where you can take a bus or a train with a universal pass, a chipped credit card, or a mobile application. The ridership data are tracked in real time, and routes are continuously optimized to meet the changing patterns of ridership. This encourages more public transit usage, instigates better environmental outcomes, and makes the city incredibly accessible to residents and tourists alike.

This trend is showing no signs of slowing, and the twenty-first century will continue to see local governments embrace new ideas faster, more efficiently, and with greater impact than large federal programs.

What does this all mean? Think for a moment about the potential of a proactive system of government, one that seamlessly delivers services for residents in response to their most pressing needs. For a futurist perspective on the potential, imagine you wake up one morning to a construction crew outside your door. When you go to investigate, you learn that a sensing system detected low water pressure from your city-owned lines. The city dispatched a rapid-response team to investigate and repair before this small issue became a main break. The leak was detected by devices that float through the city's water system to detect leaks in real time (Chandler 2014).

Farther down the street, you notice another crew repairing utility lines. The lines were scheduled for repair in the following year, but proactive city employees elevated the repairs to a higher priority. This issue was detected by systems that analyze data from city vehicles equipped with image recognition technology, enabling the city to address the problem before it became worse (Patterson, Dowling, and Chamberlain 1997).

While you are talking to the team doing the work, you notice less traffic than usual in the bike lane that is routed between your car and the sidewalk. Residents were informed about the two repair projects, and their mobile applications suggested alternative bike routes to avoid the construction areas (Verhulst 2016).

You are about to start your routine jog around the neighborhood when your fitness band sends a message about current air quality conditions. The city's air quality sensors in your neighborhood are detecting a pollen that you are particularly sensitive to, and you decide to exercise indoors.[2]

After your work out, you post a message to social media about your evening plans downtown, and the city's social media monitoring programs notice hundreds of people who say they are going to the same event. Streetlight timing is slightly adjusted in anticipation of the influx of people, and more traffic officers are dispatched to the area (Samsonowa and Remnev 2015).

The next day, you attend the final class of a computer programming certificate course. Upon completion of the final assignment, you receive an email from the city's human services department with a list of employers who are seeking applicants with your new skill.[3]

Each of these examples represents a shift in reactive city service delivery to proactive service delivery. But from experience, implementing proactive services requires a city to make proper investments in fundamental services, which I discuss in the next sections.

Building the City of the Future

Fundamentally, the city of the future is one that responds to residents' needs in a proactive way. But how would a city do it? According to Stephen Goldsmith, the proactive, or responsive, city delivers services "whenever and however citizens need it. The result is a smarter and nimbler government that better deploys its resources and attention" (Goldsmith and Crawford 2014, 7).

However, there are major prerequisites that government must address before achieving a responsive city. I contend that for cities to create and sustain a shift to responsive governing, governments must focus on five key operational areas: cultural transformation, data management, modernized performance management, and the capacity to leverage advanced analytics. In addition, cities will need to rely on networks based in both public sector organizations and philanthropic initiatives to hasten progress and achieve their goals.

Cultural transformation

Before technology, before hiring the best and the brightest, and before adequate resourcing, cities must first shift toward a problem-solving culture where ineffective practices are replaced with bold new ideas. An entrenched government culture is often the biggest barrier to success. Too often we hear from career public servants that new ideas will not work, that "we've tried that before and it didn't work," or "I could try that but it will cost a ton of money and I don't have the budget for new thinking." These attitudes are widespread and observed in nearly every project on which we have worked.

The good news is that open government and trends toward transparency are now being recognized as important tools in countering the negative effects of bureaucratic administration (Kornberger et al. 2017). Mayors across the United States participating in What Works Cities have cited bureaucratic cultural barriers as one of the biggest challenges to getting a data practice off the ground.[4] The most successful programs have avoided bureaucratic pitfalls by starting small, demonstrating the ability to have quick and efficient wins, and carefully scaling.

The following sections describe examples of successful culture change in city government, and discuss several factors that need to be addressed when seeking to institute cultural change.

Examples. Recognizing that internal capacity-building is crucial for culture change, the City of Denver created Denver Peak Performance (DPP). DPP is a training program offered to all City of Denver employees, as well as city employees from other cities around the country. The training program is part of Peak Academy, a program that trains public servants to adopt a continuous improvement philosophy in government operations.[5] Peak Academy has been cited as saving the City of Denver a significant amount of money, but, most importantly, it has been credited with boosting the morale of the public sector and affording participants the opportunity to engage in meaningful reforms.

The City of Louisville, Kentucky, established the Office of Performance Improvement and Innovation to help Louisville employees rapidly test and implement new ideas. Using "innovation" funds and a public-private partnership model, the city designed and implemented a low-cost sensor to detect fires in abandoned buildings.[6] Real-time data from remote sensors in abandoned buildings helped city officials to detect fires in places where traditional smoke detectors were not feasible. LouisStat, Lean training, and the prestigious Innovation

Award[7] are all a part of Louisville's strategies to engage the public sector in meaningful and creative ways.

Taking this cultural change to the next level, Louisville recently launched the "LouieLab," a public space for the city and community to collaborate and solve problems (Hickey 2016). The space hosts meetings, hackathons, and other events that bring the public in direct contact with the city's innovative efforts.

The City of Austin has a similar program called the "Idea Accelerator," which is an internal application for city employees. Austin's Idea Accelerator elevates new and transformative ideas from city employees.[8]

Discussion. Changing a city government's operational culture toward data-driven decision-making is a constant challenge that requires care and attention by senior leadership. Cities can no longer rely on status quo policies and practices to deliver improved results for residents in the digital age. There are several factors to consider when implementing cultural change: strategic vision, departmental silos, risk taking, and new positions.

Vision. In the absence of a clear vision or ambitious goal, a government can become rudderless. A lack of vision gives way for rapidly shifting priorities, organizational confusion, and reactive governance. The bureaucracy will retreat from reform efforts when there is a pattern of low return on investment. Staff who have experience with the fits and starts of reform will be the first to hide from new ideas.

Therefore, government needs a way to operationalize new ideas. Too often, an overreliance on pilots has led to major difficulty transforming best practices into entrenched behavior. When there is a chorus of "I don't have time to engage in that new practice" in your organization, there is a problem.

In addition, as a byproduct of term limit safeguards, government has earned a reputation as the place where good ideas go to die. Large bureaucratic systems have evolved into labyrinths of rules, policies, and regulations that serve as a deterrent to new ideas. While many of the safeguards in place are important in reducing the risk of fraud and abuse, they can also be inhibitors of progress. Government must create safe spaces that allow people to take risks, think differently, and try new ideas. This starts with a culture that is committed to a vision, energized by its mission, set up for success, and not afraid of failure.

When humans fear the message that data is conveying, even if they are not responsible for inputs, there is an incentive to create barriers to accessing data. A strong vision that is directly tied to city operations and service delivery can alleviate these data sharing concerns.

The silo effect. Cultural transformation is also made more difficult by the silo effect. Governments have created too much of a divide between information technology (IT) and programs (Latham 2016). The move to centralized IT created a number of efficiencies and added benefits to the government. However, this shift led to a growing divide between the program work and technology needs. Technologists left agencies behind, and solution-building became disconnected from service delivery.

What this has left is a bureaucracy that has major difficulty in scoping data-rich application development. Data that are created by one department often go unnoticed by other departments that could use the data for high-impact purposes. This leads to employees struggling with internal barriers as much as with the external problem being addressed.

Cities can work to break departmental silos by encouraging multidisciplinary approaches to strategic planning and operations. Setting cross-agency or cross-sector goals often works to bust silos. The key is to use a multidisciplinary approach that implicates the public sector workforce. Having an articulated goal is only the first step. The routines that are built around cross-sector frameworks must also encourage intraprogram evaluation, collective data sharing, and regular data-driven meetings that highlight the efficiencies of the work. The biggest barriers to cross sector work, real or perceived, are often due to legal concerns.

Legal roadblocks. Government legal frameworks designed to protect privacy and reduce corruption should be revamped to encourage data sharing for research and policy development. Many data efforts are hampered by government lawyers who are better at getting to "no" than getting to "yes." Cities need legal partners that understand the importance of protective law but also place a high value on data sharing and its potential impact.

The legal and policy frameworks for sharing data between agencies and the public should protect restricted information, as well as specify appropriate ways to use or transform restricted information. Current frameworks are often inflexible in accommodating productive reuse of data. Government lawyers should have access to training in both the use of data and the application of data for problem solving. The federal government should review programs such as Family Educational Rights and Privacy Act (FERPA) and the Health Insurance Portability and Accountability Act (HIPAA) in light of twenty-first-century tools for data protection, encryption, and security. Local governments should do massive regulatory reviews of implementation strategies for federal protective acts that may hamstring their ability to share data.

Cities have some legal and regulatory powers to define how data are used and shared via formal data policies. These policies reduce the uncertainty and ambiguity about who owns which city dataset, and what can be done with it. In the coming years, local government will create the need for wide ranging reforms on how data are transferred between program-level and federal-level funding streams. The federal government should study how well-worn paths blazed by decades-old reporting routines both help and hurt local governments' ability to use data.

Risk taking. Cities must create safe spaces, both physical and in policy, for teams to take risks. Sometimes just looking up from your cubicle and being given some space to examine a process that is slowing down outcomes is all it takes to facilitate problem solving. When teams are given the space to collaborate, test new ideas, and experience the benefits of their efforts, trust is built and risk taking grows.

To facilitate risk taking, cities can establish "innovation labs," taking cues from the modern library, to encourage employees and residents alike to learn new skills and find novel solutions to city problems.

New positions. Government needs to cultivate program-level positions that can translate barriers to success into technical terms. These include chief data officer, chief analytics officer, and chief innovation officer, among others. Much like the product manager role in the private sector, governments need to build the capacity to scope new programs, products, and service delivery innovations in a way that is indicative of technology modernization (Cohen 2010). This does not mean that government must stack the decks with steep technological or analytical skills. Government should leverage training programs to deepen the skills of current public sector workforces. Local governments from New Orleans to Boston are partnering with higher education institutions to expand training opportunities and invest in the skills of their people. These partnerships also facilitate low-cost labor for analytics and more sophisticated research methods.

Data management

The second key practice in developing a problem-solving culture is to begin thinking of data as an enterprise asset. Treating data in this way helps cities to organize and maintain their data for use in a variety of operational settings.

Data management is a foundational element for the purposes of implementing a responsive city, since such systems require "the development of an appropriate infrastructure of information and communications, using a common platform that enables gathering, measurement and analysis of data and the monitoring, optimization and control of all the systems involved" (García et al. 2016, 2). These principals are key to a government-wide data program. This includes all data that a government produces, not just data that will ultimately be made public. A common mistake in data governance approaches is orienting the framework around *open data*. Open data, or the readiness for data to be shared with the public, is one element of *data governance*. However, successful initiatives will be far more comprehensive than the limits placed on publicly available data.

Examples. Cities must invest in systems that allow for the seamless interaction of data and decision-making. In jurisdictions that have made this work, data governance becomes a key facilitator for interdepartmental collaboration. In addition, cities must develop the capacity to manage data at the enterprise level to benefit from advancements in technology. The following are examples of city data management practices and investments.

In New York City, the Mayor's Office of Data Analytics identified the need for a data warehousing system to connect data from all the city's departments. This system contained data from a variety of departments, including fire, building inspections, and code enforcement, among others. The unification solved the problems endemic to city data housed in disconnected systems, and allowed analysts to gain insights by combining data to make predictions about building fire hazards (Feuer 2013).

An effective use of data requires standards and uniform protocols for the sharing of data across a variety of systems, users, and infrastructures. Data should move as freely as possible between the various components of the city. To create an environment where data can move, cities are starting to think about cross-sector standards at the metadata level (Center for Government Excellence 2016a). One standard, Open311, has been implemented in dozens of cities and has opened the potential for cities to use each other's 311 data for a variety of analytical purposes.[9]

To establish the standards for how smart city components should operate, many governments have adopted data policies to guide the creation, maintenance, and publication of data for both internal and external use. This policy is developed when regular routines around data use are established through a city-wide commitment to governance (Center for Government Excellence 2016b).

Kansas City, Missouri, has implemented a data policy and a data governance team to help foster strong data management practices throughout their city organization.[10] Their formal policy specifies a workflow that covers dataset identification, issue resolution, and online publication. Kansas City also conducts a comprehensive resident satisfaction survey to collect data that informs all its data management decisions. This survey provides high-quality data that are readily available for analysis using the city's other high-quality datasets.[11]

Discussion. Over the last 20 months, GovEx visited nearly one hundred mid-sized cities as part of Bloomberg Philanthropies' What Works Cities Initiative. The charge was to collect a national baseline of the state of data practice. What GovEx discovered was that many cities have invested in IT solutions for managing and releasing data to the public, but very few have created regular routines around data and the practice of data use in their governments. This lack of routine and focus has created a hauntingly similar fatigue that performance programs are facing.

Welch, Feeney, and Park (2016) surveyed local governments to investigate the factors that lead to increased data sharing within governments, and between governments and external organizations. They provide evidence to support the hypothesis that governments are more likely to share data in coercive, persuasive, and technically competent environments. Coercive forces include laws, regulations, and policies that require city departments to share data. The persuasive mechanisms include collaborative projects between agencies and external organizations. Finally, technical capacity includes, but is not limited to, an openness toward social media, cloud-based systems, and open-source technologies. In each of the previous examples, coercive, persuasive, and technical factors were at play in facilitating city data sharing.

When a city lacks a formal data management strategy, it creates, maintains, and publishes data in an ad hoc manner. This often results in individual departments or agencies developing their own set of noninteroperable data management "silos." There are several reasons why cities are reluctant to share data: fear, cost, ownership, and priority (Conradie and Choenni 2014). Developing a strong data management program can help to address these concerns and create the conditions for interconnectivity and innovation.

The lack of connected data results in a major loss of efficiency in government, where "too many public servants working in back offices are often reduced to human APIs - retyping information from one system to another, and stuck processing the repetitive common cases that shouldn't need any human intervention at all" (Shelter 2016).

Data management does not require a large investment in enterprise IT or expensive technological solutions. People and the willingness to engage in the work drive all the key elements. Our experience through GovEx has shown that a profitable approach includes:

1. Data inventory. One centralized catalog of the data that exists across your government. Key features of a data inventory are

   a.   source of the data,
   b.   frequency of updates,
   c.   system of origin, and
   d.   data fields.

2. Create a governance committee. Governance committees, often enabled through policy or executive order, define regular participants in data governance sessions. The purpose of the sessions should generally be to

   a.   shape how data are collected,
   b.   ensure IT solutions procured by government have the capacity to share data with little friction, and
   c.   prioritize the release of data.

3. Invite the right people: Data governance committees should be staffed by others outside of IT. It is critical that participation is inclusive. Here are some suggestions of staff based on our experience in cities:

   a.   Major program subject matter experts.
   b.   Senior staff or people who have steep decision-making authority.
   c.   The public. Some local governance committees have mechanisms for citizen engagement. This can be accomplished by platforms that allow citizens to nominate data they would like released or have direct participation in the process.
   d.   Lawyers. A lawyer who can focus on protecting privacy but shares the overall goal of the program.
   e.   IT leadership.
   f.   Communications people.

4. Systems inventory. Every government should know where and how their data are stored. Ask IT team leads to provide an inventory of the different systems that produce data. Think about standardizing how data are collected across the city's vast systems.
5. Decision-making authority. Data governance committees must be able to lead and influence policy around IT investments and data standards.

Modernized performance management

While the city of the future implements the processes and practices to make responsive services possible, it is important to closely monitor program performance in real-time to ensure that operations align with outcomes. Too often, cities implement policies and disburse funding for programs without the proper mechanisms in place to track outcomes. The city of the future must invest in agile methods that will help with smarter investing and resource allocation.

Examples. The City of New Orleans has operationalized data-driven decision-making. Starting with the ambitious goal to reduce blighted properties by ten thousand units in four years, Mayor Landrieu established the interdepartmental BlightStat meetings. Recognizing the success of this approach, additional programs, such as "QualityofLifeStat" and "ResultsNOLA," were implemented to spread the use of data to other parts of the city.[12]

Jackson Mississippi is using JackStat to monitor their own blight interventions and most recently they were able to save one hundred public sector jobs by consolidating school buildings. All this decision-making occurred with a commitment to a data practice and fidelity to performance routines.

Discussion. To address the lack of insight into program success, cities have been implementing various versions of the "Stat" model over the decades. Fundamentally, "Stat," or performance management, is about bringing city decision makers from a variety of departments to a recurring meeting to review data, receive analysis, and decide on courses of action and follow up. Stat relies on strong leadership to identify priorities and maintain an ongoing routine around the use of data in enterprise-wide decision-making.

Performance management is about operationalizing successful problem-solving strategies in the daily business of government. However, there are some pitfalls to avoid when using performance management as a tool.

Reporting fatigue. Data producers and frontline employees often look at performance programs as extra work with little return. Requests for data are poorly scoped and often without context. This sentiment creates a universally felt fatigue, and data producers quickly become data hoarders. As a result, barriers to data are created as a defense against the programs, and the programs become disconnected from frontline realities and are difficult to sustain.

The traditional Stat model produced short-term results by focusing executive attention and resources on strategic priorities. However, such programs face the risk of becoming nonproductive reporting exercises that are disconnected from actual decision-making. This "reporting trap" can be caused by stakeholders who do not trust the accuracy or integrity of city data, the lack of executive buy-in, and lack of sufficient feedback loops in the decision-making process.

Mayoral turnover. Oftentimes, a new mayor is elected and wants to create a data culture in the government, but the administrative staff are data fatigued. Getting started is often the most difficult aspect of the work. Mayors know that to be competitive in the twenty-first century, they must invest in new technology, skills, and a strong data practice. However, this practice must be at the core of the way the city operates and the way decisions are made, including budget deliberation and legislative agenda setting.

Transition often sets progress back or slows the pace of a changing data culture. If the success of data innovations is tied to a particular political appointee it can also lead to political decision-making about the future of these programs. It is critical that city leadership implementing data driven initiatives get data to penetrate any bureaucratic barriers. The sooner data are valued by public sector employees on the frontlines, in programs, the more likely the data culture is to survive political change.

When establishing a data practice, cities must establish a foundational practice (governance, inventory, process) and allow for the practice to help deliver on the political leader's goal. When a new administration is elected the stakeholders should be prepared to present the practice and allow for the practice to align with new goals and outcomes prioritized by new leadership.

Concerns. Many governments and the people who power them are still emerging from an era of data-driven accountability efforts that were not collaborative and often culturally poisonous. Programs like NYC CompStat and even Baltimore's CitiStat had a reputation of being hard-nosed, aggressive, and noncollaborative. Even Hollywood contributed to the sensationalism with their depiction of CompStat in the popular Baltimore-based series *The Wire*. Bratton, the first police commissioner to use CompStat and the innovator of modern PerformanceStat, has acknowledged that collaboration is the key to successful city innovation. Programs emerging now like KCStat and ResultsNOLA have been transformed to focus on collaboration and the need to draw subject matter expertise from a large pool of experts within and outside the traditional government sector.[13]

Advanced analytics

When cities have shifted toward a culture of treating their data as an enterprise asset and instituted basic performance management practices, the next step is to implement targeted analytics projects that can quickly help to improve service delivery.

Examples. The City of Santander, Spain, built a network of street lights that optimize their light output given the volume of nearby foot traffic (Sánchez et al. 2013). This sensor-actuator system of street lights optimizes the use of electricity and provides a real-time response to residents' needs.

The City of Syracuse, New York, partnered with the University of Chicago's Data Science for Social Good program to provide technical assistance to optimize water infrastructure repairs. Using a variety of datasets including road repair and pipe infrastructure, among others, the research team was able to identify where the water department could optimize its repair schedule. The entire project is open source, and can be used by other cities for replication purposes.[14]

Discussion. Advanced analytics, and data science projects in general, are not a panacea for the issues that a city wants to address. Data science tools such as machine learning, artificial intelligence, and predictive modeling are "high-risk high-reward" tools. They can provide many benefits to service optimization and workload efficiency but can also result in high costs, privacy concerns, and issues of algorithmic bias.

Privacy. When cities engage with residents in the responsive city framework, privacy implications will inevitably arise. Cities must invest in the proper skills for public servants to ensure that they are able to understand and use data while minimizing the risk to privacy and vulnerable populations.

Information passing through a city's responsive infrastructure may include a user's location (latitude and longitude), a user's current activity (walking, running, or driving), or personal information (home address, health records). While this information is incredibly useful for the city in determining how services should be provided to residents, it has the potential to cause harm.

In this environment, sensitive information is recorded, transmitted, and analyzed with more accuracy, frequency, and granularity than ever before. These facts increase the potential for data misuse and violations of personal privacy. The Obama administration's guide, "Big Data and Privacy: A Technological Perspective," features an in-depth analysis of these privacy issues (President's Council of Advisors on Science and Technology 2014).

The data used to deliver these services are not fundamentally new to cities. Technology has just increased the volume and velocity of data collection and analysis. Regardless of the governments' ability to use data, residents must always be involved and aware of the systems, how they work, and what data they must provide to receive the service. Governments should design "opt-out" functions into these systems, and implement outreach programs to inform the public about how their data are being used.

Algorithmic bias. There are also issues with algorithmic bias. This occurs when algorithmic and data-driven processes result in prejudicial biases. These biases are not programmed into the algorithm, but they nevertheless result in negative outcomes for marginalized populations. Algorithmic bias occurs when data and processes are not properly scrutinized before they are implemented. In addition, statistical packages often make it easy for users to run a model without understanding exactly how the model works, or if the model is even appropriate for the task at hand. (For an in-depth examination of algorithmic bias, see Kirkpatrick 2016.)

The public does not trust government data, and data initiatives have been closely linked to programs that continue to create bias against vulnerable and minority populations. Failed policies like stop and frisk and inspection optimization can disproportionately impact poor, mostly minority communities. Cities must constantly be aware of the potential for bias in their collection, use, and publication of data. Without a proactive focus and attention to this issue, it is likely that data, when improperly paired with performance and decision-making, will create policies and programs that are biased. At the onset of any data program, cities must commit to protecting vulnerable populations.

Networks

Government should not be forced to do this work alone. Bloomberg Philanthropies is just one example of philanthropy's investment in building cities' capacity to use data and evidence. In addition to Bloomberg, the Rockefeller Foundation's One Hundred Resilient City Initiative, and the Arnold Foundation's support of analytics through the University of Chicago's Data Science for Social Good are just a few examples of how philanthropy is deeply committed to partnering with government to find solutions to and understand the potential impact of best practices.

Examples. These networks, which are highly effective in sharing knowledge and information, are a powerful tool for the transformation of government.

Perhaps the most useful outcome of investments in these practices is the emergence of the city network. Organizations at the helm of these multicity initiatives, like the U.S. Conference of Mayors, National League of Cities, and the National Association of Counties, should adopt common frameworks around data, discuss the potential of metadata standardization, and share best practices as often as possible. If leveraged appropriately these networks will facilitate local innovation by helping cities to understand what practices work, identify pitfalls, and insulate risk.

In addition to the networks mentioned above, the Civic Analytics Network (CAN) is playing an important role, specifically in local government data analytics, by creating linkages between cities.[15] CAN is an organization consisting of chief data officers that works to spread best practices in data analytics and data management to cities across the United States.

Discussion. Research on innovation in the private sector shows that open, collaborative, networks play an important role in innovation within a firm, as well as diffusion across the industry (Love, Roper, and Vahter 2013). These communities of governments, academic institutions, and philanthropic organizations create similar benefits for organizations and individuals seeking to transform government in the twenty-first century.

Conclusion

The key to creating the city of the future is understanding the role that data will play. But more importantly, the transformation requires investing in a public sector workforce that understands the potential of data, is willing to take some risk, and is ready for change. The U.S. public has already integrated deep data in how we buy goods and services, think about our personal futures, and connect with important people in our lives. It is time for government to accept data as a core resource and allow it to power twenty-first-century solutions.

By investing in the routine use of data, making connections between data and the outcomes that are most important to a city, and thinking about new and innovative ways that cities can accelerate success and realize their goals, the city of our future can be built.

Notes

1. See http://www.who.int/globalchange/ecosystems/urbanization/en/.

2. See cleanairpartners.net.

3. See Cityofnewhaven.com, "Welcome to the Community Services Administration."

4. What Works Cities homepage.

5. Denvergov.org, Peak Academy - Peak Performance.

6. See LouisvilleKy.gov, "City to Roll Out Locally Developed Wireless Smoke Detectors In Vacant, Abandoned Properties."

7. LouieStat is a performance management program that tracks and analyzes key performance indicators (KPIs) of success for each department. LouieStat tracks four Metro-wide KPIs (unscheduled overtime, sick leave balance, hours lost to worker's compensation, MetroCall/311 Complaints/Service Requests), as well as department-specific measures. Departments identify KPIs by answering the questions, "What results are we trying to achieve?" and "How would we know if we were achieving them?" Departments then set goals to improve performance based on an understanding of baseline data and benchmarks of who is doing this work well. Analysts evaluate performance against goals, and reports are sent to the mayor, leadership, and the department at least 48 hours before each meeting. Meetings are held regularly and are central to the city's management. Lean is a methodology that focuses on the value of services to customers and focuses on evaluating and refining processes to deliver better outcomes for customers using fewer resources. The Louisville Innovation Award is an annual award that the mayor confers to teams that are thinking in smarter ways to solve entrenched city issues. Past winners have worked on environmental reforms, public safety initiatives, and accessibility. See https://louisvilleky.gov/government/performance-improvement-innovation/metro-government-awards-continuous-improvement.

8. City of Austin Office of Innovation, "City Manager's Idea Accelerator."

9. Open311.org.

10. What Works Cities, "What Works City Feature: Kansas City, MO."

11. City of Kansas City, MO, "Citizen and Business Satisfaction Survey Results."

12. What Works Cities, "What Works City Feature: New Orleans, LA."

13. See Datadriven.nola.gov, "Results - Datadriven - City of New Orleans"; City of Kansas City, MO, "Citizen and Business Satisfaction Survey Results."
14. Data Science for Social Good, "Dssg/Syracuse_Public," GitHub.
15. Civic Analytics Network, "Civic Analytics Network | Data-Smart City Solutions."

References

Center for Government Excellence. 2016a. *Getting meta with metadata*. New York, NY: Bloomberg Philanthropies. Available from Centerforgov.gitbooks.io.
Center for Government Excellence. 2016b. *Getting started with open data*. New York, NY: Bloomberg Philanthropies. Available from Centerforgov.gitbooks.io.
Chandler, David. 19 June 2014. A new way to detect leaks in pipes. *MIT News*.
Cohen, Greg. 2010. *Agile excellence for product managers: A guide to creating winning products with agile development teams*. San Jose, CA: Super Star Press.
Conradie, Peter, and Sunil Choenni. 2014. On the barriers for local government releasing open data. *Government Information Quarterly*. doi:10.1016/j.giq.2014.01.003.
Feuer, Alan. 23 March 2013. The mayor's geek squad. *New York Times*.
García, Gonzalo Cerruela, Irene Luque Ruiz, and Miguel Gómez-Nieto. 2016. State of the art, trends and future of Bluetooth low energy, near field communication and visible light communication in the development of smart cities. *Sensors* 16 (11). doi:10.3390/s16111968.
Goldsmith, Stephen, and Susan P. Crawford. 2014. *The responsive city: Engaging communities through data-smart governance*. San Francisco, CA: Jossey-Bass.
Hickey, Kathleen. 15 December 2016. Louielab: An innovation hub for a smarter Louisville. *GCN*.
Kirkpatrick, Keith. 2016. Battling algorithmic bias. *Communications of the ACM* 59 (10): 16–17.
Kornberger, Martin, Renate E. Meyer, Christof Brandtner, and Markis Hollerer. 2017. When bureaucracy meets the crowd: Studying "open government" in the Vienna city administration. *Organization Studies* 38 (2): 179–200.
Latham, Erin. 22 February 2016. 4 Steps to eliminate data silos and unlock your data. *Government Technology*.
Love, James H., Stephen Roper, and Priit Vahter. 2013. Learning from openness: The dynamics of breadth in external innovation linkages. *Strategic Management Journal* 35 (11): 1703–61.
Patterson, Alastair M., Geoff R. Dowling, and Denis A. Chamberlain. 1997. Building inspection: Can computer vision help? *Automation in Construction* 7 (1): 13–20.
President's Council of Advisors on Science and Technology. 2014. *Big data and privacy: A technological perspective*. Washington, DC: Executive Office of the President. Available from https://bigdatawg.nist.gov/pdf/pcast_big_data_and_privacy_-_may_2014.pdf.
Samsonowa, Tatjana, and Anton Remnev. 2015. Smart events: Innovating large-scale event management with smart city solutions. Paper presented at the XXVI ISPIM Conference 2015 Budapest, Hungary, 14–17 June.
Sánchez, Luis, Ignacio Elicegui, Javier Cuesta, Luis Muñoz, and Jorge Lanza. 2013. Integration of utilities infrastructures in a future internet enabled smart city framework. *Sensors* 13 (11): 14438–65.
Shelter, Paul. 3 December 2016. My 16 months of digital transformation in Australia. *LinkedIn*.
Verhulst, Stefaan. 22 November 2016. Esri, Waze partnership: A growing trend in sharing data for the benefit of all? *Government Technology*.
Welch, Eric, Mary K. Feeney, and Chul Hyun Park. 2016. Determinants of data sharing in U.S. city governments. *Government Information Quarterly* 33 (3): 393–403.

Using Data to More Rapidly Address Difficult U.S. Social Problems

By
JEFFREY B. LIEBMAN

This article argues that the evidence-based-policy movement needs to supplement its current emphasis on program evaluations with an approach that uses data at a much higher frequency to improve the administration and impact of government-funded social service programs. Doing so offers the best chance of making significant progress in ameliorating challenging social problems. I describe how an idealized government social service agency could use data and data analysis to improve its results, review the barriers that prevent agencies from operating in this way, and outline how targeted resources and technical assistance can help to overcome these barriers. Finally, I discuss strategies for moving beyond the effective administration of siloed service programs to the improvement of population-wide outcomes, especially among individuals and families who need multiple services.

Keywords: social innovation; evidence-based policy-making; performance management; human services; what works; active contract management

Suppose our nation's goal is to demonstrate significant progress within 5 years in ameliorating a large number of social problems in individual communities and, within 10 years, to have spread the successful practices nationwide. Based on the experience of the Harvard Kennedy School Government Performance Lab (GPL), which to

Jeffrey B. Liebman is the Malcolm Wiener Professor of Public Policy at the Harvard Kennedy School, where he directs the Taubman Center for State and Local Government. He founded the Harvard Kennedy School Government Performance Lab, which has provided pro bono technical assistance to more than fifty state and local governments to improve their social programs and contracting.

NOTE: The author is grateful for support from Bloomberg Philanthropies, the California Endowment, the Dunham Fund, the Laura and John Arnold Foundation, the Pritzker Children's Initiative, the Rockefeller Foundation, and the Social Innovation Fund.

Correspondence: jeffrey_liebman@harvard.edu

DOI: 10.1177/0002716217745812

date has worked with fifty jurisdictions spanning twenty-four states, two strategies offer the best chance of achieving this goal:

- First, we need to help the state and local government agencies administering social programs use data and data analysis more effectively as a management tool to generate innovation, systems reengineering, and continuous improvement.
- Second, we need to launch, structure, and fund purposeful data-driven, community-level efforts to tackle difficult social problems in a way that breaks down funding silos and introduces accountability for population-wide outcomes.

In this article, I elaborate on these strategies in three sections. In the first section, I argue that the evidence-based-policy movement needs to supplement its current budget-oriented approach—which focuses primarily on evaluating which interventions work and encouraging governments to allocate budget resources to "proven" interventions—with an approach that uses data at a much higher frequency to improve the administration and impact of government-funded social service programs. In the second section, I present a concrete example of how an idealized government social service agency (specifically, a child welfare agency) could use data to improve the results it achieves for the population it serves. I also describe the barriers that prevent agencies from operating in this way and outline how targeted resources and technical assistance can help to overcome these barriers. In the third section, I discuss the need to move beyond effective administration of siloed social service programs to focus on achieving improved population-wide outcomes, especially among individuals and families who need multiple services. I sketch an approach that philanthropic funders could take to encourage communities to experiment with solutions to this challenge, so that we can develop models that can be adopted nationwide.

The Need for Purposeful Attempts to Achieve Better Outcomes for Target Populations

Much of the rhetoric around the use of evidence in policymaking suggests that government-funded social programs can be divided into two categories: those that work and those that do not. Under this perspective, the main point of increasing access to government data is to perform more impact evaluations so that we know which interventions to expand and which ones to defund.

The infrastructure that has been built up around the "what works" framework— the Coalition for Evidence-Based Policy Top Tier Evidence initiative, the U.S. Department of Education What Works Clearinghouse, the Washington State Institute for Public Policy Benefit-Cost Results, and the Poverty Action Lab's evaluation database, among many other examples—has been quite successful in spreading information on effective interventions. In our GPL work, we have found that in every state and local government social service agency with which we have worked, there are multiple officials who understand that some interventions in their field are "evidence based" and others are not. Moreover, although I am not aware of any comprehensive time series on the number of rigorous impact evaluations of U.S. social policy interventions completed per year, it certainly appears that the pace at which evaluation evidence is being developed is increasing and that this increase is resulting from a combination of demand-side factors (e.g., governments allocating resources based on tiered evidence standards, the philanthropic community making funding available for randomized control trials) and supply side factors (e.g., reduced costs of working with administrative data, the development of causal impact statistical frameworks that have increased researcher interest in randomization-based research strategies).

Despite all this momentum, we are still not making rapid enough progress on challenging social problems. Rates of disconnected youth, obesity, and prisoner recidivism remain high. There are still more than half a million homeless in the United States, and 30 percent of fourth graders score "below basic" in reading on the National Assessment of Educational Progress. Part of the problem is that we need a lot more innovation, experimentation, and evidence—at least twenty times what we are currently producing.[1] Most evaluations of social programs find disappointing results,[2] and a large portion of programs that look successful in an initial evaluation fail in replication. Therefore, we need to innovate and test at a much more rapid pace. Another part of the problem is that even when successful interventions are discovered, governments do not fund them at scale. Yet another part of the problem is that evidence becomes stale very quickly.[3] For example, randomized experiments in the 1970s and 1980s found that home-visiting services for low-income first-time mothers provided by the Nurse-Family Partnership (NFP) increased the spacing between first births and subsequent births. But birth control technology and Medicaid coverage for birth control has changed substantially since the original experiments were done, making them of little use in predicting the impact of those services today.[4] Finally, even the best models can fail when delivered on a large scale if staff quality and other implementation details are not sustained at the level of the original experiment.

But there is a broader issue as well. *Impact evaluations, while extremely valuable, are a relatively small portion of the hard work that needs to be done with data and data analysis if we are going to move the dial on difficult social problems.* Human service agencies need to be making greater use of data and analysis throughout their operations. Moreover, the rhetoric about using evidence to find out "what works" orients policy-makers incorrectly toward thinking that program effectiveness is a static concept and that the budget process is the primary way to achieve greater effectiveness. Instead, political leaders should be reviewing data on whether programs are doing better this month than last month (or this year than last year) and holding agencies accountable for reengineering their processes and those of their contractors to produce continually rising performance trends over time.[5]

Consider the problem of improving outcomes for a vulnerable population. Let us assume, for example, that we are leading a state health department in a jurisdiction that has one of the highest rates of infant mortality in the nation, and we have decided to focus on the objective of reducing infant mortality and the number of low-birthweight births statewide. This happens to be a policy area where there is a significant amount of evaluation evidence, as well as intervention models that have been certified as "evidence based."

There are at least four types of data analysis that are needed to tackle this problem:

First, the state needs to analyze infant deaths and low-birthweight births to *identify the entire target population* and formulate hypotheses about policy interventions that could potentially affect the problem. Where are the geographic hot spots? What fraction of the mothers are teens? What portion of infant deaths follow upon low-birthweight or premature births, and what portion result from child maltreatment? Are the mothers smokers, drug or alcohol abusers, overweight, or undernourished? What, if any, preventive services were provided to these mothers? Some of this analysis could be done with data from birth records, another portion from Medicaid claims data, another portion from health department and child welfare agency case files, and some might require pulling the medical charts of a random sample of births with bad outcomes.

Second, the state needs to use data on risk levels and intervention cost-effectiveness for specific subpopulations to *refer the right people to the right services*. Which low-income pregnant mothers should be referred to intensive evidence-based home-visiting providers, which to lower-intensity home visiting, and which to no home visiting at all? Which communities need to be targeted for public health campaigns around nutrition, exercise, and healthy infant sleep practices? Where do more resources need to be invested in drug treatment programs and teen pregnancy prevention? How can target mothers be identified early enough in pregnancy to impact birth outcomes?

Third, the state needs to *track service receipt in real time and then collaborate with service providers to minimize the portion of the target population that falls through the cracks*. Each month the state program lead should review data on what percentage of pregnant mothers referred to home visiting received services, and state program staff should meet with providers to review case files to identify reasons that target individuals failed to receive services and make changes in processes to improve the fraction of the target population that is reached. The state should also review cases with bad outcomes that were not referred to services and analyze what can be done through better outreach and targeting of services to reach the highest-risk population. And it is not just the initial receipt of services that should be tracked; progress toward program completion should be monitored as well.

At the GPL, we refer to this combination of high frequency review of data and regular collaborative meetings between government agency staff and service providers to identify opportunities for systems reengineering as *active contract management*. We contrast it with the more typical relationship between contract officers and providers that focuses on invoice processing and compliance reviews.

In the projects with which we have been involved, we have seen active contract management increase the fraction of recently released prisoners who make it to job training in New York State, improve the targeting of permanent assisted housing slots to homeless individuals in Massachusetts, reduce the lag between when a child welfare agency refers a family to emergency services and when those services begin in Rhode Island, and improve the coordination of services for the homeless in Seattle.[6]

Fourth, the state needs to *annually compare outcomes for individuals referred to different services to make decisions about how to allocate resources and adjust referral protocols going forward.* If multiple service providers are serving the same population, their results should be compared and the state should either reallocate slots to the most effective providers or convene meetings at which the higher achievers can share best practices with the others. These sorts of comparisons are not always straightforward. Results need to be adjusted to account for differences in the populations being served by different providers. Otherwise, providers who target the most difficult cases will be penalized. And short of randomization, there is no way to adjust for differences that are not measured in available data. But quite often there are opportunities to use regression-discontinuity strategies to compare outcomes for people just above and below thresholds for referral to services, and there are opportunities to replace idiosyncratic referral processes with deliberate ones that involve randomization to facilitate comparisons of relative effectiveness. Moreover, even when only unadjusted outcomes by service type can be calculated, they can be quite revealing. For example, if we observe that only 10 percent of TANF recipients referred to job training are both employed and earning more than $10,000 per year three years after training is completed, we would know that the state needs to rethink its strategy for helping this population achieve economic self-sufficiency. If we never identify self-sufficiency as the goal and never measure medium-term earnings outcomes, the state might plod along, funding slots with the same service providers, without any realization that the strategy needs to be rethought.

The overall point is that if we want to achieve better outcomes for vulnerable populations, we need to make a purposeful effort to do so. Defining the population that we are trying to reach, measuring the outcomes that we are trying to improve, and using data and analysis throughout the policymaking and service delivery chain drives the systems reengineering and continuous improvement efforts necessary to achieve better outcomes. Evaluating the impact of particular intervention models is only one part of what needs to be done.

Overcoming Obstacles to Effective Use of Data by Government Human Service Agencies

Every one of the three dozen state or local government social service agencies the GPL has worked with produces a large volume of performance data, much of them in quarterly or monthly reports mandated by the legislature or the federal government. Most of the agencies have internal performance dashboards that they review in regular meetings with senior leadership. But many of the performance metrics are highly imperfect (for example, a state labor department that focuses on the percentage of people completing a job training program who are employed immediately after completing the program, ignoring those who failed to complete the program and also failing to measure the longer-term impact on employment and earnings). And agencies find it very challenging to go beyond performance reporting to use data to drive performance improvement. This is not to say it does not happen. We have observed remarkable examples of agencies improving processes in a relatively short time when leadership and technical capacity have been aligned, but these have mostly been isolated examples of a single agency improving a single process rather than agencies that use data effectively throughout their operations to constantly improve results.

Let me illustrate some of the kinds of analyses that agencies find difficult to do. To make the examples concrete, I discuss these issues in the context of a child welfare agency; most could be illustrated in any other human services agency as well.

Improving outcomes for the entire target population, rather than focusing solely on those who arrive at the agency's front door

In annual reports of child welfare agencies, the first table often shows trends over time in reports of child maltreatment. If this trend is downward, it is interpreted as progress. But reports of maltreatment can decline either because maltreatment declines or because reporting rates decline. While all states now have processes to review child deaths, in some states these reviews continue to focus primarily on cases that occur in families that were previously known to the state human services agencies. Agencies should regularly measure all preventable child deaths in their jurisdiction as well as child injuries. If the ratio of maltreatment reports to deaths and injuries is declining, this is a sign that reporting needs to be improved. Case reviews of preventable deaths and serious injuries in families that were not previously known to the state human service agencies should ask why these families were not previously identified as needing services and what services might have prevented the incidents. Analysis should also identify geographic areas and demographic groups that are most likely to be missed by the system and target outreach to those areas and groups. The reason that these sorts of analyses are rare today is that agency program leads are in charge of managing a siloed spending program that delivers services to people identified by that program, but typically no one is responsible for whether the system as a whole is achieving the desired outcomes for the entire target population.

Evaluating the quality of decision-making on whether to do an investigation, whether to open a case, whether to refer a family to particular services, and whether to close a case

Some state child welfare agencies have very clear "structured decision-making" protocols linked to validated risk assessments that guide staff in determining when to do an investigation and when to remove a child for place-ment into foster care. Other jurisdictions give staff considerable latitude in mak-ing ad hoc judgments based on experience and expertise. But either way, state agencies should regularly evaluate whether the lines are being drawn at the right place by comparing subsequent safety outcomes (new reports of maltreatment, child deaths, child injuries) for cases just below the thresholds for doing an inves-tigation or opening a case to those just above the thresholds. If subsequent safety outcomes are poor for those just below the thresholds, then the threshold should be lowered. If subsequent safety outcomes are very good for those above the threshold, it may be worth experimenting with raising the threshold to see if those families do similarly well even with a more limited set of in-home services but without a formal case being opened. To facilitate such analysis, it may be necessary to collect data on the subjective assessments of risk levels by agency staff making the decisions so that those cases that are near the threshold can be identified.

Focusing on outcomes rather than volume of service metrics

While all child welfare agencies that GPL has worked with have strategic plans that focus on the goals of safety, permanency, and child well-being, they take a wide variety of approaches when designing the data dashboards that they review in their regular senior staff meetings. In particular, it is quite common for these meetings to focus on volume of service metrics, rather than measures of safety, permanency, and child well-being. Common metrics are the size of the caseload, the number of case closings, and the number of children referred to different types of services. Agencies often focus on volume metrics because these metrics determine the rate at which the agency exhausts its annual budget allocation, and how large the caseloads are for social workers. While monitoring volume metrics is important and can lead to decisions that affect the quality of services delivered, when leadership attention is focused exclusively on volume metrics, opportuni-ties are missed to improve service delivery and outcomes.

Interpreting implications of data in a way that can drive operational improvements

We regularly observe meetings at which agency leadership is looking at the right data, but not asking the right questions about them and at which the staff are presenting data, but do not offer any useful interpretation of what the data mean.[7] For example, a histogram might be displayed of the distribution of social worker caseloads, showing a mode of approximately twenty and that 90 percent of caseworkers have caseloads between fifteen and twenty-five. Everyone will nod when the data are presented each month and say "the range of caseloads is interesting, maybe we should do something to reduce it," but no one asks any operationally relevant questions. Are the large caseloads all from a single regional office that is understaffed? Is the heterogeneity in caseloads across caseworkers appropriate with some caseworkers given a larger number of low-intensity cases and others given a smaller number of higher-intensity cases? Is it resulting from some caseworkers failing to do the paperwork to close inactive cases promptly? It would be straightforward to check in with field office managers about outliers and reasons for this heterogeneity and, if necessary, to pull a sample of cases to sort out what is going on. But this does not happen, and so data are presented month after month without any useful interpretation or follow-up.

Collaborating effectively with service providers outside of government to make sure services are delivered effectively

As I mentioned briefly, government social service agencies rarely do a good job of managing their contracts with private sector social service providers. This is the problem with which the GPL has the most experience helping agencies. To date, we have helped governments to improve their contracting processes for homelessness services, child welfare services, prisoner reentry services, adult basic education services, workforce development services, early childhood home visiting services, pre-K services, and juvenile justice services. Typically, governments contract for services without identifying the strategic purpose they are trying to achieve, and simply pay for slots in programs. They usually fail to measure the outcomes achieved by contractors or to build effective outcome reporting or performance incentives into contracts. Most importantly, they typically fail to actively manage provider performance once contracts are executed. In our work, we help government agencies to track in real time whether individuals referred to services actually receive services, whether the individuals are progressing successfully through the service model, and what their subsequent outcomes are. We help agencies to set up regular (monthly or quarterly) meetings with service providers to review performance metrics and to discuss how the government and the providers can collaborate to achieve better results. For example, in Rhode Island we have helped the state child welfare agency there establish monthly "active contract management" meetings with the four large providers of front-end family preservation services to review performance data and conduct deep dives on issues where the group thinks systems reengineering can produce better results for children and families. The key elements of the active contract management approach are high frequency data-driven purposeful efforts to improve outcomes implemented in such a way that a culture of collaboration develops between government agencies and service providers.

Comparatively evaluating different types of services to rethink the service mix

We find that agencies fall into patterns in which they contract every year for the same set of services with the same set of providers and miss opportunities to alter the service mix to achieve better results. For example, we worked in one state in which rates of placement in long-term congregate care had been steadily rising for more than a decade in large part because the state had reduced spending on in-home services that could enable families to stay intact. In another state, referrals to a long-established in-home service offered by four providers had declined over five years to substantially less than contracted capacity, leaving the service providers (who were compensated largely based on families served) scrambling to cover their fixed costs. In yet another state, there was a bureaucratic backlog that prevented new families from getting approved as foster care providers, resulting in long stays of children in congregate care. Regular review of rates of referrals to different types of placements and services and regular tracking of cases in which a child or family is referred to a less optimal service because the first choice service did not have available slots can help to direct attention to resource misallocation and to bottlenecks that need to be eliminated. And comparing outcomes for similar individuals referred to different services can help to inform decisions about which services are most effective (and most cost-effective).

These examples are not exhaustive of all the ways social service agencies could improve results through better use of data, but my hope is that they are sufficiently concrete to provide an understanding of the potential for data and data analysis to be used to improve results for priority populations.

There are two main obstacles that are preventing this work from occurring: First, many agencies lack leadership with a time horizon that is sufficiently long to prompt performance improvement projects, that is philosophically oriented toward using data to drive change, and that is willing to bear the stresses associated with driving change. Second, many agencies lack staff with the combination of spare capacity, expertise, and desire necessary to lead data-driven reform projects. In some cases, there are several people in the agency who could lead this kind of work, but they are already occupied more than full time, making sure the trains run on time and all the required quarterly and annual reports are produced. In other cases, there is no one around with the ability to look at data and ask questions about them in the way that is necessary to drive reform. In still other cases, agency leadership fails to empower the capable analysts to roam beyond their narrow silos to address cross-cutting issues; analysts and program specialists need to collaborate effectively. And in still other cases, the capable personnel decline to take on challenging reform projects because the initiatives require extra work and involve risk taking.

There are other more minor obstacles that sometimes arise.[8] For example, some agencies have farmed out data management to private contractors and can only regain access to the agency's own data by paying a large fee to the contractor. In other cases, data warehouses have been set up at local universities, and the gatekeeper to that data becomes a bottleneck. Sometimes agencies have seven-year-old computers meant for word processing and cannot easily procure even a $1,000 work station and a copy of Stata to use for data analysis. Other times outcomes data need to be obtained from a different state agency or a federal agency, and the lawyers for the various agencies operate in a risk-adverse, "it is not permitted" mode rather than in a problem-solving mode. Such "legal" bottlenecks invariably get solved not by further negotiations between lawyers, but by intervention from an agency head or state budget officer who directs the lawyers to start operating in problem-solving mode. Finally, while most of the necessary data matching and analysis are simple, occasionally there is the need for technical assistance that can allow an agency to perform a more advanced statistical analysis than an agency can perform on its own. But the key point is that in most projects the data matching and data analysis per se are not very hard. What is hard is overcoming inertia and resistance to change and making sure there are people in the agency who are capable of looking at numbers and asking the right operational questions about them.

In thinking about how to assist agencies in overcoming these obstacles it is important to focus both on sustainability and on replication. Technical assistance needs to be provided in a way that allows agencies to continue doing whatever the assistance enabled, even after the assistance ends. Ideally, a technical assistance project that helps a government to do a data-driven management reform not only allows an agency to continue to implement that particular reform, but also to undertake additional projects on its own, without further technical assistance, based on the learning that occurred from during the initial reform. On the replication front, the human service agencies in all fifty states (and many counties and cities) are all essentially in the same business. In theory, a successful data-driven management reform can be transported to other jurisdictions quite easily. In practice, the GPL has found that even when all the steps are known from doing a project in one jurisdiction, the resources necessary for replicating a project in a second jurisdiction can be 70 to 80 percent of what they were in the initial jurisdiction.[9] The hardest parts of reform work are getting leadership and other agency staff to buy into the project, training staff in taking an analytical approach, and building relationships with service providers and other community actors. To a first approximation, all this work needs to be done from scratch in each new jurisdiction. What does improve in replication is one's confidence that the process will produce the desired results.

How can we rapidly increase the number of government social service agencies making effective use of data? There are things that the technical assistance community already knows how to do and simply needs the resources and focus to achieve and things that we still need to find better models for. Organizations such as the Annie E. Casey Foundation, Pew Center on the States, the National Governor's Association, and the Harvard Kennedy School GPL have shown that various mixes of on-site and remote technical assistance can help a willing government to successfully implement a reform project. While there are important lessons that have been learned along the way—how one verifies that a government really is committed to a project, what one can do to increase the chance that the project gets completed in six months rather than in two years, and how to maximize the probability that a new way of doing business sticks after the technical assistance is complete—there are now known techniques for providing technical assistance that result in successful execution of reform projects in government human service agencies. This is not to say that the work is easy; overcoming inertia and deliberate resistance to change is hard. But if we had a willing agency head, it would be relatively straightforward to provide them with four outside full-time equivalents (FTEs) who could work with four internal FTEs to implement a project that aimed to purposefully use data to reengineer a large number of their systems over a two-year period to achieve better performance (one might want more than four FTEs for a complicated agency such as Medicaid and fewer for a relatively straightforward one such as TANF). One could imagine doing this in two jurisdictions for each of the twelve or so main state human service agencies (they would not need to be the same jurisdictions for all twelve agencies). At the end, we would have templates that could be brought to the other forty-eight states.[10] There are also good existing models for how to share best practices across jurisdictions once the best practices have been developed—models of peer learning, executive education, cohort-based technical assistance and the like.

What currently seems harder is to provide state human service agencies with the human capital necessary to continue to do data-driven reforms on their own once the technical assistance ends. Strong human capital would also greatly facilitate the spreading of best practices once they are developed, because there would be able and willing people in each jurisdiction to implement the new models—we would not have to provide dedicated FTEs to each via outside technical assistance.

Thankfully, the scale of this challenge is not that large. Suppose our goal was to have four data-focused leaders in each of the twelve key social service agencies in each of the fifty states. That is only 2,400 people who need to be recruited and trained: 480 a year if we want to achieve this in 10 years and assume 50 percent turnover. Including the human service agencies in the fifty largest cities might increase the target number by 50 percent. The best models for how to do this lie in cities such as Boston, Denver, and Louisville, which have started by hiring a few pioneer data-focused individuals. The pioneers have helped to create a culture that attracts other young workers with analytic talent.[11] Denver and Louisville have also made systematic efforts to train up a large fraction of their existing staff alongside attracting new talent.

One could imagine a state making a dedicated effort to bring in an initial cadre of a dozen analytically oriented new staff members and spreading them across the human service agencies. While they would initially be somewhat isolated within their agencies, they would have both an interagency peer network and a cross-jurisdiction peer network. And over time as the group within their jurisdiction grew from twelve to forty-eight, they would have new peers within their agencies and have found allies among the existing employees, and the culture around the use of data would shift.

Put simply, it seems to me that we are in a place in which with a purposeful effort to inject data-driven management approaches, we could greatly improve the administration of our most important social programs nationwide in a relatively short period of time. I am optimistic that by improving the administration of these programs we would make major progress in addressing difficult social problems, but that is an unproven hypothesis at this point based largely on observing how far from the frontier we are right now, and therefore how much low-hanging fruit there appears to be.

Breaking Down Silos with Data-Driven, Outcome-Focused, Community-Level Collaboration

Many of our most difficult social problems cross agency boundaries, and families often receive services from multiple agencies. A problem with how social services are often delivered today is that each service provider is focused on providing units of a specialized service, but no one is accountable for thinking holistically about what it would take to get the individual or the family to an overall successful outcome. This tunnel vision exists within government human service agencies as well. Most agencies are organized around program managers who are accountable for making sure their program dollars get spent and for counting how many individuals receive services from their program, but no one is responsible for tracking and managing the overall well-being of the target population.

I had a conversation recently with an expert in a child welfare agency about the challenge of obtaining substance abuse treatment for parents whose addictions were leading to neglect of their children. The child welfare agency would refer such parents to the state's substance abuse program, but when a parent failed to show up for treatment, the substance abuse program would simply cross the parent off their list of individuals who were interested in treatment without thinking of the case as one that still needed attention. Too often, social service agencies are structured in these myopic ways—focused on the administration of their own programs not on making progress on population outcomes.

We need to make progress in four different areas to address the problem of silos.

The first and simplest is that agencies, as discussed here, need to properly define the population that is their target, measure outcomes for the full target population, and manage their operations to improve those outcomes. They need to break down the silos and unit-of-services focus within their particular agencies.

Second, we need explicit cross-agency collaborations that allow multiple programs spread across multiple agencies to jointly define the target populations and outcomes they are trying to affect and whose teams meet regularly to review data and spot opportunities to troubleshoot, collaborate more effectively, and improve performance.

Third, we need to experiment with efforts to identify the highest-need families in a jurisdiction and to provide appropriate case management that connects the families to the right mix of services. My GPL recently published a case study about the UK Troubled Families Program that has been applying this approach nationwide in the UK (see Economy and Gong 2017).

There is also a large research project that needs to be done to inform this approach. Some jurisdiction should look at all the individuals who had really bad outcomes—children involved in the juvenile justice system, children who were maltreated, children who were expelled from school, and so on—and map out how many different families these cases represent, what the overlap is between those showing up as problem cases in different systems, the first time a human service agency became aware of a problem with the individual or family, and where the first opportunity to intervene occurred. Then we need to develop predictive models to inform early intervention efforts that appropriately balance the risks of overproviding and underproviding services.

Fourth, we need to find ways to channel the momentum being produced through collective impact efforts such as the Strive Partnership so that they actually change how services are being delivered on the ground. The collective impact movement has correctly observed that better collaboration and a results-focused orientation are needed not only within government but with all the partners in a community—including philanthropic foundations, employers, and school districts—who impact outcomes for children and other vulnerable populations. But even when there is considerable high-level buy-in for these efforts, it has been hard to translate this buy-in into improvements in service delivery. In some cases, the challenge appears to be that the collective impact effort is not being driven by the entities that control either the funding or the data, and GPL's best current hypothesis is that these initiatives will be more successful when the entities that control the data and the funding—typically government agencies— are at the center of these initiatives.

I have written previously about what I call the "10-year challenge," which could be a framework for bringing about the data-driven, outcomes-focused, community-level collaborations that I believe are necessary to move the dial on complex social programs (Liebman 2013). A funder, either the federal government or a large philanthropic foundation, would choose one or more social problems on which it wanted to make significant progress; examples could be reducing recidivism among ex-offenders, raising third-grade test scores among low-income children living in high-poverty neighborhoods, preventing high-risk youth from dropping out of high school, retraining individuals who have been unemployed for more than nine months, increasing the rate of community college completion, reducing obesity-triggered diabetes, eliminating chronic and/or family homelessness, or helping developmentally disabled youth make successful transitions into the adult workforce, among many others. All the problems would be ones where the specific individuals in the population to be served can be identified and baseline outcomes can be established; these two factors will provide an observable baseline against which improvement can be measured.

Through a grant competition, ten communities would be selected for each problem in an effort to transform outcomes for the specific population within 5 to 10 years. In a first step, the funder would issue planning grants of approximately $250,000 each to several dozen communities that were interested in putting together proposals. Then ten communities would be selected for more substantial funding based on how likely the proposed project is to make significant progress in addressing the social problem, the potential for the project to yield rigorous evidence about what works, and the extent to which the approach demonstrated by the project could be spread nationwide. Although it would be terrific if all ten communities were successful, the real goal would be to discover two or three transformative approaches for each policy problem—solutions that could then be developed and implemented nationwide. In the original proposal, I suggested that average-sized projects would spend $10 million a year on services and serve approximately one thousand to two thousand individuals (with flexibility depending on the nature of the intervention and the size of the community and of the target population). I suggested that the primary funder (the federal government or a philanthropic foundation) would cover one-third of the costs of the intervention, state and local governments would need to agree to providing another one-third, and private community partners would be required to cover the remaining third. In addition, each chosen jurisdiction would receive $1 million per year for technical assistance on data analysis and evaluation. In total, this initiative would cost the primary funder approximately $40 million per year for 5 to 10 years per social problem. Clearly all these numbers can be adjusted by varying the number of people served and the number of communities working on solutions to each problem.

Final Words

The modern era of social-policy development and evaluation dates back to the late 1960s when large datasets and randomized experiments began to be used regularly to evaluate federal policy initiatives. Decades later, we have a better sense of what works to address certain social challenges, but we are still very far from where we need to be. We still lack proven, cost-effective, scalable solutions to most social problems, and, despite significant government investment, we are failing to make sufficiently rapid progress in addressing our most serious challenges. Today, if a governor were to ask his or her policy advisors for a state-wide program that could cut recidivism among individuals recently released from state prison by one-third, or a program that could raise the employment of welfare recipients by 10 percentage points, there is no intervention currently available for those advisors to offer the governor that has more than a 50 percent chance of working. Even in early childhood education, where the evidence of successful interventions is strong, if the governor were to ask for an initiative to eliminate half of the gap in third-grade test scores between more- and less-affluent students, it is far from certain that an initiative could be designed and implemented to achieve that target with what we know today.

Part of the reason we lack solutions to many social problems is that the problems are hard and human beings and their social environments are complex. But it is also the case that our current mechanisms for funding and evaluating social programs do not produce a culture of continuous learning and improvement; nor do they generate opportunities for fundamental reengineering of systems to produce better results. Sustained purposeful efforts to actually move the dial on a particular social problem in a particular community are rare. My conjecture is that if we take advantage of the great expansion in the availability of data and analysis tools to actually try to move the dial on social problems in a data-driven, outcomes-focused way, we might find that we succeed.

Notes

1. Bridgeland and Orszag (2013, 63) estimate that "less than $1 out of every $100 of government spending is backed by even the most basic evidence that the money is being spent wisely."

2. For example, Baron and Sawhill (2010, 21) report that nine of ten evaluations of entire federal social programs found "weak or no positive effects."

3. The social entrepreneur George Overholser has observed that "evidence melts like ice cream." See Overholser (2014).

4. The GPL provided technical assistance to the state of South Carolina on a project that is expanding funding for NFP and providing a platform for a new randomized evaluation of the impact of NFP. We are also assisting two other states that are developing similar projects.

5. There is a parallel between my argument and recent developments in federal management policy. The Bush administration's Program Assessment Rating Tool (PART) focused on systematically assessing whether each government program was achieving its goals and was often perceived by agencies and congressional committees as a mechanism to apportion programs into those that were worth keeping and those that should be eliminated (Moynihan 2008). The Obama administration's performance.gov approach focused on tracking and improving performance trends. See Metzenbaum (2009) for an influential presentation of these ideas, and Metzenbaum and Shea (2017) for a recent assessment.

6. Further details on the Seattle project are available in Azemati and Grover-Roybal (2016).

7. See Behn (2014) on the difference between creating a white elephant performance dashboard and actually undertaking a data-informed performance leadership strategy. Behn notes that in contrast to the popular expression, data do not in fact speak for themselves.

8. See Goerge (this volume) for an insightful discussion of barriers researchers face in trying to access state government administrative data.

9. Perhaps the clearest demonstration of this is in our pay for success/social impact bond work. There are now sixteen pay-for-success projects in the United States. The GPL has provided government-side technical assistance on ten of them. But even though we understand all the steps are necessary to implement a project and have done it many times, it is still taking at least two years from conception to service delivery in these projects. Certain steps in the process—getting decisions from government decision-makers, obtaining legislative authority, helping local service providers become comfortable with the pay-for-success model and able to understand the financial implications of increasing the scale of their operations, setting up the data systems necessary to track outcomes, and waiting for investors to be recruited—need to be done anew in each project.

10. Bloomberg Philanthropies' What Works Cities initiative provides a good example of how to do multijurisdictional technical assistance at scale. See Blauer (this volume).

11. On the Boston example, see Steve Poftak (2016). On Denver, see Brian Elms (2016). See Blauer (this volume) for a broad vision of how cities might make better use of data in the future.

References

Azemati, Hanna, and Christina Grover-Roybal. 2016. *Shaking up the routine: How Seattle is implementing results-driven contracting practices to improve outcomes for people experiencing homelessness.* Cambridge, MA: Harvard Kennedy School Government Performance Lab.

Baron, Jon, and Isabel Sawhill. May 2010. Federal programs for youth: More of the same won't work. *Youth Today.*

Behn, Robert D. 2014. *The PerformanceStat potential*. Washington, DC: Brookings Institution Press.

Blauer, Beth. 2017. Building the data city of the future. *The ANNALS of the American Academy of Political and Social Science* (this volume).

Bridgeland, John, and Peter Orszag. July/August 2013. Can government play moneyball? *The Atlantic*.

Economy, Christina, and Gloria Gong. 2017. *UK Troubled Families Programme: Lessons from local authorities*. Cambridge, MA: Harvard Kennedy School Government Performance Lab.

Elms, Brian. 2016. *Peak performance: How Denver's Peak Academy is saving money, boosting morale, and just maybe changing the world*. With J.B. Wogan. Washington, DC: Governing.

Goerge, Robert M. 2017. Barriers to accessing state data and approaches to addressing them. *The ANNALS of the American Academy of Political and Social Science* (this volume).

Liebman, Jeffrey. 2013. *Building on recent advances in evidence-based policymaking*. Hamilton Project. Washington, DC: Brookings Institution.

Metzenbaum, Shelley H. 2009. *Performance management recommendations for the new administration*. Washington, DC: IBM Center for the Business of Government.

Metzenbaum, Shelley, and Robert Shea. 11 January 2017. Memo to the president: Performance accountability, evidence and improvement. Government Executive.

Moynihan, Donald P. 2008. *The dynamics of performance management: Construction information and reform*. Washington, DC: Georgetown University Press.

Overholser, George. 9 September 2014. Statement of George Overholser. Hearing on Social Impact Bonds and Families in Need. House Committee on Ways and Means Subcommittee on Human Resources.

Poftak, Steve. 2016. *City Hall's data and technology journey: Using data to improve the lives of citizens*. Boston, MA: Rappaport Institute for Greater Boston.

Section III: Comprehensive Strategies

The UK Administrative Data Research Network: Its Genesis, Progress, and Future

By
PETER ELIAS

This article describes the ways in which UK administrative data are becoming more widely available for research. I outline the historical context of these developments, detail the network infrastructure that has now been put in place and discuss the continuing legal measures that are required to bring this network to fruition. I focus on the lessons that have been learned as work has progressed, drawing on this experience to elucidate some principles that may have relevance to similar attempts to promote better access to and linkage between administrative datasets in different cultural and legal settings.

Keywords: networked data infrastructure; administrative data; data access; data security

This article reports on research infrastructure developments in the UK, designed to facilitate and improve record level access to administrative data. I describe how over the last two decades, access to data for research purposes has moved from being unreliable, haphazard, and unregulated, to a situation in which all those involved, from data holders to the general public, have a clearer understanding of the needs of the research community and in which researchers

Peter Elias is a research professor at the Institute for Employment Research, University of Warwick, UK. His research interests include higher education and the labor market, processes of occupational change, and the evaluation of large scale labor market programs. Over the past 10 years he has worked closely with the UK Economic and Social Research Council, involved in the development of a research data infrastructure within the UK.

NOTE: I would like to thank Vanessa Cuthill and David Hand for comments and advice on earlier drafts of this article. Additionally, reviewer advice and feedback was most helpful in improving earlier drafts. The views expressed are the sole responsibility of the author.

Correspondence: Peter.Elias@warwick.ac.uk

DOI: 10.1177/0002716217741279

can plan their research and be confident that access to administrative data will be granted.

My aim is not to portray these developments as a specific model for others to emulate. Rather, I seek to highlight the problems that have been addressed in establishing this new access regime and to derive the lessons learned. What were the main obstacles to improve access, and how were they tackled? Does the new system provide researchers with access without placing a large burden on them? How does it sit alongside other structures that have been set up to provide research access to specific datasets? What has it cost so far, and how does this compare with the scientific benefits expected from this infrastructure?

The article is structured as follows. In the next section, I describe earlier attempts to improve person-level access to administrative data in the UK. What was accomplished, how successful were these attempts, and how did this translate into the approach adopted in 2012 when work began in earnest to establish the Administrative Data Research Network (ADRN)? After that, I describe the taskforce that was set up to examine the barriers to access that researchers had faced when seeking access, recommending how these barriers could be lifted through the creation of a new networked infrastructure. In the third section, I detail the way in which these recommendations were enacted through the creation of the ADRN, looking at what it has achieved in its first two years of operation. This section draws also on recent and independent reviews of its activities. What are the main problems it now faces, and what should be done to improve the ADRN, thereby further realizing the research value of administrative data?

The fourth section examines in some detail how a better understanding of the needs of data providers has impacted upon the early work of the ADRN. Following that discussion, I highlight the lessons learned, drawing on this experience across the UK to signpost the ways in which others might chart a roadmap toward improved access to administrative data. But the barriers to access and data linkage that researchers are likely to face will be legal and may also be "cultural," in the sense that data holders have over many years developed particular approaches to data sharing for research. Such hurdles are both country and agency specific, as will be made evident from the differing degrees of success in developing data access arrangements across the four countries of the UK and the slow rate of progress toward access to data held by particular government departments. Bearing this in mind, the lessons taken from the UK can only be drawn at the level of principles, not specifics. These principles are enunciated in the concluding section.

Earlier Attempts to Improve Access to Administrative Data

The digitization of government administrative records commenced in the UK in the 1960s, with the advent of mainframe computers, card readers, and line printers. Data held in these computers was designed for administrative purposes only. Information derived from such data and placed into the public domain was aggregated, usually across time periods, and was generally months out of date at the time of publication in official statistical gazettes. Access for research purposes unrelated to these administrative functions was generally not regarded as a legitimate function for those collecting and processing such records.

In the late 1970s and through the following two decades, government departments and agencies began to appreciate the research value inherent within their large and growing databases and started carrying out research, usually to inform service delivery, using unit-level statistical records for which they had responsibility. These activities were either conducted in-house, by their own research teams, or were "bought in" services provided by contracted researchers, often involving university research teams with expertise in computer programming and statistical analysis. Access for external research purposes was rarely granted, a situation that was further confounded by the fact that there is no centralized statistical authority within the UK that could provide a more regulated approach over access to person-level administrative data. Most departments of government retain such control, except for information deemed to be "national statistics" (a term that refers to an aggregate statistic that achieves a certain level of quality, defined by a Code of Practice, rather than raw data per se). Some departments of government cover the whole of the UK (e.g., taxation, social security, defense), others are specific to each country of the UK (e.g., education, justice, health). To complicate matters further, there are three national statistical authorities, each covering population, the economy, and society (see Box 1).

BOX 1
The National Statistical System in the UK

The United Kingdom has devolved responsibilities for the collection, processing, and publication of statistical information to its constituent countries.

In Scotland, the national statistical authority is National Records Scotland (https://www.nrscotland.gov.uk/statistics-and-data/statistics).

For Northern Ireland, these tasks are the responsibility of the Northern Ireland Statistics and Research Agency (http://www.nisra.gov.uk).

In England and Wales, the Office for National Statistics (https://www.ons.gov.uk) has this responsibility, and it also acts as the coordinating agency for UK-wide statistical information.

By the turn of the century, many researchers were becoming aware of the research potential of the vast amounts of data that had been accumulating within government departments. For their part, government departments and agencies were being urged to engage in cross departmental data sharing to improve service efficiency. On the research front, reports commissioned as part of the UK National Data Strategy[1] detailed numerous datasets that could prove to be valuable research assets if access procedures could be improved (Smith et al. 2004;

Jones and Elias 2006). These reports listed some of the more successful efforts that had been made by researchers, both within government and academia, to improve research access to particular types of data (see Box 2 for an example). An influential report published in 2008 stressed the need for data holders to have a better understanding of their legal powers to share data, given that this was widely recognized as a major obstacle (Thomas and Walport 2008).

BOX 2
The National Pupil Database

The National Pupil Database (NPD) is described as "one of the richest education data-sets in the world, holding a wide range of information about students who attend schools and colleges in England" (See http://www.adls.ac.uk/department-for-education/dcsf-npd/?detail). The NPD combines annual examination results of pupils with information on pupil and school characteristics and is an amalgamation of a number of different data-sets, including attainment data from key stages in a child's education, and school census data, which are linked using a unique identifier for each pupil.

These data are held by the Department of Education in England. Access was promoted through a user group that was set up and previously (2006–2013) organized by Simon Burgess, Director of the Centre for Market and Public Organisation (CMPO) and Harvey Goldstein, Professor of Social Statistics at the Centre for Multilevel Modelling.

Despite the difficulties that some have experienced, the user group has been successful in promoting research access to these data. More than eighty publications were listed by the Administrative Data Liaison Service (http://www.adls.ac.uk/ADLS-hub/publications/?dept=DfE&ds=229&search_submit=1).

Encouraged by these reports and the growing demand for access to administrative data for research from the academic research community, in 2006 the UK Economic and Social Research Council (ESRC) agreed to fund both an Administrative Data Liaison Service (ADLS) and a Secure Data Service (SDS). These were established in 2008. The former did not provide access to administrative data; instead, it worked as a repository for metadata relating to the wide variety of datasets held by government departments and of potential interest to social scientists. The ADLS rapidly became a "first stop shop" for researchers seeking to discover whether any administrative data were potentially available that could meet their research needs. The SDS was set up to mirror a similar secure data laboratory established by the Office for National Statistics,[2] initially holding unit-level records for organizations on the national business register. It has since expanded its holdings and developed remote access technology to the highest security levels required by government departments.

The success of these services was notable. Awareness was raised within the research community of the potential of the wide variety of administrative data that government departments held. Secure access to such data could now be guaranteed. Despite these efforts, progress on data sharing and record matching across different data sources and in different parts of the UK was patchy. In part, this was a consequence of legal barriers—some very real and others perceived by data guardians in their attempts to interpret complex laws—and of the unsatisfactory procedures that had evolved in an ad hoc manner to respond to requests from researchers for access to unit-level data. In Scotland, with a different legal system and where there existed a high degree of trust between data guardians, significant progress in linking individual-level data was being made.[3] This was not the case in England and Wales. While there was a general understanding among data holders and researchers of the need to protect data subjects from any misuse or misappropriation of data about them, mistakes had sometimes been made, due mainly to errors in data processing or through the use of subcontractors providing data processing services. For example, for an evaluation of a particular employment program, individual-level data on many thousands of program participants were supplied under contract to a university-based research team, complete with names and addresses of all participants.[4] These errors, together with a number of widely reported losses of millions of personal data records,[5] led to a situation where all government departments took steps to minimize any exchanges of personal data with other agencies. Research use of administrative data came to a virtual standstill in many departments from 2008 (see Smith et al. 2004). Nonetheless, the ADLS had been established, and the SDS[6] was open for business at this time. The stage was set for change.

The administrative data taskforce

In September 2010, a new chief executive took up post at the ESRC. With his background in longitudinal data linking, based in the more progressive data access environment that existed in Scotland, one of his first acts was to revitalize efforts to improve access to administrative data across the UK. The first major breakthrough came in May 2011. At a meeting convened by the Wellcome Trust, senior social scientists, research funders, data holders, and government statisticians met to discuss the scientific value of linked administrative records.[7] It quickly had become clear that, in the medical sciences, new legislation, coupled with the centralization of digital records from various parts of the National Health Service, was revolutionizing the opportunities for ground-breaking research. Strategic plans were developed for the exploitation of such data. This was not the case for a range of administrative data of interest to social scientists (e.g., tax, social security records). Consequently, a taskforce was established to determine why this was the case and to make recommendations to improve research access to such data. Membership of the taskforce was drawn from data guardians within government departments, research funding organizations, the private sector, and the Information Commissioner's Office.[8] The terms of reference for the taskforce are shown in Box 3. The taskforce worked to address its terms of reference by focusing on three areas: legal and ethical challenges to data access, public acceptability of improved access for research, and models for data access and linkage. It was also tasked to advise on the cost implications of recommendations for improved access.

BOX 3
Administrative Data Taskforce (ADT)

The ADT seeks to propose new mechanisms and collaborative agreements to enable and promote the wider use of administrative data for research and policy purposes.

Terms of reference

The key roles of the taskforce were:

- identification of potential benefits and risks from increased research use of administrative data;
- the development and introduction of common procedures to provide more efficient research access to administrative datasets;
- clarification of the legal situation governing the research use of routine data;
- clarification of when consent is required and what consent procedures should be used;
- identification of possible need for legislative change to improve research access to administrative data for research;
- the development of agreed methods for data linkage;
- procedures to raise public awareness of the benefits arising from research use of administrative data and data linkage; and
- identification of likely resource implications arising from increased research use of administrative data.

Some secondary priorities for the taskforce could include:

- further development of a "metadata authority" to assemble and disseminate information relating to the use of administrative data for research, for details of data linkage procedures, and for the preservation of information relating to the quality of various administrative datasets as research resources;
- agreement regarding the potential preservation and reuse of linked data;
- guidance on data access, including the use of "safe-settings" and how the research environment should be controlled; and
- proposals for how the quality of administrative data may be assessed.

The Administrative Data Taskforce (ADT) worked quickly. Within one year of its formation in 2011, the taskforce reported its findings (ESRC 2012), noting in particular that even in those instances where successful data linking and sharing of administrative data had been achieved, the process was often very slow.[9] There was evidence that a number of funded research projects had been abandoned due to the lack of support from data holders after access had been agreed to in principle.

The report made a number of important recommendations relating not just to the provision of a new research infrastructure but, more importantly, to issues about the governance of research access; the legal situation; the ethics of data sharing for research; and the need to build trust between researchers, data holders, and the general public. Specifically, this translated into:

- The establishment of new facilities in each of the four countries of the UK (to be called Administrative Data Research Centers [ADRCs]), together with a UK governing board and a UK information service (to be called the Administrative Data Service [ADS]) as the point of entry for research applications to gain access to administrative data. These research centers and the new service were to form the backbone of the new ADRN.
- A call for new legislation to clarify the legality of data sharing between departments and with others, particularly for those agencies established by statute and without expressed powers for data sharing.
- The creation and implementation of a single UK-wide accreditation process for researchers wishing to gain access to administration data.
- A strategy for public engagement.
- Sufficient resources to provide all of the above.

The government response was supportive (Department for Business, Innovation and Skills 2013), essentially endorsing the recommendations of the taskforce. Funding to facilitate implementation of the recommendations was announced. Shortly after funding was announced from the Department for Business, Innovation and Skills, a technical group was formed to advise the ESRC on the appropriate technical and infrastructure design and to publish a report (Elias 2013), which led to the commissioning of four administrative data research centers, one in each country of the UK, together with an advisory, liaison, and coordination service (encapsulating the Administrative Data Liaison Service set up five years previously and called the Administrative Data Service).

The usual approach to commissioning a research infrastructure is for the process to be managed by the research councils on behalf of the science ministry releasing the funds. In this manner, independence from government funding is maintained, while the scientific merit of various bids to construct the infrastructure is evaluated by senior scientists who are vetted to ensure they have no affiliation to those bidding. A different model was required in this instance. The cooperation of government departments was vital to the success of the ADRN, and there was a role to be played by the various statistical authorities of the UK. To this end, the three statistical authorities of the UK were invited to state how they would work with the centers once these had been commissioned and to produce a bid for funds for such participation. The major government departments were invited to nominate representatives to join the commissioning panel, which was chaired by an academic and included international expertise.

Commissioning of the four centers and the service was completed by fall 2013. The big question now was, Would it work?

The Administrative Data Research Network

The decision to commission one administrative data research center in each country of the UK was more than simply a gesture toward the increasingly devolved nature of the four countries of the UK. It recognized that progress in developing research access had been moving forward at a better pace in Scotland, Wales, and Northern Ireland than was the case in England.[10] This was not a consequence of the different legal systems in these countries, but more a reflection of their smaller and more integrated administrative departments of government. The groundwork performed for the taskforce had established that knowing the people involved in data sharing activities and having trust in them was a major factor in facilitating data access and linking. One of the aims of the newly established ADS was to explore these differences and to determine how best practice could be spread across the network.

As the new centers and the coordinating ADS were being set up, agreement was reached with the UK Statistical Authority (UKSA, an independent body operating at arm's length from government, accountable to the UK Parliament and with oversight responsibilities for the three statistical agencies of the UK) to provide a home for and to service the governing board for the network. Given its independence from government, this gave the network a degree of authority as an official independent UK body without it having to be established via an Act of Parliament.

The governing board met first in April 2014 and immediately identified a number of strategic issues for the board members to consider, including:[11]

- public confidence;
- legal issues;
- demand and capacity; and
- data quality.

On the legal front, progress was much slower given the complexity of the legal issues to be addressed and the need to ensure that the privacy lobby in the UK (an amalgamation of interest groups with concerns about the potential invasion of privacy that data sharing and matching could foster) was consulted and that their concerns could be reflected in the proposals being developed. The Cabinet Office (the department responsible for the development of new legislation) began a process termed "open policy making" in April 2014, concluding this in April 2015 with the publication of a policy paper (Cabinet Office 2015). This paper recommended that "any public body that needs it [should have] the necessary power to engage in trusted third party data shares with one or more sources for the purpose of research," and "[this power] should only be used when all the bodies involved in the data share, other than the data sources, are accredited bodies." This is a vital power for those administrative departments of government and agencies established by statute, given that they have no power to share data for research unrelated to their administrative functions.

In spring 2016, the Cabinet Office published a consultation on the potential section of a new Data Sharing Bill and included clauses informed by the open policymaking discussion to improve access to administrative data for research purposes. The consultation responses provided the necessary confidence for Ministers to prepare a bill to be presented to Parliament. The bill was placed before Parliament in July 2016. This bill, known as the Digital Economy Bill, is broader and includes many aspects of the digital activity of government and its arms length bodies, but sections designed to facilitate sharing for research purposes and also sharing for statistical purposes have been included. These sections were subject to scrutiny as the bill progressed through the UK Parliament. It received royal assent on April 27, 2017.[12]

Reviewing the work of the ADRN

The ADRN has made considerable progress by bringing a coherent approach to access to and the use of administrative data for research. The composition of the governing board means that issues identified can be acted upon quickly and communicated back to data holders if necessary. Concerns about data security can be addressed in a way that is acceptable to all data providers. Training is given to researchers who wish to gain access to secure data (see Box 4). The board has formed an approvals panel, consisting of data holders, senior academics, lay members, and an expert in data privacy and confidentiality, which acts to vet all research proposals planning to use the ADRN as a resource. The approvals panel undertakes its work in accordance with the following criteria:

   i.   an outline of an acceptable process for review of the ethical implications;
  ii.   clear understanding of and approaches to address any potential privacy issues;
 iii.   a feasible project for being undertaken in the ADRN with the data proposed;
  iv.   a project of sufficient scientific merit to warrant the use of ADRN resources; and
   v.   a convincing case is made for potential public benefit.

The fifth of these criteria reflects the fact that, for most of the applications to undertake research using administrative data, the data subject may not have consented to such use.

The board also helped to establish what is named the National Statistician's Data Ethics Advisory Committee[13] to ensure that ethical approval can be given for research proposals from government departments and third-party organizations. Unlike universities, most bodies such as these do not have any ethics committees set up to review and provide ethical safeguards for the subjects of research.

The ADS, with the four administrative data research centers, has been receiving applications for research, approving proposals, and training researchers in procedures for access to data in a secure setting. The network has promoted its work through YouTube videos, special events held around the UK, at annual

---

BOX 4
National Training for Accreditation of Researchers

Before they can access sensitive and/or potentially "disclosive" data via the Network—or indeed any other major UK data services—researchers have to undertake the National Training for Accreditation of Researchers, including passing a post-training test.

The training has been developed by a consortium of UK data services:

- Administrative Data Research Network
- HMRC Data lab
- ONS Virtual Microdata Laboratory
- UK Data Service (Secure Lab).

Other data services are expected to join the program in the future.

Trust in researchers is essential, so the program has been designed to make sure that they behave safely and responsibly when accessing detailed data. With this in mind the training covers two main areas:

- The legal responsibilities (and expected behavior) of researchers accessing detailed data. They learn about the "five safes": safe researchers, safe projects, safe settings, safe outputs, and safe data; as well as the legal and procedural background of UK data access and their role and responsibilities in data protection.
- Output disclosure control. In this module researchers learn about Statistical Disclosure Control, how a disclosure might happen and how to avoid disclosive outputs.

SOURCE: https://adrn.ac.uk/media/1190/newsletter-final_web.pdf.

---

conferences, as well as critically ensuring that the network data security conforms to the standards required by data holders. By May 2017 the network had received more than eighty project requests, with two being rejected by the approvals panel.[14]

Review of the ADRN commenced in mid-2016. Although the network had been under close scrutiny by its governing board, all major infrastructure projects funding from UK capital funding are subject to a formal and independent review process known as "gateway review."[15] Earlier reviews had focused on the progress made by the ADRN in establishing the infrastructure. The review in mid 2016 centered on the delivery of the benefits realized by the investment. It concluded that "the key risk relates to the availability of UK wide data."[16]

This risk derives from the difficulties that researchers have continued to experience in gaining access to linked data from a number of major government departments holding UK-wide data on individuals, including tax records, social security records, and driver and vehicle license records. Within the devolved parts of the UK (Scotland, Northern Ireland, Wales) the network was performing well. But without similar success with these important UK-wide sources of administrative data, it would not achieve the vision set out in the taskforce report in 2012. What was the problem? The answer to this question requires a deeper understanding of the needs of data providers.

Understanding the needs of data providers

Faced with a request to allow research access to data, data providers will consider four factors: the legality of the request, the public benefit (including the ethics of using the data they hold for a purpose that does not align with any consent for reuse given by the data subject), the resources involved in meeting the request, and the risks that they are exposed to if they meet the request. Each of these factors is examined in turn.

Many would regard the legality of a request as a key obstacle to data sharing. Data protection laws are designed to provide data subjects with safeguards against any inappropriate use of their data. In so doing, the concept of *personal data* is invoked, where personal data are defined as any data relating to a living person which identify them or have the potential to identify them given the detail they contain. Data can be legally shared for research purposes if the risk of revealing the identity of an individual is minimized. The legal basis for sharing data then hinges upon how this risk is assessed and whether the risk of disclosure of identities has been minimized sufficiently (see Box 5).

There are some data types for which the legal basis for sharing is much more explicit than is established via data protection legislation. In the UK, some data providers are organizations established by statute. In other words, they exist because of a body of laws that states what they can do. Anything not listed as a lawful activity of a statutory body is *ultra vires*. For example, the UK taxation authority, Her Majesty's Revenue and Customs (HMRC), was established by an Act of Parliament in 2005.[17] This act allows HMRC to disclose information to other organizations or persons when the disclosure is "made for a purpose of the Revenue and Customs" (Commissioners for Revenue and Customs Act 2005, section 18, subsections (1) and (2)). Given this stipulation, HMRC can only release data for research if the research can be construed as a purpose of HMRC by, for example, improving the efficiency of tax collection methods. This is a severe limitation that has had to be addressed via a change in the law. Nonstatutory bodies, such as the Department for Work and Pensions, already possess the right to share data,[18] but have shown a degree of reluctance in this respect.

The issue of consent from data subjects for reuse of social and economic data collected for a specific administrative purpose has not been seen as a restricting factor by data holders. It is generally recognized that, as long as the research that forms the basis of the data request has some public benefit, then it is in the wider public interest to reuse data for this purpose.[19] The problem is how to define *public benefit*. This can only be assessed on a case-by-case basis, to examine the potential benefits that could derive from research findings, weighing these against the privacy rights of the individual or organization whose data are to be reused for proposed research. The ADRN effectively hands the task of balancing of benefits and rights to its approvals panel, who in turn requests an initial assessment from the research proposer. This situation may change with the adoption in 2016 by all member states of the European Union of a new regulation on data privacy,[20] which is enforceable from May 25, 2018. Recognizing the need to ensure that the work of the ADRN is trusted by the public, much work has to be

---

BOX 5
Data Protection Legislation in the UK

In the UK, the principal legislative instrument governing the collection, sharing, transmission, and processing of electronic records is the Data Protection Act 1998. This set
out eight data protection principles:

1. Personal data shall be processed fairly and lawfully.
2. Personal data shall be obtained only for one or more specified and lawful purposes,
   and shall not be further processed in any manner incompatible with that purpose
   or those purposes.
3. Personal data shall be adequate, relevant, and not excessive in relation to the purpose or purposes for which they are processed.
4. Personal data shall be accurate and, where necessary, kept up to date.
5. Personal data processed for any purpose or purposes shall not be kept for longer
   than is necessary for that purpose or those purposes.
6. Personal data shall be processed in accordance with the rights of data subjects
   under this Act.
7. Appropriate technical and organizational measures shall be taken against unauthorized or unlawful processing of personal data and against accidental loss or destruction of, or damage to, personal data.
8. Personal data shall not be transferred to a country or territory outside the European
   Economic Area unless that country or territory ensures an adequate level of protection
   for the rights and freedoms of data subjects in relation to the processing of personal
   data.

The second principle would appear to preclude reuse of administrative data for research
purposes, but the Act also states that reuse for research is permissible provided:

- that the data are not processed to support measures or decisions with respect to
  particular individuals, and
- that the data are not processed in such a way that substantial damage or substantial
  distress is, or is likely to be, caused to any data subject.

Such data can be processed only for research purposes and can be kept indefinitely if:

- they are processed in compliance with the relevant conditions [as above], and
- the results of the research or any resulting statistics are not made available in a form
  that identifies data subjects.

---

done to promote the work of the network and its value while ensuring that data
about individuals and organizations are kept secure and handled in ways that
ensure that confidentiality is maintained.

The resources involved in meeting a request for data access are not trivial. The
data holder must have knowledge about the conditions under which data will be
held and analyzed, and must be confident that the data analysts will proceed with
due diligence, paying particular attention to the scope for inadvertent disclosure

of identities. Some subsettings may be required for data extraction and proce-dures agreed to for safe data transfer, both of which may require significant resources. The role of the ADRN is to streamline this process and ensure effi-ciencies that minimize these costs as far as the data provider is concerned by providing secure data transfer; ensuring that data are held in safe centers; vetting and approving projects and researchers; and in some cases providing resources to data holders to assist with data extraction, documentation, and data transfer.

The major difficulty facing any public sector data provider is the evaluation of the risks to which they will be exposed if they grant access for research. Data holders in the UK have a statutory responsibility to prevent the disclosure of the identity of individuals for whom they hold data, except in certain defined situa-tions (see Box 5). While the ADRN and the ADS operate to minimize such risk through the use of safe data centers, remote secure access technologies, and the use of trusted third parties for data linking and output vetting procedures, data holders may still consider the risk too high. One small error can be perceived as having powerful negative consequences for the public trust in that organization. Understanding and meeting this need has been one of the main functions of the ADS.

Given the efforts that have been made by the ADRN and the ADS to mini-mize the risk of disclosure, it appears illogical for data providers to have concerns about disclosure risks. However, although an independent approvals panel may have given the green light for a specific project, and ethical clearance has been obtained, the data holder may take the view that a particular piece of research may reflect negatively on its own performance. Simply refusing to provide data for a specific research project could draw unwarranted attention to the data pro-vider. If this is the case, the best perceived course of action for the data provider is to restrict or withhold access to all data to the ADRN.

The board of the ADRN has reacted vigorously to the report arising from its gateway review. Specific government departments have been identified as data owners who may require additional assistance, requesting timetables for delivery of data to projects already approved, and providing extra support to these depart-ments if necessary.

Taking Stock: What Has Been Created and What Has Been Learned?

For any research infrastructure that is just two years old, stock taking can be only partial. The infrastructure is maturing and could take up to five years to reach its full potential. With new legislation now in place that will affect its operation, and plans to address data access issues, this assessment of what has been achieved must be regarded as provisional.

The first question to ask is the counterfactual: What would the research com-munity now have if this new facility for access to administrative data had not been created? The answer to this is clear. For some data types, there was already an established network, user group, or set of procedures that could provide research access. An example of this was given in Box 2. For these data sources, researchers may argue that they now face a more bureaucratic access regime. But many such data sources are accessed via a closed network, not open to researchers outside of certain institutions. To gain access to the data, those researchers often had to sign a contract with the data owning department and sit within that department, so there were limitations and barriers even to them.

The role of the ADRN is to improve on the methods and procedures for access by providing added value, particularly through linking to other datasets held by different departments and agencies, improving metadata, and providing training and support. New safe access facilities and investment in technical infrastructure would not have happened without the ADRN. The network is sharing knowledge and expertise and, crucially, providing a repository for this information as administrative data change with the changes to the administrative processes that generate them. So, the answer to the first question is that the research community has an improved environment for research and analysis of administrative data.

Is a cost/benefit analysis of the infrastructure development feasible? This is a more difficult question to address. The costs are known and lie in the region of $20 million for a five-year investment.[21] Institutional support is also provided by the higher education institutions that house the centers in the ADRN and the ADS, which may total an additional $5 million in capital spend and staff support. The direct employment generated by this investment is less clear. Each center lists between thirty and fifty staff, but some are from the contributions of established academic staff who would otherwise be engaged in academic activities. A best guess would put the direct employment associated with this investment at thirty to forty full-time posts. While this may be an interesting statistic to some, the benefits should not be measured in this way. The benefits are the gain to society in having more effective and efficient policymaking through the improved research evidence that the infrastructure is providing. It is as yet too early to address this issue, but it must remain firmly on the agenda as the work of the ADRN progresses.

Could there have been another way of developing improved access? This is an intriguing question and one with which the taskforce grappled as it formulated its recommendations to create the ADRN. The most obvious alternative approach was to let the four countries of the UK set up their own arrangements for data access independently of each other. This view was voiced within the taskforce given that Scotland had already made substantial progress in setting up procedures for access to and linkage between datasets held by Scottish departments of government. However, this approach was roundly rejected given that it would not necessarily promote best practice procedures across the four countries of the UK. It also did little to address the issues relating to access to administrative data that were not the responsibility of the devolved administrations (for example, defense, taxation, social security, UK security, and driver/vehicle licensing).

There is a related question about the effectiveness of the design of the coordination and management structures within the ADRN. To establish a "network" and to allocate the funding provided by the UK government science ministry within a challengingly short timescale (the ESRC would usually take nine months or more to commission research infrastructure of this size, but government budgetary requirements constrained this period to four months), a collaborative network of equals was established, with no one director of the ADRN (there are five directors) having seniority over others. Furthermore, no consortium or other agreement was put in place to bind together how the ADRN centers and ADS operate. With hindsight, although the speed of commissioning and unique nature of this structure led to these decisions, a network of this size and complexity seeking to change the relationship between data custodians in government and researchers needed strong leadership from a single overall director and agreements designed to bind all parties to such a management structure. The ADRN is succeeding despite this, with steps now being taken to address this weakness by appointing one center director as the overall director of the network.

There have also been challenges in engaging at the most senior level with government departments and negotiating access agreements with these departments. The position of a data access negotiator has been created and filled by an individual who has worked with senior civil servants and has in fact come from a data owning department, thus providing another step to address some of the ongoing challenges. If these two positions had been in place from 2013, there would have been challenges but possibly not as many as the ADRN has faced. Arguably the lack of a senior leader has held back recognition of the ADRN as a single unified and expert network within government circles.

Has it been successful in achieving its objectives? The answer to this question must be a qualified yes. There are access issues that remain to be solved, and new legislation to contend with in terms of its implications for research access to administrative data, but the direction is positive. Compared with other major investments in research data, the capital costs are relatively low, and the potential for the production of well-informed policies based on the reuse of existing data is high. However, with the limited number of projects currently being facilitated by the ADRN, the ongoing running costs may not be regarded as value for the money.

What have we learned from this experience? Here, the focus must be on the most critical elements that have driven forward the successful implementation of the research infrastructure. Four factors stand out: governance, coordination, engagement, and review.

The governance of the ADRN has been a major force in ensuring that it will meet its objectives. The composition of the governing board, which is made up of senior representatives from data holders, funders, key executives from the network, representatives from the statistical authorities of the UK, lay members, and senior academics, gives the board a powerful voice. But it is not just the constitution of the board that has helped. Positioning the board within the independent UK Statistical Authority, a body that reports directly to the UK Parliament and not to the science ministry, means that the governing board can escalate problems to the UK Parliament if it finds it necessary to do so. It should be noted also that the board operates without a statutory framework. It has not been set up through a legislative process, relying instead on the power of collective voice to carry out its mission. The governing board continues to monitor the progress that the network is making toward implementation of the recommendations made by the taskforce. Two important issues remain to be resolved, access to the network's resources by the private sector and the issue of data retention. The latter reflects the fact that the taskforce had concerns that retention and reuse of linked data could lead to a situation where the network was holding vast amounts of personal information from individuals. But most government departments view the continued creation and destruction of linked datasets as wasteful, with no ongoing investment in data assets. With the agreement of data owners, this approach to retention is now being explored.

Coordination of the network has been an important aspect of its success. The four centers have a degree of independence, but they are bound by a commitment to share expertise; to adopt a common outward identity on the web and in publications; and to adopt the same procedures they use for project approval, output vetting, and so on. This would have been difficult to establish without the ADS, the service that provides cohesion to the network. The ADS represents the four research centers on the governing board, placing it in a strong position relative to the centers.

Engagement, with the general public, data holders, academics, and lawmakers has been exemplary. This is an unusual activity for academics, more comfortable with the production of papers rather than YouTube videos and Twitter feeds, but it has proven to be popular, particularly the short animated YouTube videos.[22]

Independent review of the work of the ADRN has been most helpful in alerting the board to the priorities it must make in its governance arrangements, particularly the need for stronger overall direction of the network. Rather than reacting to what researchers want, there needs to be a stronger focus on key departments and datasets, with development of a strategy for the proactive promotion of certain datasets.

Conclusion

The four factors discussed above provide some general principles that transcend the particular situation existing within the UK. First, and most importantly, the UK experience has indicated the need for any network of this scale and complexity to have a *single, dedicated, full-time director*. This role is critical to success and requires the competence of an individual with the requisite knowledge and expertise to command the respect of all members of the network as well as those organizations it must negotiate with. Without such a director, the UK network has had to rely on its governing board. This should not be the role of a governing board, which should, instead, be keeping its eye on the long-term strategic aims of the network, its overall costs, and its potential benefits.

A second principle relates to the *coordination of the network*. With many different functions, such as training, data security, provision of data and metadata, promotion of the networks activities, and active liaison with researchers, there is potential for these activities to vary across a large network. Close coordination helps to provide all users of the network, whether as researchers or data providers, with a common experience.

Related to the need for coordination is the *promotion of the identity of the network*. With no market forces to determine success or failure, it is incumbent of those in receipt of public funds or grant income to ensure that the services they are seeking to provide are recognized as having value by researchers and by the public. Promotion of the facilities that such a network can provide does not come naturally to many academics, but the UK experience has shown that this helps to convince data holders, researchers, and the general public that there is much potential for valuable research through the exploitation of administrative data.

Finally, the role of a governing board needs careful consideration. While the governing board of the UK ADRN has had to tackle problems that should have been the responsibility of a director for the network, it now is operating as it should to *monitor the long-term strategic development* of the resource and to ensure that it will provide value for money as a major data research infrastructure.

How these principles can be applied to similar networks in different environments will depend upon many constraints, such as those operating through legal systems, via the requirements of funding organizations and via the different types of support that academic institutions can offer. Above all, strong leadership for a network sits as a priority.

Notes

1. In 2004, the Economic and Social Research Council (ESRC, one of seven research councils in the UK and the main funding agency for research in the social sciences) decided to adopt a more strategic approach to the development of data resources for research in the social sciences. The first *National Data Strategy* was published in 2006. This strategic approach has continued, with publication of the third strategy in 2013 covering the period 2013–2017; see http://www.esrc.ac.uk/about-us/policies-and-standards/national-data-strategy/.

2. Known as the ONS Virtual Microdata Laboratory; see https://www.ons.gov.uk/aboutus/whatwedo/paidservices/virtualmicrodatalaboratoryvml.

3. A good example is the Scottish Longitudinal Study, linking population census and health statistics.

4. Data supplied for analysis of a program known as Employment Zones; see Elias (2003).

5. While these losses were not related to requests for access to administrative data by researchers, they caused such a degree of public consternation that all forms of data movement became severely restricted.

6. Now known as the UK Data Service Secure Lab (https://www.ukdataservice.ac.uk/use-data/secure-lab).

7. "Linking Data: New Scientific Possibilities for the Biomedical and Social Sciences in the Digital Age," Frontiers Meeting, Wellcome Trust, London, 16–17 May 2011.

8. The government agency responsible for the enforcement of the UK Data Protection Act 1998, and also responsible for Freedom of Information.

9. An example of this is the data sharing agreement between the Ministry of Justice, the Department for Work and Pensions, and Her Majesty's Revenue and Customs, which took two years to establish. See https://www.gov.uk/government/statistics/experimental-statistics-from-the-2013-moj-dwp-hmrc-data-share.

10. The Taskforce Report uses an example to make this point.

11. UK Statistics Authority, Administrative Data Research Network Board, "Strategic Issues for the ADRN Board and Forward Planning," Paper ADRN (14) 03 (2014).

12. See www.legislation.gov.uk/2017/30/contents/enacted/data.htm. As a consequence of this new legislation, the governance arrangements for the ADRN are changing. See https://www.statisticsauthority .gov.uk/wp-content/uploads/2017/06/ADRN-05-06-2017.pdf).

13. See https://www.statisticsauthority.gov.uk/national-statistician/national-statisticians-data-ethics-advisory-committee/.

14. Reasons for rejection were insufficient potential public benefit and/or insufficient scientific merit.

15. See http://webarchive.nationalarchives.gov.uk/+/www.dh.gov.uk/en/Managingyourorganisation/ Gatewayreviews/DH_121642 for information about the gateway review process. The review team focusses on the progress of major projects, not their scientific achievements.

16. UK Statistics Authority, Administrative Data Research Network Board, Minutes of the Tenth Meeting of the Board, 12 July 2016.

17. Commissioners for Revenue and Customs Act 2005.

18. There is an arcane distinction here between statutory and nonstatutory government bodies. The former are established by an Act of Parliament. The latter are vestiges of the Crown and reflect the historical ministries set up by the advisors to a king or queen. They continue to exist to this day via what is termed the "royal prerogative" and have all the rights that a private citizen has, including the right to share data with others subject to the restrictions placed on private citizens. This right is termed a "permissive right" in that the government body is not obliged to release data, but may do so in accordance with the legal restrictions covering the processing of personal data.

19. In collaboration with the Office for National Statistics, the ESRC funded an enquiry into the public acceptability of establishing the ADRN; see http://www.esrc.ac.uk/public-engagement/public-dialogues/ public-dialogues-on-using-administrative-data/.

20. Regulation (EU) 2016/679 of the European Parliament and of the Council of 27 April 2016 on the protection of natural persons with regard to the processing of personal data and on the free movement of such data, and repealing Directive 95/46/EC (General Data Protection Regulation). Despite the fact that the UK will leave the EU, it is highly likely that this regulation will be transposed into British legislation.

21. This is the direct investment cost from the UK Science Ministry to the Economic and Social Research Council over the period October 2013 to September 2018, to support the capital spend and staff salaries at a number of UK higher education institutions, as well as the funds paid over to the three statistical authorities of the UK and the UK Statistical Authority for their roles in supporting the network.

22. See, for example, https://adrn.ac.uk/for-the-public/about-us/.

References

Cabinet Office. 2015. *Conclusions of civil society and public sector policy discussions on data use in government*. Report on the Open Policy-making Process. London: Cabinet Office.

Department for Business, Innovation and Skills. 2013. *Improving access for research and policy: The government response to the report of the administrative data taskforce*. London: Department for Business, Innovation and Skills.

Elias, Peter. 2003. Do employment zones reduce unemployment? An analysis based on administrative microdata. In *The wider labour market impact of employment zones*, eds. Chris Hasluck, Peter Elias, and Anne Green, 51–74. Research Report 175. London: Department for Work and Pensions.

Elias, Peter. 2013. *Administrative data taskforce: Report of the technical group*. Swindon: UK Economic and Social Research Council.

Economic and Social Research Council. 2012. *Improving access for research and policy: Report from the administrative data taskforce*. Swindon: UK Economic and Social Research Council.

Jones, Paul, and Peter Elias. 2006. *Administrative data as a research resource: A selected audit*. Report to the UK Economic and Social Research Council. Coventry: University of Warwick.

Smith, George, Michael Noble, Chelsie Antilla, Leicester Gill, Asghar Zaidi, Gemma Wright, Chris Dibben, and Helen Barnes. 2004. *The value of linked administrative data for longitudinal analysis*. Swindon: UK Economic and Social Research Council.

Thomas, Richard, and Mark Walport. 2008. *Data sharing review report*. Report to the Prime Minister and Secretary of State for Justice. Available from http://webarchive.nationalarchives.gov.uk/+/http:/www .justice.gov.uk/docs/data-sharing-review.pdf.

From SkyServer to SciServer

Twenty years ago, work commenced on the Sloan Digital Sky Survey. The project aimed to collect a statistically complete dataset over a large fraction of the sky and turn it into an open data resource for the world's astronomy community. There were few examples to learn from, and those of us who worked on it had to invent much of the system ourselves. The project has made fundamental changes to astronomy, and we are now faced with the problem of ensuring that the data will be preserved and kept in active use for another 20 years. In redesigning this very large, open archive of data, we made a system that is able to serve a much broader set of communities. In this article, I discuss what we have learned by rebuilding a massive dataset that is available to an increasingly sophisticated set of users, and how we have been challenged and motivated to incorporate more of the patterns of data analytics required by contemporary science.

By
ALEXANDER S. SZALAY

Keywords: astronomy; open data; sky surveys; databases; collaborative science

The unprecedented amount of observational, experimental, and simulation data is transforming the nature of scientific research. As more and more datasets are becoming public, those of us who are interested in data ubiquity need to find the right ways not only to make the data public, but accessible and usable. Yet our techniques have not kept up with this evolution. Traditionally scientists were moving the data to their computers to perform the analyses. With increasingly large amounts of data this is becoming difficult; as a result, scientists are learning how to "move the analysis to the data," that is, executing the analysis code on computers co-located with the

Alexander S. Szalay is the Bloomberg Distinguished Professor at the Johns Hopkins University. He is a cosmologist, also working on open scientific data. He built the archive of the Sloan Digital Sky Survey. He is a fellow of the American Academy of Arts and Sciences.

Correspondence: szalay@jhu.edu

DOI: 10.1177/0002716217745816

data repositories. In a digital world, we have to rethink not only the "data lifecycle" as most datasets are accessible via services, we also need to consider the "service lifecycle."

The data from Sloan Digital Sky Survey (SDSS) is one of the first examples of a large open scientific dataset. The data have been in the public domain for more than a decade (Szalay et al. 2000). It is fair to say that the project and its archive have changed astronomy forever, showing that a whole community of scientists are willing to change their approach to data and analytics, if the data are of high quality and presented in an intuitive fashion. The continuous evolution and curation of the system over the years has been an intense effort, and has given us a unique perspective on the challenges involved in operating open archival systems.

The SDSS is one of the first major open eScience archives. Tracking its evolution has the potential to help the whole science community to understand the long-term curation of such data, and see what common lessons emerged for other disciplines facing similar challenges. These new archives not only serve flat files, like a spreadsheet or a text document and simple digital objects like images and videos, but they also present complex services. The toolkits change, the service standards evolve, and even though some services may have been cutting edge 10 years ago, today they may be dated. To support the increasingly sophisticated client-side environments, the services need active curation at regular intervals.

Scientists in many disciplines would like to compare the results of their experiments to data emerging from computer simulations based on "first principles." Starting from a simple set of initial conditions, we apply the laws of nature to move the system forward to a state comparable to our observations and experiments. This tells us whether we have used the correct laws and approximations, and about the correctness of the initial assumptions. This requires not only sophisticated simulations and models, but that the results of the simulations also be made available publicly, through an easy-to-use portal. Turning simulations into open numerical laboratories where anyone can perform their own experiments and integrating and comparing experiments to simulations are nontrivial challenges in data management. Not every dataset from simulations has the same lifecycle. Some results are transient and need to be stored for a short while to analyze, while others become community references, with a useful lifetime of a decade or more.

In many areas, like environmental science, another challenge is the enormous complexity of the datasets involved. Various physical scales interact in a complex fashion; we have physical, chemical, biological factors all contributing to the observed phenomena. For example, the processes in the soil are affected by large-scale weather patterns, rainfall, on scales of many kilometers; but the local accumulation of water depends on local geographic features on meter scales, the soil properties are affected by the chemical composition and grain size on centimeter scales, and the decomposition is dominated by the microbes on the scales of a few microns. Much of these data reside in small files, such as the spreadsheets and tables collected in laboratories, in contrast to the large data collections like SDSS. These form the "long tail" of scientific data. Often, scientists would like to cross-correlate the data in these small objects with each other as well as with the large online databases.

The progression through these challenges forms the story told in this article. We feel strongly that the framework developed for astronomy, and used for over a decade by the SDSS, captures the way scientists should approach scientific data, and our tools form a set of generic building blocks out of which many new applications can be built. In the sections below I describe these components, how they fit together, and how they can be generalized to solve a variety of problems.

Our data and services span a wide range in terms of their age: the SDSS data are quite far along in their lifecycle; after 20 years they face a set of different curation issues than services that have been in operation for 5 years (turbulence, cosmological simulations, sensors), and different from newly built applications. We discuss the history of our ongoing efforts, and describe our goals, and the objectives and methods applied to the problems.

SDSS is the first among the large scale eScience projects where the instruments are now approaching the end of their life, but the data will still be used, possibly for decades to come. We find ourselves at a place where we have to invent the best solution that serves the long-term needs of our user base.

The Origins

The Sloan Digital Sky Survey

The SDSS was one of the first large-scale digital surveys of the sky. The goal was to perform a high-resolution, five-color imaging of the northern sky, and based upon our own images, collect spectra of the brightest one million galaxies and a few hundred thousand stars and quasars. All data were to be open and public, after a six-month proprietary period.

The project was started in 1992, and expected to end in 2000. The total budget was to be $25 million, about $10 million on the telescope, $10 million on the instruments, $3 million on the mountain operations, and $2 million on the software.

The telescope started operating in 2001, and we finally completed the survey as originally proposed by 2008. The final cost was more than $100 million, with close to a third of this spent on software development, data processing, and data management. The original projections for the data in the mid-1990s were that we would collect about 10 terabytes (TB) of raw imaging data, process them as they arrive, with maybe an additional full reprocessing toward the end. We projected the total volume of the database to be about 0.5TB, which was quite a big number in 1992. The final tally of all the low-level data that need to be preserved for long-term use is about 150TB, the current size of the main database is 15TB, with an additional 20TB of supplementary databases, such as additional time-domain data. This was all made possible with the eventual delays in the survey, where Moore's Law (the power of computers doubles every 18 months) helped us to reprocess the data much easier as we understood various systematic errors better, and Kryder's Law (the capacity of disks is doubling every 13 months) enabled us to store much more of the data as they were collected and processed. One of the lessons learned for future surveys was the fact that in projects like the SDSS the *capital investment is in the software and the computational hardware became disposable.*

The SDSS was amazingly successful. There are now more than seven thousand refereed papers published, with well over 350,000 citations. Many more papers were from outside the collaboration than by the survey participants, and the published papers have exceeded our imagination.

Initially, there was a lot of distrust in the astronomy community whether SDSS would truly release their data as promised. It took several years to convince the astronomers that we stood by our promises—we have never missed a data release. In the end, most of the proprietary periods were close to zero, and those of us who were creating the dataset were almost always getting the data at the same time as the public. In the beginning, people did not believe that we were able to process the data well enough in an automated environment. Much of the astronomy software at the time still required that an astronomer directly issue interactive commands. This was unacceptable for a uniform processing of a large fraction of the sky, and represented one of the biggest unforeseen challenges for the project. Creating such an automated pipeline that required essentially no human interaction to process millions of images required much more code to be written than previously envisaged.

There was very little precedent that we could rely upon, and we had to make things up as we went along, rather quickly, as the data went online and usage grew quickly. We had to figure out how to deal with reproducibility. New data were added every few nights. We decided to adopt a model where the public data releases happened once a year, and once released, they never changed. This meant that a query submitted to a particular data release, say DR3, will always return the same result. While DR4 and later contain all of DR3, and more, each of the data releases was treated as a separate edition of a book. When a new "edition" was released, we did not take the old ones off the shelf. This enabled students, who started their thesis with a particular data release, to remain consistent and papers published on an earlier data release can be fully reproduced by re-running the queries on the original version of the database. Today we are at DR15 and counting. All data releases are still up and available at Johns Hopkins University. We have completed the imaging survey of the available sky, and turned off the main imaging camera and now are only taking spectra.

The data releases presented an interesting challenge. Data come in at an approximately linear rate, assuming no significant changes are made to the detectors. This means that from year one to year two the data are doubling, but after that the relative change is much smaller. The total amount of data that we have to store is approximately quadratic: $1 + 2 + \ldots N = N(N - 1)/2$. Of course, we always store several copies of the most current data: right now, we are serving six different instances of DR13 and later. We can relax this somewhat for the older, less used versions. As the price of storage is constantly dropping, with larger and larger disks, we found that the second year was the hardest to accommodate from the perspective of hardware expenditures. The evolution of storage technologies has far outpaced the rate of 20 years' linear-rate data collection.

Jim Gray and the SDSS archive

Alex Szalay and Ani Thakar, in collaboration with Jim Gray (Microsoft), have spent much of the last two decades working on the archive for the SDSS. The archive was originally built on top of an emerging database technology, but after a few years it became clear that the users would want to have a very flexible query environment with a lot of ad hoc queries, which this system could not support well enough. As a result, we have started to develop our own (very limited) additions to the query capabilities of the system.

It was around this time, when we met Jim Gray of Microsoft. Jim liked to say that the "best collaborators are the desperate ones," as they are ready to change the way they approach a problem. We were desperate at that point. After a few meetings, Jim advocated for a more traditional relational database, consisting of tables of columns and rows—a much more mature technology. He made the point that a few programmers in an academic environment cannot successfully compete with the thousands of developers at Microsoft, Oracle, and IBM, and we should spend our efforts on creating the additional "business logic" related to astronomy, and use an off-the-shelf commercial platform with a robust engine. These are all based on SQL, the Structured Query Language: the standard, portable way to query databases. This advice set us on the trajectory that we have followed ever since.

The project has revolutionized not just professional astronomy but also the public's access to it. Although a substantial portion of the astronomy community is using the SDSS archive on a daily basis, the archive has also attracted a wide range of users from the public (Singh et al. 2006): a scan of the logs showed more than 4M distinct IP addresses accessing the site. The total number of professional astronomers worldwide is only about fifteen thousand. Furthermore, the collaborative CasJobs interface has more than eight thousand registered users—almost half of the professional astronomy community.

SDSS (2000–2005) and its successors SDSS-II (2005–2008) and SDSS-III (2008–2014) have an extraordinary legacy of mapping structure across a vast range of scales, from asteroids in our own solar system to quasars more than 10 billion light years away. These surveys have produced data that have supported 7,000 papers with more than 350,000 citations. The SDSS has several times been named the highest impact project, facility, or mission in the field of astronomy, as judged by number of citations of associated refereed journal articles (Banks 2009; Madrid and Macchetto 2009). The SDSS was the source of the most highly cited astronomy article in the years 2000, 2002, 2005, and 2008 (Frogel 2010). Within the collaboration there have been more than 120 SDSS-based PhD theses, and outside the collaboration there have been many more. Its publicly available, user-friendly tools have fueled a large number of undergraduate and even high-school projects and research papers.

In 2007 we played a key role in launching the Galaxy Zoo citizen science project (Lintott et al. 2008) in which online volunteers—members of the public, most of whom had no prior experience with scientific research—were asked to visually classify SDSS images of nearly a million galaxies. Today, Galaxy Zoo has more than 200,000 volunteers, who have collectively classified each of the million galaxies between 9 and 50,000 times. Galaxy Zoo has been featured by many of the world's best-known and respected news organizations (BBC, the *New York Times, Nature*, etc.), showing how active scientific research can attract a large and involved nonexpert population. But Galaxy Zoo users have contributed more than just raw image classifications. One of the most unexpected and successful parts of the project was the way in which citizen scientists used SkyServer tools to learn more about the galaxies they were asked to classify. In two cases, these efforts by citizen scientists led to published original research in astronomy journals (Lintott et al. 2009; Cardamone et al. 2009).

The 2.5-meter Sloan telescope in Apache Point, New Mexico, remains the most powerful wide-field spectroscopic survey facility in the world today. To capitalize on this resource, a collaboration of 186 astronomers and physicists from sixty-five institutions have organized the SDSS-IV program, conducting a broad survey of our Milky Way Galaxy, the population of nearby galaxies in the local universe, and the large-scale structure of the universe as a whole. SDSS-IV will operate from July 2014 to July 2020. It will marshal imaging data from multiple telescopes and wavelength regimes to identify targets for follow-up spectroscopy.

Evolution during the Early Years

The SkyServer usage log database

One of the most useful byproducts of the SDSS data has been the usage logs that we have kept since the very beginning of the project: every web hit and every single query have been logged since the archive was opened. The log database today is over 3TB, and contains rich historical information about how astronomers learned to access a virtual telescope (Singh et al. 2006). This has resulted in an amazingly rich and useful resource not only for SDSS scientists and project managers, but since the dataset is available to anyone, many other projects and researchers have found it extremely valuable. Next generation large astronomy surveys like Pan-STARRS (Heasley et al. 2007) and LSST (Becla et al. 2006) have used this data to plan their data management infrastructure and services, and several other groups in astronomy and computer science have downloaded the entire dataset for analysis. The SDSS log data was the subject of a PhD dissertation at Drexel University in Human-Computer Interaction research (Zhang 2011). We receive on average one or two requests per month to download the SDSS log data, especially the SQL query logs since this is perhaps the only such large dataset of SQL usage in existence. The SDSS has several mirrors over the world (UK, Brazil, India, China, Hungary). Their logs are harvested every night and aggregated into our main log database. On the main SDSS SkyServer web page there is a link to some cumulative counts from the log DB. The most current values are 2.4 billion web hits, and 364 million free-form SQL queries.

Parallel loader environment

The raw data are transformed into a common loadable format by a set of specific plug-ins. The data come in blocks, typically a few tens of gigabytes (GBs) at a time. Each block is transformed into a set of files in a single directory tree, with checksum files stored in each directory. For larger datasets this is a brutal data-parallel operation. The results of the data transformation process are picked up by the parallel loader (Szalay, Thakar, and Gray 2008). The loader scales to an arbitrary number of machines. It performs a two-phase load. First, for each block, we create an empty database with the same schema as the main system, and load the whole block. During the load process, broken into tasks, steps, and phases, we generate a detailed log at each granularity. The state of all jobs can be tracked visually using the load monitor interface.

Some of the tasks in the workflow described by a DAG (directed acyclic graph) perform a very detailed integrity check and data scrubbing, looking for out-of-band data. The data rows in each block get tagged by a load-ID unique to the block, so that combining this with the loader logs allows us to track each row's provenance. The two-phase load has proven to be invaluable, as data errors were caught well before the bad data could have contaminated the main database. It turns out that the load performance of a typical database server, running on a good file system, is not I/O- but rather CPU-limited, due to the various page formatting and checksum calculations. We found that on a high-end SQL server machine, using an array of SSDs and thirty-two cores, we were able to achieve load speeds in excess of 1GB per second using thread parallelism. Once data are in a DB page format, copying the DB files to other machines is only limited by the hardware performance.

The web interface

Early on we decided to move away from the solely form-based interfaces to the archive, where users are only allowed to enter certain parameters on a particular predefined search pattern through a web page, but they are not allowed to change the pattern itself. We decided to have a highly visual interactive front end, based on the available browsers at the time. This era is still remembered as "browser hell," as the existing web browsers had rather incompatible functionalities and commands. Internet Explorer and Netscape were still not capable of stylesheets, their javascript implementations were rather different. In the end, we built the website using our own abstract API for rendering various items, which were mapped onto their native implementations when a web page was loaded. This approach saved us a lot of headaches. Some of the functions are still there, but we are in the process of gradually replacing them with HTML5 canvas, and other more modern components. Based upon Jim Gray's Terraserver experience, and the emerging MapQuest, we created a clickable map of the sky, with image mosaics built server side from precomputed color images.

Free-form SQL queries

After about a year we visited the National Center for Biological Information (NCBI) for a few days. During this visit, David Lipman, the NCBI director showed us an article arguing against form-based interfaces to biological databases. The author felt that these interfaces, designed by a programmer and not by a scientist at the cutting edge, restrict the patterns of how data can be explored, thus limiting the scope of possible science. He suggested that there should be a back-door, enabling "anything and everything goes" type of creative query.

We decided to open the database for free-form SQL queries. Many people cautioned us against this, arguing that no astronomer would want to write SQL queries and that we would be constantly hit with denial of service attacks. We did it anyway and much to our amazement we found that neither of those predictions came true: astronomers embraced SQL remarkably quickly, and there were no major abuses of the interface.

To help astronomers to learn SQL, we posted the twenty queries that came out of early discussions. We first displayed the original question or problem definition written in plain English, then showed the SQL implementation that executed the query. Finally, in about a page or so we explained why the query was written the way it was shown. This enabled the astronomers to look for a query that was close enough to what they wanted to do, first do a cut and paste, run it, and start modifying it step-by-step, until they arrived at their results. Over the years we have added another fifteen query patterns to the pool. We have also built a step-by-step tutorial to teach the basics of the SQL.

Maturity and Production

The CasJobs/MyDB collaborative environment

As traffic on the SDSS archive grew, many users were running repeated queries and extracting a few million rows of data. The DB server delivered such datasets in 10 seconds, but it took several minutes to transmit the data through the slow wide-area networks. We realized that if users had their own databases at the server, then the query outputs could go through a high-speed connection, directly into their local databases. This improved system throughput by a factor of ten. Furthermore, we have built an asynchronous (batch) mode that enabled queries to be queued for execution and results to be retrieved later at will.

The CasJobs/MyDB batch query workbench environment was born as a result of combining these "take the analysis to the data" and asynchronous query execution concepts. The name "CasJobs" comes from "CAS (Catalog Archive Server)" and (batch) "jobs." CasJobs builds a flexible shell on top of the large SDSS database. Users are able to conduct sophisticated database operations in their own space: they can create new tables, perform joins with the main DB, write their own functions, upload their own tables, and extract their value-added datasets to their home environment. The system was an overnight success.

For redundancy, we had three identical servers containing the active databases. By studying the usage patterns, we realized that the query length distribution was well represented by a power law. Hence, we split the traffic into multiple queues served by different servers, each handling the same aggregate workload (O'Mullane et al. 2004). Each query can be submitted to a "fast," "medium," or "long" queue, returning the result into a MyDB table. The user can then process the derived result further, run a multistep workflow, or extract the data. Everything that a user does is logged. This set of user-controlled databases form a very flexible tier on top of the rigid schema of the archive. This resolves the long-standing tension between stability and integrity of the core data and the flexibility for user creativity.

As users became familiar with the system, there were requests for data sharing. As a result, we added the ability to create groups and to make individual tables accessible to certain groups. This led to a natural self-organization, as groups working on a collaborative research project used this environment to explore and build their final, value-added data for eventual publication. GalaxyZoo, which classified over a million SDSS galaxies through a user community of 300,000, used CasJobs to make the final results world-visible, and CasJobs also became a de facto platform for publishing data. We added the capability for users to upload their own datasets and import them into their MyDBs for correlation with the SDSS.

SQL extensions

Over the years, we have developed a design pattern to add domain specific extensions to the SQL server, using CLI integration. Our code for spatial indexing was used in the "shrink-wrap" production version of SQL Server 2005 (Fekete, Szalay, and Gray 2006; Budavári, Szalay, and Fekete 2010). The idea is to take a class library written in one of the .NET languages (C++, Java,C#), store a binary instance of the class as a binary datatype, and expose the object methods as user-defined functions (UDFs). The SQL server makes this very convenient, since unlike many other database platforms like MySQL, it allows for table-valued UDFs. One can then pass the binary object as a parameter to the function and execute the method, or access the property.

We have 236 UDFs supporting detailed astronomy knowledge, like conversion of cosmological coordinates in a curved space to angles and radial distances. Also, we have built an astronomy-specific spatial index, representing spherical polygons with extreme accuracy over the whole sky, with a relational algebra over the regions, and fast indexing capabilities to find several million points per spherical region in a second.

For large numerical simulations much of the data are in multidimensional floating point arrays. We have built such a User Defined Type for SQL Server, which is used for all our simulation databases (Dobos et al. 2011). We will develop a generic module that repartitions the data in a large array into smaller blocks organized along a space-filling curve, adds the custom metadata header, and writes these out in native binary format for optimal SQL server load performance.

Schema and metadata framework

The schema for the database is contained in a set of DDL files. These files are quite complex; they not only contain the code to generate the database and the associated stored procedures and user defined functions, but in the comment fields of the scripts they contain rich metadata describing the schema elements, including physical units, enumerations, indexes, primary keys, and short and long descriptions. A parser can extract this information at different granularities (object, column) and create a set of metadata tables that can be automatically loaded into the database. This ensures that all the schema and related metadata are handled together in an automated fashion, similar to the approach originally employed by Donald Knuth, when he created TeX. The database will then contain all the up-to-date metadata and these can be queried and displayed using simple functions and dynamic web services. This tool is quite robust and mature and has been in use for more than 14 years.

Branching Out to Other Disciplines

The SkyServer genealogy

The template for the SDSS archive is now being used within astronomy by several projects and institutions beyond JHU (STScI, Fermilab, Caltech, Edinburgh, Hawaii, Portsmouth, and Budapest). The technologies and concepts used for the SDSS archive have also been used beyond astronomy. Using the same template, we have built databases for a growing number of other disciplines. Such databases include those for turbulence (Li et al. 2008), radiation oncology (McNutt et al. 2008), environmental sensing and carbon cycle monitoring (Szlavecz et al. 2006), and, most recently, a prototype for high-throughput genomics (Wilton et al. 2015). The databases built for cosmological simulations are revolutionizing how astronomers interact with the largest simulations.

Open numerical laboratories

Worldwide, there is an ongoing effort to build an exascale computer. However, fewer and fewer codes will scale to millions of cores, and as a result, fewer people will use these ever larger machines. There will be an increasing gap between the wide science community and the top users. It will be increasingly important to create science products that can be used by a much wider pool of users, otherwise community support will dwindle. There is already an increasing demand from the broader science community to access the largest numerical simulations. While only our largest supercomputers are capable of creating such simulations, their analysis, especially if the data will be publicly accessible, requires a different type of architecture.

To date, the usual way of analyzing somebody else's simulation is to download the data. With PB scale datasets, this will not work. We are experimenting with a new, immersive metaphor for interacting with large simulations by using a large number of virtual sensors that can be placed in a simulation, anywhere at any timestep. They can also be set to send a data stream in real physical quantities. Imagine how scientists could launch mini accelerometers into simulated tornadoes, emulating the movie *Twister*. We have successfully implemented this metaphor for our turbulence data, and are now porting it to the cosmology simulations.

In this approach, one can create a so-called immersive environment, in which the users can insert virtual sensors into the simulation data. These sensors can then feed data back to the user. They can provide a one-time measurement, they can be pinned to a physical (Eulerian) location, or they can "go with the flow" as comoving Lagrangian particles. By placing the sensors in different geometric configurations, users can accommodate a wide variety of spatial and temporal access patterns. The sensors can feed back data on multiple channels, measuring different fields in the simulation.

This pattern also enables the users to run time backward, something that is impossible in a direct simulation involving dissipation. Imagine that the snapshots are saved frequently enough that one can interpolate particle velocities smoothly. Sensors can back-track their original trajectory and one can see where they came from, all the way back to the initial conditions. This simple interface can provide a very flexible, yet powerful, way to do science with large datasets from anywhere in the world. The availability of such a 4D dataset "at your fingertips" and the ability to make "casual" queries from anywhere are beginning to change how we think about the data. Researchers can come back to the same place in space and time and be sure to encounter the same values.

The Twister metaphor mentioned above was implemented in the Turbulence DB eight years ago. The Turbulence DB is the first space-time database for turbulent flows, containing the output of large simulations, publicly available to the research community (Perlman et al. 2007). The 27TB database contains the entire time-history of a 1024^3 mesh point pseudo-spectral Direct Numerical Simulation of forced Navier-Stokes equations representing isotropic turbulence. One thousand and twenty-four time-steps are stored, covering a full "large-eddy" turnover time of model evolution. We have built a prototype that serves requests over the web for velocities, pressure, various space derivatives of velocity and pressure, and interpolation functions. The data and their interface are used by the turbulence research community and have led to about 100 publications to date. To date we have delivered more than 36 trillion data points to the user community. In a recent paper on MHD, trajectories were computed by moving the particles backward in time, something that is impossible to do in an in situ computation and only enabled by interpolation over the database (Eyink et al. 2013).

A similar transformation is happening in cosmology. The SDSS SkyServer framework was reused for the Millennium simulation database (Lemson and the Virgo Consortium 2006). The database has been in use for more than 10 years, has hundreds of regular users, and has been used in nearly 700 publications. The database contains value added data from a simulation originally only containing 10B dark matter particles. A semi-analytical recipe was used to create mock galaxies in the simulations, and their hierarchical mergers were tracked in the database. The merger history was used to assign a plausible star formation rate to each galaxy, which in turn can be used to derive observable physical properties. The database contains several such semi-analytic scenarios and has been expanded with data from three other simulations, one of which contains 300 billion particles.

Environmental science

Environmental data are complex; combine biological, physical, and geological measurements; and are heterogeneous in space and time. The data are fragmented, and as various scientists focus on specific variables and store data in isolated file systems, integration becomes a significant challenge. A great deal of effort has been spent to make environmental data more accessible. A common feature of these networks is that they have largely focused on data accessibility through metadata catalogs where investigators can search data by keyword, project name, investigator name, and so on.

Our pilot system focused on integrating data on various spatial and temporal scales to answer science questions related to the soil ecosystem. LifeUnderYourFeet (Szlavecz et al. 2006) has been continuously collecting soil moisture and temperature data since 2008, and soil respiration data since 2010. We used the SciServer framework to integrate data at national and local spatial scales and to correlate soil measurements in space and time for various climatic, atmospheric, meteorological, and anthropogenic conditions and scales.

Toward a Sustainable Solution: The SciServer

Consolidating the evolution

Over the first 12 years of the SDSS archive we have incrementally evolved the system, avoiding major architectural changes. The SDSS data with all the additional science projects have been created at a cost of well over $100 million. They are widely used by a diverse community, and are generating new papers and supporting original research every day.

But the services are showing signs of aging; while the data are still very much alive, they will still be used 15 years from now. To prepare for the future, we need to consolidate and reengineer the services, to make them more sustainable and inexpensive to operate. To do this, we have endeavored to convert the SkyServer to the SciServer, a generic, modular set of building blocks that can be connected in several ways.

New building blocks

FileDB. Relational databases have shown their value to the scientific community. The SDSS Database (Thakar et al. 2008) was a forerunner, showing how the community was willing to take the step of learning SQL to access a database. However, data volumes are reaching the limits of what can be managed within relational databases with reasonable effort. For example, it takes a week to load a typical Turbulence database. To avoid this bottleneck, we built a system that allows raw data from the database to be linked, using indexes, without ingesting them into the database. We wrote custom functions that can access the file system, but can be called from ordinary SQL. These functions are exposed as table-valued, user-defined functions and are accessible through standard SQL queries. Their performance is as good as native DB calls.

ScratchDB. We have enabled the CasJobs system to have many other contexts, not just the SDSS data versions (right now we have all the previous data releases from DR1 through DR9) but also other astronomical collections. We will also bring the simulations and environmental datasets into the federation. Uploaded and derived data (and the related metadata) will automatically show up in the user's MyDB. For large scale intermediate data, the small user space is not quite enough. For example, a custom cross-match of large astronomical catalogs, like SDSS and GALEX, might require several 100 GBs if not TBs of disk space. This cannot be done today. We resolve this problem with a new MyScratch layer between the static contexts and the MyDBs, with tens of TB of storage, both in flat files and as large databases.

Advanced scripting. Our users, both in SDSS and in the numerical laboratories have become quite artful in using database queries. They use SQL tools not as a hammer, but rather as a violin, and they generate "nice music." But with the emergence of Python, sophisticated machine learning algorithms, libraries, and packages have become available, and the users are now keen to use these with the same ease of interactivity as SQL. A typical use case would start with an SQL query returning tens of thousands of objects with a particular spectral property. However, the user would then like to go back to the raw data (spectra in this case) and run her own tools and algorithm written in Python.

To facilitate this, we built two add-ons: one is SciServer Compute, a set of servers providing about 100 virtual machines, always available, that can be used to start Jupyter/iPython notebooks, within Docker containers. These are preconfigured with the database interface tools, and users can run their SQL queries out of Python. Furthermore, all the raw data files of SDSS (about 150TB) are wrapped into a data container, so access is trivial. The Jupyter environment also enables Matlab and R, which are relevant for our engineering and Biostats/genomics users. Several of our interactive numerical laboratories (Turbulence, Ocean Circulation, N-body) are now using both Python and Matlab bindings.

SDSS Futures

Consolidation of the SDSS versions

We aim to integrate the SDSS-IV results with the legacy data from earlier stages: SDSS-I, SDSS-II, and SDSS-III, including a large (14,555 square degree) imaging survey of the sky with follow-up optical and near-infrared spectroscopy. Currently, because the SDSS-III project proceeded under a different organizational structure than SDSS-II, the SDSS products have branched into two distribution sites. For SDSS-IV, we plan to reintegrate this distribution under a single archive that includes all the legacy data and documentation, as well as the new data, integrated under the reengineered and enhanced version of SciServer. The proven flexibility and extensibility of the Sky/SciServer framework makes it possible to integrate these new data in a coherent and scientifically powerful fashion. The total data volume of the survey, combined with the legacy data, is projected to be around 400TB, with the final reduced catalogs around 15 to 20TB. In addition, these final reduced catalogs will consist of several different flavors of data—optical and near-infrared spectra and several different types of imaging data (optical, near- and mid-infrared). Finally, the combination of imaging and spectroscopic coverage maps will form a complex pattern on the sky that will need to be described quantitatively for science, and that the spatial tools of the SkyServer have been designed to track.

The data lifecycle

We often talk about the data lifecycle, and its phases. As the SDSS project is probably nearing its data acquisition end, we have to think carefully about the long-term sustainability of the data archive, and how it will be curated and preserved. Given that its usage shows no signs of decreasing, we need to consider that the data will support good science for another 20 years. How can we support such a long lifecycle, where does the support come from, and where will the data reside? It is time to start thinking about what happens to the data after the sunset of the observations.

We can see three distinct phases. In Phase 1 observations are still happening. As long as the SDSS telescope is still taking data, the archive is part of an active data collection effort. Phase 2 starts once the telescope is shut down. The archive needs to be kept alive, but the data do not grow any longer. Over a five-year period during this phase we need to consolidate the services as much as possible. This must be done by the team currently operating the archive. During the following five years of Phase 3, the archive must be handed off to an organization that can operate on a good economy of scale, and whose sustained existence is guaranteed, independent of the individual datasets. One of the possibilities we are considering is to identify a set of university libraries, which are willing to undertake this task of maintaining the archive and operate a help desk. This phase will continue as long as there is continued use of the archive and one can justify its existence based upon scientific value generated.

The service lifecycle

However, during the 20 years that we have been working on the SDSS archive and now the SciServer, we have learned about the service lifecycle as well. The SDSS archive and now the SciServer are much more than just a simple file-store. The data are served through a set of sophisticated, smart services, which offer a lot of server-side functionality. In 2001 we built the first web services deployed in a science setting, but now many of these APIs and interfaces are obsolete. Computing has undergone several major paradigm shifts. Over the last 20 years we went from a lot of different technologies, with their own special acronyms: CORBA to The Computational Grid, to Web Services, Grid Services, then the Cloud, and most recently to Data Lakes. No matter what, this dynamic evolution is going to continue, and it is difficult to predict what the world of distributed computing will look like even five years from now.

There is also natural aging. Technology has improved significantly since we built our first services; the first web services in science were built for SDSS by us. While several improvements have been implemented over time, it is important to rethink the methodologies in the context of the new, evolving Internet. Smarter client-side web interfaces are possible today using HTML5 and JavaScript, which are standard and quickly became widely accepted. These modifications will enable our new infrastructure to perform some of the processing steps in the browsers rather than overloading the servers. Smarter clients will work efficiently with new services; by now, REST has replaced SOAP almost everywhere. Asynchronous messaging protocols will make the infrastructure more robust against the glitches in communications. Behind the web server we will build a universal application layer that uses proper scheduling mechanisms to handle the large volume of complex user jobs. Load balancing will be realized on all levels by partitioning and parallel execution of the tasks over a cluster of database servers.

From queries to file extractions, everything will be prioritized and executed in the most efficient way by schedulers that keep track of data locality and use the closest copies in the distributed database system. The next generation execution environment will be based on workflows, whose state can be persisted in a database. Thus long-running and expensive scientific analyses can be suspended and resumed, making the framework more resilient and the system management much easier.

All that we can do today is to prepare for these changes to come, and reorganize the underlying services and APIs in such a way, that they are maximally modular and independent, so that future upgrades and improvements will be as painless as possible. Building the database schema to be maximally portable enabled us to move from one database system to another, until we settled on SQL Server. In the SciServer we are extending this philosophy, and we have further modularized the whole environment, and incorporated design patterns going beyond astronomy. That it was very easy to bring new science use cases, even related to social science, into the SciServer validated our approach beyond our initial hopes.

Community response

In just a few years these datasets have earned the trust of the astronomy community and have been heavily used. Starting with the Turbulence project, we introduced the notion of interactive, database-centric tools into other science domains. The initial reaction from the turbulence community was rather skeptical: they felt that they could analyze their own data more effectively than through our database approach. However, others in the research community did not feel this way.

Many researchers started to access the data in our system and do their research in the open numerical laboratory. For instance, experimentalists could place tracer particles as measurement devices inside the numerical space-time data in our numerical laboratory and calibrate their measurement techniques. Mathematicians could find seeds of possible singularities in the partial differential equations. These scientists represent a cross-section of the research community that had real difficulties accessing large datasets from simulations prior to the JHTDB. The availability of our open numerical laboratory has led to many results and papers by researchers all over the world, having been used for over one hundred published papers on turbulence, for example. In 2015 the number of points has exceeded 12 trillion, and recently, it had reached 56 trillion.

A similar transformation is happening in cosmology. The SDSS SkyServer framework was reused for the millennium simulation database (Lemson and the Virgo Consortium 2006). The database has been in use for more than eight years, and has hundreds of regular users, and has been used in nearly seven hundred publications. The set-oriented SQL makes it remarkably easy to formulate very complex aggregate queries over the temporal history of various subsets of galaxies and create samples that can be compared directly to observations.

Conclusion: The Cost and Price of Data

In every new community with which we have engaged, it takes about three to five years to overcome the initial skepticism, and for us to demonstrate that our interactive approach to large-scale problems is more scalable than the traditional ones. We have to earn the trust of the community—by giving them open access to high quality data and easy to use tools that mesh well with how they analyze their data.

It is also clear that none of the domain communities understand the subtle differences between the value of data, and the cost of data, and the cost of archiving. The value of data is relatively easy to grasp, we make new discoveries based upon these datasets, write new papers, share them, combine them with other datasets, and they provide a solid foundation for reproducible results.

It is much harder to define the price of data. On one hand, one can argue that the price of the data is the cost to build and run the instruments. Many of today's large data collections in this sense have cost hundreds of millions of dollars (SDSS), if not billions (LHC). On the other hand, one can argue that a typical NSF grant of $100,000/year is considered high quality if it produces two papers in a good, refereed journal annually. By this token, the value of a paper is about $50,000. Of course, not all science support goes into the individual grants, at least an equal amount goes into various national facilities, both physical and computational. Let us double this number, and estimate the value of a good scientific paper to be about $100,000. By this measure, the SDSS data have, to date, resulted in more than 7,000 refereed publications, and this has a "monetized value" of $700 million. At the same time, the total cost of all the SDSS projects combined has been less than $200 million, making it very cost-efficient.

We also need to consider the cost of archiving. On one hand, we can calculate the physical costs, power, disk drives, curation personnel, servers, and so on. In astronomy, the typical annual operating cost of a telescope is around 5 to 10 percent of the capital investment. Everyone accepts this. At the same time, we are still shocked if the cost of maintaining an archival dataset is a few hundred thousand dollars, often a small fraction of 1 percent of the capital cost of acquiring it. Yet these archival datasets will generate a disproportionally high value in terms of new publications, for several decades to come.

These large, open datasets, analyzed by a much broader range of scientists than ever before, using all the tools of the computer age, are creating a new way to do science. We cannot predict where they will lead, but it is already clear that these technologies have brought and will bring about dramatic changes in the way we do open science and make new discoveries.

References

Banks, Michael. March 2009. Impact of sky surveys. *Physics World*.

Becla, Jacek, Andrew Hanushevsky, Sergei Nikolaev, Ghaleb Abdulla, Alexander S. Szalay, Maria Nieto-Santisteban, Ani R. Thakar, and Jim Gray. 2006. Designing a multi-petabyte database for LSST. *Proceedings of the SPIE* 6270:62700R.

Budavári, Tamas, Alexander S. Szalay, and George Fekete. 2010. Searchable sky coverage of astronomical observations: Footprints and exposures. *Publications of the Astronomical Society of the Pacific* 122:1375–88.

Cardamone, Caroline N., Kevin Schawinski, Marc Sarzi, Steven P. Bamford, Nicola Bennert, C. Megan Urry, Christopher J. Lintott, William C. Keel, John Parejko, Robert C. Nichol, et al. 2009. Galaxy Zoo green peas: Discovery of a class of compact extremely star-forming galaxies. *Monthly Notices of the Royal Astronomical Society* 399:1191–1205.

Dobos, Laszlo, Istvan Csabai, Milos Milovanovic, Tamas Budavari, Alexander. S. Szalay, Marko Tintor, Jose Blakeley, Andrija Jovanovic, and Dragan Tomic. 2011. Array requirements for scientific applications and an implementation for Microsoft SQL Server. Paper presented at EDBT/ICDT Workshop on Array Databases, Uppsala, Sweden.

Eyink, Gregory, Ethan Vishniac, Cristian Lalescu, Hussein Aluie, Kalin Kanov, Kai Bürger, Randal Burns, Charles Meneveau, and Alexander S. Szalay. 2013. Flux-freezing breakdown in high-conductivity magnetohydrodynamic turbulence. *Nature* 497:466–69.

Fekete, George, Alexander S. Szalay, and Jim Gray. 2006. Using table valued functions in SQL Server 2005. Paper presented at the MSDN Development Forum.

Frogel, Jay A. 2010. Astronomy's greatest hits: The 100 most cited papers in each year of the first decade of the 21st century (2000–2009). *Publications of the Astronomical Society of the Pacific* 122 (896): 1214–35.

Heasley James N., Maria Nieto-Santisteban, Alexander S. Szalay, and A. Thakar. 2007. The Pan-STARRS object data manager database. *Bulletin of the American Astronomical Society* 38:124.

Lemson, Gerard, and the Virgo Consortium. 2006. Halo and galaxy formation histories from the millennium simulation: Public release of VO-oriented and SQL-queryable database for studying the evolution of galaxies in the ΛCDM cosmogony. Available from https://arxiv.org/abs/astro-ph/0608019.

Li, Y., Eric Perlman, Minping Wan, Yunke Yang, Charles Meneveau, Randal Burns, Shi-Yi Chen, Alexander S. Szalay, and Gregory Eyink. 2008. A public turbulence database cluster and applications to study Lagrangian evolution of velocity increments in turbulence. *Journal of Turbulence* 9 (31): 1–29.

Lintott, Christopher. J., Kevin Schawinski, William C. Keel, Hanny Van Arkel, Nicola Bennert, Ed Edmondson, Daniel Thomas, Daniel J. B. Smith, Peter D. Herbert, Matt J. Jarvis, Shanil Virani, Dan Andreescu, Steven P. Bamford, Kate Land, Phil Murray, Robert C. Nichol, M. Jordan Raddick, Anze Slozar, Alexander S. Szalay, and Jan Vandenberg. 2009. Galaxy Zoo: Hanny's Voorwerp, a quasar light echo? *Monthly Notices of the Royal Astronomical Society* 399:129–40.

Lintott, Christopher J., Kevin Schawinski, Anze Slosar, Kate Land, Steven P. Bamford, Daniel Thomas, M. Jordan Raddick, Robert C. Nichol, Alexander S. Szalay, Dan Andreescu, Phil Murray, and Jan Vandenberg. 2008. Galaxy Zoo: Morphologies derived from visual inspection of galaxies from the Sloan Digital Sky Survey. *Monthly Notices of the Royal Astronomical Society* 389:1179–89.

Madrid, Juan P., and F. Duccio Macchetto. 2009. High-impact astronomical observatories. *Bulletin of the American Astronomical Society* 41:913–14.

McNutt, Todd R., Thomas Nabhani, Alexander S. Szalay, Theodore Deweese, and John Wong. 2008. Oncospace: EScience technology and opportunities for oncology. *Medical Physics* 35:2900–2901.

O'Mullane, William, Jim Gray, Nolan Li, Tamas Budavari, Maria Nieto-Santisteban, and Alexander S. Szalay. 2004. Batch query system with interactive local storage for SDSS and the VO. In *Proceedings of the ADASS XIII, ASP Conference Series*, eds. F. Ochsenbein, Marc Allen, and Daniel Egret, 372–76.

Perlman, Eric, Randal Burns, Yi Li, and Charles Meneveau. 2007. Data exploration of turbulence simulations using a database cluster. In *Proceedings of the Supercomputing Conference* (SC'07). doi:10.1145/1362622.1362654.

Singh, Vic, Jim Gray, Ani R. Thakar, Alexander S. Szalay, Jordan Raddick, Bill Boroski, Svetlana Lebedeva and Brian Yanny. 2006. *SkyServer traffic report: The first five years.* Microsoft Technical Report, MSR-TR-2006-190. Redmond, WA: Microsoft.

Szalay, Alexander S., Peter Kunszt, Ani R. Thakar, Jim Gray, Donald Slutz, and Robert Brunner. 2000. Designing and mining multi-terabyte astronomy archives: The Sloan Digital Sky Survey. In *Proceedings of SIGMOD 2000 Conference*, 451–62.

Szalay Alexander, Ani R. Thakar, and Jim Gray. 2008. The sqlLoader data-loading pipeline. *Computing in Science and Engineering* 10:38–48.

Szlavecz, Katalin, Andreas Terzis, E. Razvan Musǎloiu, Josh Cogan, Sam Small, Stuart Ozer, Randal Burns, Jim Gray, and Alexander S. Szalay. 2006. *Life under your feet: An end-to-end soil ecology sensor network, database, web server, and analysis service.* Microsoft Technical Report, MSR-TR-2006-90. Redmond, WA: Microsoft.

Thakar Ani R., Alexander S. Szalay, George Fekete, and Jim Gray. 2008. The catalog archive server database management system. *Computing in Science and Engineering* 10:30–37.

Wilton, Richard, Tamas Budavari, Ben Langmead, Sarah J. Wheelan, Steven L. Salzberg, and Alexander S. Szalay. 2015. Arioc: High-throughput read alignment with GPU-accelerated exploration of the seed-and-extend search space. *PeerJ* 3. doi:10.7717/peerj.808.

Zhang, Jian. 2011. Data use and access behavior in eScience: Exploring data practices in the new data-intensive science paradigm. PhD thesis, Drexel University, Philadelphia, PA.

Maximizing the Use of Integrated Data Systems: Understanding the Challenges and Advancing Solutions

By
DENNIS CULHANE,
JOHN FANTUZZO,
MATTHEW HILL,
and
TC BURNETT

State and local governments are seeking to use their health, education, and human services administrative data to address major social problems. As they attempt to move forward to develop and use integrated data systems (IDS), they have encountered substantial challenges. The Actionable Intelligence for Social Policy (AISP) team at the University of Pennsylvania targeted four common sets of challenges to IDS use: IDS governance, legal agreements, technology and data security, and data standards. The purpose of this article is to present the results from a year-long convening of four panels of national experts in each of these key topic areas. The results specify the greatest IDS challenges in each of these areas, and develop state-of-the-art responses to innovate the IDS field. It discusses how these solutions promote more effective, efficient, and routine use of IDS that are scalable to advance the IDS field beyond these current limitations in practice.

Keywords: integrated data; governance; administrative data; social policy; public policy

Currently, the federal government spends nearly $4 trillion per year on behalf of its citizenry (U.S. Government Publishing Office 2016). And the United States' population is larger and more diverse than ever. There are now more than 323 million people living in the United States, who speak more than 350 languages (U.S. Census Bureau 2015). With the

Dennis Culhane is the Dana and Andrew Stone Professor of Social Policy at the School of Social Policy and Practice at the University of Pennsylvania. He is a co–principal investigator (PI) of Actionable Intelligence for Social Policy (AISP). His primary research expertise is in the field of homelessness.

John Fantuzzo is the Albert M. Greenfield Professor of Human Relations at the Graduate School of Education at the University of Pennsylvania. He is also a co-PI of AISP. His primary research expertise is in the areas of early childhood risk, early childhood education, and Head Start.

Correspondence: culhane@upenn.edu

DOI: 10.1177/0002716217743441

national debt growing to more than $20 trillion, there is pressure to address more complex social problems with less. Yet only 20 percent of Americans would describe government programs as well run, and just 19 percent of Americans trust the federal government most of the time (Pew Research Center 2017). Americans want a responsible government, one that delivers more effective and efficient services to its citizens and abides by ethical standards of conduct (Kettl 2009). But what hope is there to improve government within a context of growing need, limited resources, and low public confidence?

Responding to this challenge, the Office of Management and Budget (OMB) and the United States Congress have called for the cross-sector use of government-collected administrative data to inform social problem-solving processes that lead to evidence-based policy. This resulted in the passage of H.R. 1831 in March 2016, establishing the Commission on Evidence-Based Policymaking. The goal of the commission is to figure out how administrative data from federal programs can be integrated and made available to facilitate "program evaluation, continuous improvement, policy-relevant research, and cost-benefit analyses by qualified researchers" (U.S. Congress 2016). It also seeks to make recommendations on what type of "data infrastructure" and "database security" can best support these objectives.[1]

Fortunately, there is a robust national movement at the state and local levels to use integrated, individual-level administrative data across public service systems to address vexing social problems (Fantuzzo and Culhane 2015; Lane 2016; Heidbreder 2016; Jennings, Hall, and Zhang 2012). This is critical because the role of the federal government is largely to redistribute funds to state and local governments, which possess the actual assets required to deliver and tailor services to the needs of their constituencies (Perlman 2010).[2] Since many of the important decisions about government service provision are ultimately made by states and local jurisdictions, sustainable program evaluation, policy analysis, and planning processes are needed at this level. State and local integrated data systems (IDS) have demonstrated their ability to fulfill this function by engaging cross-sector stakeholders across administrative silos and creating the legal and collaborative infrastructure to make longitudinal, cross-system analyses possible on a routine basis. When education, health, and human service records are successfully linked at the individual level, a broader range of relevant factors and outcomes can be examined longitudinally for entire populations. For example, in 2016, Los Angeles County administrators from multiple agencies wanted to determine how they could better coordinate programs to address homelessness and to examine their spending on this population. They were able to quickly

Matthew Hill is the former executive director of AISP at the School of Social Policy and Practice at the University of Pennsylvania. He is currently a senior research fellow at the University of Massachusetts Amherst Center for Heritage and Society.

TC Burnett is the associate director of AISP at the School of Social Policy and Practice at the University of Pennsylvania. Her work covers a wide range of topics related to integrated data systems, as well as the administration and management of AISP activities.

accomplish this by using L.A. County's long-standing integrated data system to look at county service provision to the homeless population. County administrators found that, across just six agencies, almost $1 billion was spent in 2015 on services to individuals experiencing homelessness. More specifically, they were able to determine that just 5 percent of individuals experiencing homelessness accounted for 40 cents of every dollar spent by the county on homelessness services (Wu and Stevens 2016). Armed with this information, the county enacted strategic policy and programmatic changes to better focus outreach and services to these individuals to decrease both county spending and homelessness (County of Los Angeles, Chief Executive Office 2016). As evidenced through the example of L.A. County, integrated data systems provide state and local government with actionable evidence to inform decision-making. The use of established IDS offers a promising avenue for government leaders to improve decision-making and generate more effective data-driven solutions for policy and practice.

Recognizing the potential of these IDS to produce cross-sector actionable intelligence for government leaders, and the complexity they represent, the MacArthur Foundation provided funding to the University of Pennsylvania to establish a network of integrated data systems to study the best practices of well-established state and local IDS in the United States. University of Pennsylvania researchers identified high-functioning IDS with strong track records of using integrated cross-sector administrative data to address complex social problems in their jurisdiction. Sites were determined using a key-informant process. University of Pennsylvania researchers contacted administrators of known integrated data sites, a federal human services research sponsor, and other university researchers that were identified as having potential knowledge of integrated data system sites. These individuals were asked to identify integrated data systems that met the following three criteria: (1) contains data from multiple agencies, (2) the IDS was developed to serve a general purpose rather than to complete a one-off research project, and (3) the IDS links data at the individual level. Responses were then used to generate the convenience sample of sites (Culhane et al. 2010). These included state IDS sites (Florida, Michigan, and South Carolina), as well as county- or city-level IDS sites (Allegheny County [Pittsburgh], Cook County [Chicago], Cuyahoga County [Cleveland], Los Angeles County, and Philadelphia) that produce, in a sustainable real-time manner, actionable intelligence to advance social problem solving in government.[3] With a network in place, AISP researchers studied the best practices across these exemplary IDS sites. A principal finding in the AISP Network study was the necessary and sufficient contribution of four critical *core components* of effective IDS operations required for data-driven solutions: IDS governance, legal agreements, technology and data security, and data standards (Fantuzzo and Culhane 2015).

Discovering these critical, common components of effective IDS sites is a significant accomplishment, but it is just the beginning. There is more work to be done to fully develop the potential of effective and efficient IDS use to foster ongoing quality improvement of government public services. The next important step is to consider the greatest challenges or barriers in establishing each of these essential IDS components, and to then search for existing state-of-the-art responses to these challenges to advance the field of IDS practice. With the support of the Laura and John Arnold Foundation, AISP established four panels of national experts for each of the IDS core components. Panel members were selected based on current public sector or academic leadership experience in the governance, legal, technology, or data-related aspects of IDS development. They were charged first with identifying the major barriers to IDS use related to each of these components. Once this had been done, each panel was tasked with recommending innovative solutions to effectively address these challenges. The purpose of this article is to present a summary of the expert panels' findings. This work presents viable next steps in IDS development by showing how to concretely address current challenges. Taken together, these recommendations have the potential to increase the speed, scalability, and sustainability of effective IDS.

IDS Governance

Governance is the foundation of IDS use. The governance of IDS refers to the people, policies, procedures, and technologies required to manage the operations of an IDS under the charge of an executive government leader such as a mayor or governor. A governing board, which consists of a group of key stakeholders, is typically appointed to oversee the operations of the IDS. They supervise how the IDS is used to accomplish high priority research and evaluation inquiries with the aim of improving public services.

The challenge: Public mistrust of data integration

The biggest challenge in the governance of an IDS is *public mistrust* of government's ability to safeguard the personal information found in an individual citizen's administrative records. The public fear is that the perceived risks of integrating the administrative data of individuals across public service agencies are far greater than the benefits. We live in an era of low public trust in government. This is particularly true regarding American's confidence in government's ability to protect their personal data. According to a recent Pew Research Center report on *Americans and Cybersecurity*, only 12 percent of respondents said they were "very confident" government agencies can keep their records private and secure, and half reported that they do not trust the federal government to protect their data (Pew Research Center 2017). Moreover, the public perception is that this situation is getting worse, with nearly half of those surveyed reporting that their personal data are less secure now than compared to five years ago.

This general fear and mistrust is fueled by news stories of government surveillance and "unmasking" of the identity of citizens, and media reports of increasing data breaches of private records stored by national retailers, insurance companies, and financial institutions. These fears are further intensified by anecdotal stories about the potential of combining government datasets stripped of personal identifiers with publicly available data to reveal the identity of citizens in these de-identified government records. In one highly publicized case, a computer scientist was able to use zip code information contained in voter rolls to reidentify individuals (including the governor) in an "anonymized" dataset on state employee hospital visits released by the Massachusetts Group Insurance Commission (Anderson 2009).

These public fears about the unauthorized use of data records pose a real threat to using personally identifiable information in a government operated IDS to foster evidence-based improvements in public services. Public mistrust is a real challenge to IDS governance, and it calls us to directly respond to this challenge by intentionally prioritizing innovative ways to enhance the ethical uses of IDS (Stiles and Boothroyd 2013). The following section considers the advancements proposed by the expert panel on governance. These concrete strategies are aimed at making both the real benefits of IDS use and the safeguards that can be put in place to minimize risk of personal data use more evident to the public.

Opportunities

The adage *"the best defense is a good offense"* captures the spirit of the experts' recommendations for IDS governance. Our expert panel on governance recommended taking very proactive and transparent steps to build public trust and confidence in IDS use by establishing the ethical use of personal information to advance the social good (Gibbs et al. 2017). This starts with grounding all IDS operations in the bedrock ethical principles of using human participants' data in research—*beneficence, autonomy*, and *justice* (Fantuzzo and Culhane 2015).[4] First and foremost is the ethical principle of *beneficence*. This superordinate principle asserts that all research uses of an IDS must be high-priority uses that are in the best interest of the persons being served. This means that the benefits of participation are clear and that they exceed the risks. Next is the principle of *autonomy*. Autonomy ensures that the beneficent uses of personal information respect the dignity of all participants and give the public an active voice in IDS decision-making (governance). Finally, speaking directly to public mistrust is *justice*. This principle respects all the public laws that protect the rights of participants and demonstrates that the use of individuals' information is reasonable, nonexploitative, and identifies and minimizes risks. The following three subsections outline concrete recommendations from the governance expert panel on how to incorporate these tried-and-true principles of ethical conduct into the modus operandi of IDS governance.

Advancing beneficence. The AISP governance expert panel's report appropriately introduces concrete ways to advance the *beneficence* of IDS use. This starts with the realization that the IDS will only operate effectively if at its inception there is a clear articulation of its purpose and expected benefits to the public. This takes the form of collaboratively constructed *mission* and *vision* statements. So much of the existing public fear and mistrust about IDS is associated with ignorance and confusion that results from the lack of any direct communications to the public. Developing a transparent and straightforward mission statement will communicate why the IDS exists, what the IDS does, and who does what for whom. A mission statement should be constructed with all the relevant stakeholders to provide a "we" consensus justification of the beneficence of the IDS's existence in a state or local jurisdiction. Such a statement must underscore and make visible the core purpose and mechanisms of the IDS to use public resources to achieve more effective and efficient public services. The mission statement is an assertive step toward dispelling myths and fears about IDS, but it is not sufficient on its own. It must be accompanied by a coconstructed vision statement. The vision statement is a simple declaration that describes in plain language the end goal of the IDS and points to the long-term expected benefits of IDS operations. The vision statement makes evident to all how the IDS will ultimately benefit the clients being served by the participating public agencies; the citizens of the community; the government leaders and policy-makers in the community that will use the actionable intelligence it provides; as well as other communities, both national and international, that can use the research and evaluation knowledge resulting from the IDS. The expert panel report underscores the importance of developing these clear and honest consensus statements of *What is it?* and *How it will benefit us?* as key to establishing *beneficence* as a cornerstone of ethical IDS use.

Advancing autonomy. The AISP governance expert panel's report also provides clear guidance to actualizing the ethical principal of *autonomy*, through engaging relevant stakeholders in the design, launch, and governance of an IDS. Autonomy emphasizes the significance of providing for and respecting the public *voice* and *choice* of relevant stakeholders as a means of concretely building trust among all the key participants in IDS use. All too often, mistrust, fear, and resistance are generated when individuals or groups feel that others are doing something important that impacts them that they have no ability to influence. Their resistance ("No!") may in fact be a negative expression of their autonomy—voicing reasonable concerns that have not been yet been considered. To effectively address resistance to IDS use in a state or local jurisdiction, we must *partner with resistance* (Fantuzzo, McWayne, and Childs 2006). Core to the principle of autonomy is the *practice of respect* for the distinctive perspectives of all relevant stakeholders (Fantuzzo 2015). As recommended by the panel, this first involves the recognition of key contributors and beneficiaries and then the creation of an inclusive process that allows for their points of view to influence the decision-making about the routine use of the IDS.

The panel's report provides guidance for how to identify and include key stakeholders. It lists four major stakeholder categories to consider that are involved distinctively in effective IDS operations: government executive leadership, frontline service providers, researchers and data analysts, and the public (i.e., both the direct beneficiaries of the services and the community at large). Identifying key stakeholders within these categories is essential to inviting the most interested and capable stakeholders to serve on the various boards and advisory groups that are necessary to the ongoing governance process of the IDS.

Once stakeholders across categories have been identified and prioritized with respect to their ability to contribute to the governance of the IDS, plans should be made to engage them. This is an important consideration of where their voice and distinctive contributions would most benefit the various activities of the IDS. The sum of these functions include the whole range of work executed by those involved in the governance process of the IDS: (1) inaugurating the IDS with mission and vision statements; (2) generating the various legal agreements that permit the integration of individual data across agencies for IDS use; (3) establishing the integrity of the data infrastructure and analytic capacity to conduct research projects; (4) determining the priorities for IDS research projects to improve services; (5) monitoring and overseeing the successful completion of those projects and ensuring that the results are translated into actionable intelligence in accord with the IDS mission and vision statements; and (6) communicating, in an open and transparent way, to the public what has been learned and its contribution to more effective and efficient public services. The aim here is to draw upon all those stakeholders who are interested and able to contribute to the robust "we" of IDS use. Here our aim is to achieve equality of respect by recognizing that respect is "not something we possess, but an ongoing ethical practice that requires a sincere effort" (Fantuzzo 2015, 85).

Advancing justice. The ethical principal of *justice* in IDS governance builds upon the principals of *beneficence* and *autonomy*. Establishing the purpose and benefits of IDS use and inclusion of all relevant stakeholders must be followed by a written agreement ensuring that there are ethical and legal safeguards in place governing all the concrete policies and procedures of IDS use. Here, justice is codified in the memorandum of understanding (MOU) agreement, which is signed by all the key contributors involved in IDS use. The MOU sets forth the core features of the IDS structure and conduct, and defines the legal rights and responsibilities of each party within the IDS in a just manner. The MOU provides the collaborative foundation for how the "we" of the IDS will achieve the benefits of the IDS. The MOU accomplishes three important objectives. First, protecting the private information of individuals being served by the respective service agencies participating in the IDS is made a top priority. Second, it respects the rights and responsibilities of the agencies that collect private information during the course of service provision to use these data to inform how they can improve the quality of the services they provide. Third, it affirms the "we's" commitment to beneficence and autonomy by making its policies, procedures, and accomplishments transparent and open to the public at large. In this way, the MOU is both an ethical and a legal document that upholds equal burden and equal benefit of IDS use.

IDS Legal Issues

The second major core component of IDS is legal issues. IDS utilize the personal information found in government administrative data records to improve public services. These data are originally collected by government agencies through the routine provision of programs and services. The agencies hold and use this information in the context of existing laws. It is therefore essential to understand the legal issues related to IDS use.

The challenge: Too many red lights

Fundamentally, the purpose of law in a society is to govern and guide actions and relations among and between persons, organizations, and governments to protect the valued liberties and rights of members of that society from unreasonable intrusions by persons, organizations, or government. The law at its best provides *freedom within form*. It regulates transactions to protect liberties and can be equated to traffic lights in a big city, which use red and green lights to permit many individuals to move about the city freely with minimal harm. The red lights protect citizens from the impulses of other drivers, and the green lights permit citizens to get to their destinations while also regarding the rights of other drivers. A driver's license signifies that an individual knows the law and is willing and capable of abiding by it. Therefore, to a naïve, uninformed person the legal component of IDS should be equally simple—just identify the laws that govern the use of the personal data collected by the government, and give the government a license to integrate and use these data in accordance with the existing laws to regulate IDS use. This sounds like a simple, linear, and rational process. However, this does not reflect the reality of the complex and often irrational world of twenty-first-century America. Therefore, our contemporary context poses significant legal challenges to IDS use.

There are two prevailing forces that beset lawyers and generate legal challenges to state-of-the-art IDS use. They include (1) the unprecedented crisis of public mistrust surrounding government's use of personal data; and (2) the unprecedented, though complex, opportunities to use IDS to make substantial improvements in government health, education, and human services. As we mentioned, there is currently a substantial lack of public trust in government's ability to safeguard personal data. As a result, there is a predisposition to be cautious by legal counsel in government agencies. Fears of litigation; long-standing cultural trends; norms and policies within government agencies against sharing; as well as overly conservative interpretations of federal, state, and local laws all point to a "no" red-light, legal response (Petrila et al. 2017, 6). Unfortunately, this climate of "many reasons to say no" is a breeding ground for myths, misinterpretations, and half truths about the risks associated with IDS use. More importantly, it diverts attention from the benefits of how IDS can contribute to a more innovative, effective government.

To complicate matters further, the effectiveness and utility of an IDS is enhanced when there are more data partners and community stakeholders involved throughout the life of the IDS projects. This translates into "more opportunities mean more complexity." From a legal perspective, this makes the formulation of comprehensive MOUs very complex and time-consuming, with many moving parts to regulate—many complex actions and relations among partners. This requires an experienced general counsel that understands the intricacies of the relatively new and burgeoning world of big data and legally sanctioned IDS uses. It also requires an extraordinary amount of time to negotiate and finalize these complex agreements. All this may be too much for the typically overburdened legal counsel in government service. The nature and amount of knowledge, experience, and time required to craft these complex agreements creates a sizable burden for existing legal counsel. This burden further challenges and thwarts effective IDS use and increases the likelihood of a "no," or red-light legal response.

Opportunities

As highlighted above, the value of the law within society is to promote liberties within a social contract that governs, guides, and regulates the expression of those liberties for the social good of all. This important freedom within form is actualized by both red light *and* green light applications of the law. The challenges presented above reflect primarily red-light applications of the law designed to prevent or minimize risk. Absent is the counsel and leadership to promote liberties and to pursue opportunities amid risks that have the potential to yield the greatest good for the greatest number of citizens. Heineman, Lee, and Wilkins (2013), in a paper titled, *Lawyers as Professionals and Citizens: Key Roles and Responsibilities in the 21st Century*, draw our attention to three distinct roles that lawyers should play in the twenty-first century. These roles are technical expert, wise counselor, and effective leader. A lawyer, for example, as legal technician (or technical expert) makes a specific application of existing law to a particular set of facts. Here the implication is that there is always a specific legal answer to a given situation. We want the technician's answers to be a simple yes or no, even though the problem may be immensely complex and convoluted. However, such a stance causes us to look less to the *wise counsel* or *effective leader* roles in the legal profession. To appropriately address the legal challenges of IDS and advance government innovation, we need to call upon these roles. IDS use in government has the potential to advance evidence-based decision-making needed to improve the quality of care and services received by millions of citizens. As such, it necessitates the highest levels of functioning from our legal professionals. The AISP legal issues expert panel report invokes all three roles to lay out concrete steps to address these contemporary legal challenges. Fortunately, in constructing the report, the expert panel exercised *effective leadership* and pointed to "green light" responses and pathways forward.

At the outset, the legal issues expert panel report asserts that the primary purpose of IDS use in federal, state, and local government is to achieve more effective, efficient, and responsive government by facilitating the core government functions of audit, evaluation, research, and evidence-based practice in public programs and policy. At this time, we are not proposing IDS use for the day-to-day operations and case management of individual clients in public service agencies. This specific type of individual, client-level information sharing across agencies almost always requires that the individual consent to having his or her personal data shared for these purposes. In the context of this article, IDS use is focused on linking thousands of individual records across multiple agencies to achieve a broader view of a social problem and policy solutions for entire service populations. Here the primary aim is to study services to enhance them and generate more effective policies in an ongoing data-driven process. The AISP Legal Issues Expert Panel (LIEP) vision of the legal profession's contribution to IDS use is to identify appropriate legal regulation of IDS to maximize IDS as a means to improve evidence-based practice while minimizing privacy and data security risks. Therefore, the preamble of their wise counsel is that the legal issue is no longer *whether* we should integrate data to drive data-based decision-making, but *how* to integrate data such that we address existing legal barriers and concerns to realize the spirit of the law. To accomplish this charge, the legal issues expert panel report seeks to expose myths of IDS use, explicate permissible uses in federal law, and demystify the legal agreements that govern IDS use.

Expose myths and explicate permissible uses. Pervasive public mistrust and fear of litigation are the breeding grounds for misinterpretations and myths about IDS use. The LIEP report identifies the most common arguments posed by legal counsel in opposition to IDS data sharing across agencies and provides clear legal responses to refute these misconceptions. The first misconception is, "This is not legal." As the LIEP report explains, such an assertion is not true because IDS use is legal. All federal and most state laws authorize data sharing for appropriate governmental and research purposes. The LIEP report provides a detailed review of the existing federal laws to illustrate the legal pathways to legitimate use. Another set of common objections involves issues of individual rights, such as, "This (IDS use) requires obtaining individual consent to re-disclose data, which is not administratively feasible and it pits individual interests against societal interests." Again, this is not true because most data privacy laws allow the agency holding the data to use or share that data, including personal identifiers, for research or policymaking purposes without obtaining individual consent. The LIEP report argues that the perceived conflicting interests reflect a false dichotomy. While individuals have a strong interest in data privacy, they have an equally strong interest in effective and efficient government programs and policies. A well-constructed IDS preserves individual privacy through policies and procedures. At the same time, it helps to ensure that government carries out its functions to the highest quality.

Another set of legal oppositions involves misconceptions of how IDS is a threat to the participating public agencies. Examples include, "This (IDS use) exposes us to too much liability … we are going to get sued"; or "This is not a well-accepted practice; it is uncharted and unsanctioned territory placing us at risk." These often push the agency to a "no" response, but such objections are not true. First, major data privacy laws not only allow and encourage data sharing for these purposes, but they also do not contain private right of action for individuals to sue over a data breach or misuse of private data (Petrila et al. 2017). To say that IDS use in government is uncharted territory is also false. IDS exist throughout the United States, and are endorsed at the federal and state levels. The LIEP report points to the AISP national network of existing IDS sites, which consists of local- and state-level IDS that include more than 26 percent of the U.S. population.[5] Adding further evidence to this is the fact that, in 2016, the Evidence-Based Policymaking Commission Act of 2016 (H.R. 1831) became law. Its goal is to promote IDS. Additionally, the National Conference of State Legislatures has prioritized opening government data for public use, including integrated data (Petrila et al. 2017).

Finally, the LIEP report cites two major legal misconceptions that directly exacerbate Americans' fears of government, cybersecurity, as well as governmental ability to manage the (perceived) overwhelming complexity of IDS use in government: "It (IDS use) is too big for government to handle, and it makes a serious data breach more likely." Again, the LIEP report points to the exemplary IDS sites in the AISP network, some of which have been operating for more than 30 years, that, to date, have zero security breaches. It can be done and done well if the IDS is well constructed and uses the best data security practices. High-quality IDS place a premium on data security and formulating legal agreements that maximize beneficial use while minimizing risks to personal data breaches. We devote the remaining sections of this article to addressing how to demystify IDS use and innovate IDS operations to lessen the burden on personnel (including legal counsel) and foster economically sustainable administrations of IDS in government.

Demystify foundational IDS agreements: MOU and DUL. Both the ethical and legal principles addressed in the governance and legal issues' reports require that legal counsel has an adequate understanding of the operations and laws related to an IDS, experience in negotiating and drafting IDS data sharing and data use agreements, and the time and resources to continually develop and monitor these agreements going forward. The LIEP report proposed three responses to legal challenges. It addresses the legal content, process, and structure of the foundational legal agreement documents of an IDS—the MOU and the data use license (DUL). The MOU is the bedrock agreement among the lead IDS agencies and data contributors. It is coconstructed by the IDS stakeholders, and it codifies both the legal rights and responsibilities of each party in the IDS and the procedures and policies that govern sanctioned IDS operations. The DUL is the other basic legal agreement in an IDS. The DUL details the terms and conditions under which a researcher, evaluator, or outside party may gain access to data from the IDS related to a project conducted in partnership with the governing body of the IDS.

The three advancements proposed by the LIEP report are designed to demystify the MOU and DUL legal agreement processes and reduce the burden on government legal counsel (Petrila et al. 2017). The report first specifies the content of these agreements by generating a checklist of information that legal counsel needs to obtain to craft the MOU and DUL. This checklist comprises a set of key questions that relate to laws and regulations governing IDS use. For example, "What are the legal, regulatory, and administrative policies governing the specific types of data involved in the IDS and provide applicable citations?" "What are the specific categories of data to be shared and with whom?" "Are there any restrictions (legal, regulatory, administrative, or other) regarding who can be an authorized user of the data?" Next, the LIEP identifies the logical steps in the process of gathering information, negotiating agreements among those involved in IDS use, and finalizing the written agreements. This process involves major categories of work related to understanding the data sources to be included, identifying the specific data elements to be integrated, gathering all the laws and regulations associated with those elements, considering safeguards related to access and usage, identifying access restrictions and usage requirements, and composing agreements such that they can be comprehended by all partners before signing.

The LIEP report also provides annotated templates of MOU and DUL agreements, and points to online exemplars of these agreements from AISP IDS sites across the United Stata. These templates and examples of existing agreements provide legal counsel with a valuable framework to move forward. The final proposal of the LIEP report is to develop standardized legal agreements (i.e., these annotated templates of agreements) endorsed by recognized legal authorities and legal organizations. This would save an enormous amount of time and reduce the burden on state and local general counsel. The legal leadership of LIEP provides a clear green-light pathway forward to actualizing the benefits of IDS use in government.

IDS Technology and Security

At first glance, the dual charges of the Commission on Evidence-Based Policymaking seem incompatible: to increase access to administrative data for establishing the evidence base for social policy, and to increase the protection and security of these data. But, perhaps counterintuitively, the only way to increase access and use of administrative data will be through the adoption of increased security for these data. As noted previously, among the key objections that agency administrators and attorneys use to argue against data sharing is the fear that making data accessible will increase the risk of a data breach or the reidentification of protected personal information. Indeed, the relatively slow rate at which jurisdictions have been adopting integrated data systems reflects this basic fear. Through the implementation of all four panels' recommended innovations, the security and safety of data sharing can be greatly enhanced. A thorough and thoughtful adoption of standards can enable a community to provide appropriate assurances—both to agency leadership and to the public—that these data integration efforts can be undertaken in a way that safeguards private information.

As with the enhanced governance and legal standards, technology innovations are also making data sharing much more secure by greatly reducing, if not eliminating, the potential risk for data breaches and reidentification risks. Secure research platforms for data sharing have proliferated in several fields, specifically with respect to protected health, education, employment, and social services data. Many countries in Europe, provinces in Canada, states in Australia, and

New Zealand all provide authorized users with access to linked administrative data for approved projects. They have also adopted similar technological approaches and procedural safeguards that point a way forward for jurisdictions in the United States. To facilitate that roadmap, we surveyed these countries, convened an international conference in November 2016, and charged the AISP technology and data security expert panel (TDSEP) to recommend a set of technology-based solutions to greatly reduce the barriers to the implementation of integrated data systems in the United States.

Challenges

Beyond the governance and legal challenges that state and local agencies seeking to share data face, the practical challenges of sharing data in a secure and safe manner create additional barriers. While sharing data between two agencies under the same government auspice, and possibly using a shared secure platform, may seem relatively safe, sharing data with external evaluators and researchers is inherently more complex. Secure file transfer protocol (FTP) and encrypted file transfers can provide some increased security, but having the data travel outside the direct control of the government agencies responsible for these data creates an increased risk that the data can be stolen or otherwise shared with unauthorized people or for unauthorized purposes. Similarly, the risk of reidentification grows because data can be manipulated or linked with other data sources for this purpose.

States and local governments are also suspicious of big information technology (IT) projects, and with good reason. The typical IT project in government involves a complex and time-consuming procurement process. Costly consultants must be retained simply to draft the appropriate specifications for a procurement. Contractors propose and build highly customized solutions at enormous costs. Typically, government agencies are then tied to these contractors for the life of the system, and must reengage them at high costs to make even basic modifications. Legislatures are wary of such projects for all the apparent threats. From our survey of existing integrated data systems in education, health, and human services, sites report that the more sophisticated platforms cost between $2.5 and $4 million to develop. Only some states and a handful of localities have budgets that permit them to build such costly systems, and even jurisdictions with the capacity to fund them are reluctant to engage contractors to build highly customized solutions given the high future attendant service costs.

AISP's work with state and local governments has also revealed what is perhaps the most important resource constraint that they face in developing systems of data sharing and collaboration: workforce capacity. Governments are often working with threadbare staff. The last two decades have seen a shedding of government workers across the board, but especially in the areas of research and evaluation. Not only are attorneys and general counsel offices overwhelmed and overworked, and thus reluctant to take on new work related to IDS MOUs and DULs, but the agency staff to which the operational aspects of this work would fall are often equally overworked. Simply undertaking a single data-sharing agreement between two agencies—the simplest use case—can take nine months to a year to execute. The prospect of having to process multiple requests across multiple departments, and to manage simultaneous transactions with both internal and external analysts, all the while maintaining data security and proper oversight of projects, is unimaginable with current staffing capacities. Technological innovations will be required to make the integrated data system process move at a vastly different scale and efficiency, and to offer genuinely actionable intelligence in a timely manner.

Opportunities: An open source, shared technology solution set

The TDSEP report proposes a shared set of technology solutions that simultaneously address data security, cost, and transaction management challenges that confront jurisdictions seeking to develop an integrated data system (Patterson et al. 2017). Recognizing that states and local governments have many data integration needs, and that no single system can or should be burdened with the responsibility of meeting the diversity of needs and possible uses, they propose a specific archival approach comprising a thin stream of data that would be updated periodically (quarterly or yearly) and that would be designed to meet the specific needs of program evaluators, policy analysts, and researchers. TDEP recommends an open-source set of solutions, consisting of two primary components. The first component, "DataHub," would standardize the technology and workflow processes for acquiring, storing, linking, and provisioning the data. The second component, "Clearinghouse," would manage the transactions associated with processing data requests, managing secure access, and providing oversight of approved projects and users.

The solution set proposed in the TDSEP report includes specific features designed to address the data security concerns of agency administrators. Through the adoption of state-of-the-art encryption methods, the data would be encrypted by source agencies in transit to the DataHub, and at rest within the system, so that personal identifiers are not attached to records. Tools would be available to the system administrator for creating customized linked research datasets to the specifications of an approved project and user. Research datasets would be made available to evaluators and analysts through a secure portal, through which queries could be sent and run against the data. The statistical output generated from these queries would be run through an automated disclosure filter, designed to ensure that only aggregate data with minimum cell size limits are returned to the analysts. Analyst queries would also be monitored to make sure that queries conform with approved purposes. Of course, a manual disclosure review for final output is also possible. Analysts would not be able to view record-level data; however, simulated, record-level data views could be generated to verify statistical output. Each jurisdiction would have its own instantiation of the DataHub, with physical and technical control over the data and server. While some sites may eventually seek cloud-based solutions, TDSEP's assessment of state and local governments' preferences has identified a robust consensus for site-based physical and technical controls over their data; DataHub is designed to provide that.

The Clearinghouse platform will operate as a website that will standardize the workflow processes associated with end user data requests and project execution.

The site would be configured to appear as the portal to a given DataHub installation, or, in a future phase of the initiative, to enable multisite, cross-jurisdiction data requests. The Clearinghouse would provide metadata through the jurisdictional DataHub. Evaluators and researchers would submit requests for projects using a standardized form. Once a designated governing board approved a project, a data use license would be generated for the signature of the end user and their sponsoring institution (countries surveyed only permit universities and approved research institutions access to microdata). The DUL would specify the data elements and research questions that have been approved, and the time period for which data access will be permitted, as well as other responsibilities and safeguards required of the end user and their institution to protect against unauthorized uses of the data and related sanctions for violations (usually lifetime refusal of future access, in addition to financial and legal penalties for the institution and end user). AISP is also planning to create a tutorial on the laws and ethics related to the analysis of administrative data, which end users may be required to complete. Once approved, the Clearinghouse would provide user authentication and electronic certification, permitting the analyst to access her or his designated research dataset. One important feature of the Clearinghouse is that it would also permit researchers to submit approved external datasets for linkage to the DataHub. Queries would be submitted via the Clearinghouse, and the statistical output would be provided via the secure portal at the specified DataHub. The automated and possible manual disclosure review would screen output for approval. The Clearinghouse would host a results forum so that evaluators, project sponsors, IDS administrators, and data source agencies could discuss results and data interpretation issues before any findings are made public. Similarly, public forums for specific topics would be hosted for the discussion of results and papers by subject matter experts, policymakers, and other interested parties. Last, the TDSEP has recommended that the Clearinghouse include a mechanism for jurisdictions and funders to post requests for proposals, or a notice of research priorities, to which evaluators could respond. The site would also manage financial charges for access to research datasets, standardize contracts, and invoice end users, thereby avoiding the bureaucratic site-specific procurement and payment processes that can often slow projects.

The solutions proposed in the TDSEP report would be commissioned and overseen by a governing board comprising jurisdictions seeking to adopt this common solution set, as well as experts in computer science and evidence-based policymaking. The governing board would also be responsible for developing a business plan.

IDS Data Standards and Minimum Datasets

IDS data challenges

Jurisdictions collect thousands of data elements across scores of datasets as part of their administrative duties. However, only a fraction of these data is of sufficient quality for research and evaluation. Given that administrative data are not typically collected with these uses in mind, great caution must be exercised in selecting data elements that are reliable and valid. Moreover, tremendous variability exists in the data elements collected by state and local governments, making cross-site comparisons, let alone simultaneous multisite analysis, potentially problematic.

A further challenge is that the diverse data sources in an IDS need to be organized in a way that facilitates an understanding of what data are available. Viewed as a series of one-off, or program specific, data siloes, the data potentially available to an IDS can seem vast and overwhelming. The specific program uses addressed by a given dataset can also seem so particular as to require years of experience and domain-specific knowledge to understand their peculiarities. Moreover, state and local variations in data definitions and even different measures in varying datasets for some of the same variables create significant challenges for data managers and administrators seeking to provide meaningfully curated research datasets.

Opportunities

The data standards expert panel (DSEP) was charged with identifying the most promising data from across education, health, human services, justice, housing, and workforce programs that could be incorporated in a state or local government's IDS. Recognizing that the data holdings of these entities are large and complex, the DSEP was asked to consider which datasets are most likely to be common across jurisdictions, which data elements within them are most likely to be governed by federally mandated minimum data standards and definitions, and which data elements are most likely to be valid and reliable for research purposes. To fulfill this charge, the DSEP first developed a conceptual framework for organizing these diverse data holdings. They surveyed the data sources of existing IDS to create an inventory of the optimal candidates for inclusion in a robust IDS data model that would meet their criteria for universality (or near universality) across the United States, reliability, and validity. They also developed a data schematic to classify the types of data most commonly held in these datasets. Last, they considered some of the issues that should be addressed in the repurposing of administrative data for research.

DSEP adopted a life course conceptual framework to structure the recommendations provided in their report (Wulczyn et al. 2017). Data about citizens begin with the birth certificate and end with the death certificate. In between, there are data about infancy and early childhood, including immunizations, early intervention testing and screening, and early childhood education and enrichment programs. Data from school districts track entry and progression through school, including attendance, achievement, special education status, standardized test scores, and disciplinary actions. Social programs for children, including child welfare investigations and out-of-home placements, and juvenile justice placements, record special services to children and youth at risk. The transition to adulthood is recorded through higher education datasets, as well as workforce training programs. Employment and earnings data are available through state labor department records. Special population data, for adults and children who experience homelessness, for example, are collected across the life course, as are public assistance receipt and assisted housing participation. Inpatient and emergency room services are tracked by state "all payer" datasets. Some programs for people with disabilities, including vocational rehabilitation programs, are tracked, as are placement in assisted living and nursing home care.

The DSEP inventoried all these data sources, surveyed the data holdings of existing IDS sites, and rated the data on their accessibility for a given IDS installation. The results of these efforts are listed in their final report, which also includes an appendix of the candidate data sources, the types of data held within them, and their likely utility for an IDS (Wulczyn et al. 2017). While a given agency may track hundreds of variables, the DSEP report identifies the relatively small subset that is likely to be nationally standardized (or approximately so), provided that it is subject to mandated federal minimum data requirements, and with prescribed data definitions. Not surprisingly, the data elements with the highest reliability tend to be those that are audited because they are associated with tracking service provision, billing, and payment. The DSEP report also provides a schema for classifying the types of data likely to be found in these datasets to improve the ease of understanding by potential data requestors (Wulczyn et al. 2017). These include distinctions for persons, types of service encounters, dates associated with services, places or providers for services, and exit codes or destinations.

Finally, the DSEP report considers how communities can address some of the data management issues associated with repurposing administrative data for research and evaluation. Data managers must consider the historical legacy of various data sources, how to reconcile conflicting pieces of information from one or more data sources, how to conduct and document record linkage approaches, and how to assess the quality and completeness of various data elements (Wulczyn et al. 2017). Each of these involves careful assessment by the data management staff of an IDS. The report presents some best practice guidance, and AISP hopes to create a community of experts in this area who can share their experiences to advance the collective understanding and appreciation for the data that can be most effectively used to generate actionable intelligence.

Conclusion

Our growing and diverse nation faces a myriad of social challenges. States and local governments administer dozens of major social programs intended to meet these challenges. However, they have limited knowledge about the people they serve, the impacts programs have, and the best ways to improve the effectiveness of these programs. In most cases, the lack of data is not the problem. Instead, there is a lack of collaborative dialogue among the public agencies that serve the population, the service providers who deliver the programs, the researchers and subject matter experts with domain knowledge, and the public whose needs are to be addressed. That lack of collaboration extends to—and is partly the result of—the lack of data-sharing across agencies. As a network of advanced IDS practitioners, AISP has identified the four key domains for IDS development and operations. The expert panels commissioned in each of those domains have identified the most common challenges to institutionalized data sharing procedures and the recommended solutions to those challenges. The resulting reports, summarized here, provide a roadmap for states and local governments to more quickly and readily adopt best practices for IDS implementation, including guidance for how to address the complex legal and governance issues that set the framework for dialogue and collaboration. A recommended set of technology solutions would enable communities to adopt a low-cost and shared approach to doing this work, while maintaining site-specific governance, authority, and control over their data and how they are used. By adopting a national data model, jurisdictions can further engage in multisite collaborations with data that have known generalizability, reliability, and validity. With these reports, the path forward is clearer and the barriers reduced, and hopefully many more communities will be able to adopt IDS-based approaches to actionable intelligence, thereby improving the quality of life of their citizens through more effective and efficient public services.

Notes

1. The commission was also charged with determining the kinds of administrative data that are ultimately relevant for program evaluation and policymaking, and how to make these data available to researchers through a clearinghouse. See https://www.govtrack.us/congress/bills/114/hr1831/text.

2. States and counties spent more than $2.5 trillion in direct general expenditures for government services in 2012, the majority of which went to education, health care, and social safety net programs. When intergovernmental transfers are factored in, including federal funds, those expenditures increased to more than $3.5 trillion. See http://www.urban.org/policy-centers/cross-center-initiatives/state-local-finance-initiative/projects/state-and-local-backgrounders/state-and-local-expenditures.

3. Since 2008, nine additional jurisdictions have been added to the AISP network.

4. See the Belmont Report, https://videocast.nih.gov/pdf/ohrp_belmont_report.pdf.

5. See https://www.aisp.upenn.edu/aisp-network/.

References

Anderson, Nate. 2009. *"Anonymized" data really isn't—and here's why not.* Ars Technica. Available from https://arstechnica.com/tech-policy/2009/09/your-secrets-live-online-in-databases-of-ruin/.
County of Los Angeles, Chief Executive Office. 2016. *Homelessness initiative recommendations.* Los Angeles, CA: County of Los Angeles, Chief Executive Office. Available from http://file.lacounty.gov/SDSInter/bos/supdocs/101295.pdf.
Culhane, Dennis P., John Fantuzzo, Heather L. Rouse, Vicky Tam, and Jonathan Lukens. 2010. Connecting the dots: The promise of integrated data systems for policy analysis and systems reform. *Intelligence for Social Policy* Working Paper, Philadelphia, PA.

Fantuzzo, John. 2015. Towards a "what if" class: Practices of respect as the aim of teaching ethics to court-involved youth. *Teaching Ethics* 15 (1): 83–86.

Fantuzzo, John, and Dennis P. Culhane, eds. 2015. *Actionable intelligence: Using integrated data systems to achieve a more effective, efficient, and ethical government*. New York, NY: Palgrave Macmillan.

Fantuzzo, John, Christine McWayne, and Stephanie Childs. 2006. Scientist-community collaborations: A dynamic tension between rights and responsibilities. In *Handbook of ethical research with ethnocultural populations and communities*, eds. Joseph E. Trimble and Celia B. Fisher, 27–49. Thousand Oaks, CA: Sage Publications.

Gibbs, Linda, Amy Hawn Nelson, Erin Dalton, Joel Cantor, Stephanie Shipp, and Della Jenkins. 2017. *Principles and practices for ethical and effective ids governance: Setting up for success*. Philadelphia, PA: Actionable Intelligence for Social Policy, University of Pennsylvania.

Heidbreder, Brianne. 2016. Change and continuity in the study of state and local governance: A conversation with Ann Bowman. *State and Local Government Review* 48 (1): 63–71.

Heineman, Ben W., William Lee, and David B. Wilkins. 2013. *Lawyers as professionals and citizens: Key roles and responsibilities in the 21st century*, 1–84. Cambridge, MA: Center on the Legal Profession, Harvard Law School.

Jennings, Edward T., Jeremy F. Hall, and Zhiwei Zhang. 2012. The American Recovery and Reinvestment Act and State Accountability. *Public Performance and Management Review* 35 (3): 527–49.

Kettl, Donald F. 2009. *The next government of the United States: Why our institutions fail us and how to fix them*. New York, NY: W.W. Norton & Company.

Lane, Julia. 2016. Big data for public policy: The quadruple helix. *Journal of Policy Analysis and Management* 35 (3): 708–15.

Patterson, David, Ken Steif, Niall Brennan, Andreas Haeberlen, Aaron Schroeder, and Adam Smith. 2017. *Technology and data security expert panel report*. Philadelphia, PA: Actionable Intelligence for Social Policy, University of Pennsylvania.

Perlman, Bruce J. 2010. Governance challenges and options for state and local governments. *State & Local Government Review* 42 (3): 246–57.

Petrila, John, Barbara Cohn, Wendell Pritchett, Paul Stiles, Victoria Stodden, Jeffrey Vagle, Mark Humowiecki, and Natassia Rozario. 2017. *Legal issues and agreements expert panel report*. Philadelphia, PA: Actionable Intelligence for Social Policy. University of Pennsylvania.

Pew Research Center. 2017. *Americans and cybersecurity*. Washington, DC: Pew Research Center.

Stiles, Paul G., and Roger A. Boothroyd. 2013. *Ethical uses of administrative data for research purposes*. Philadelphia, PA: Actionable Intelligence for Social Policy. University of Pennsylvania.

U.S. Census Bureau. 2015. *Census Bureau reports at least 350 languages spoken in U.S. homes*. Available from https://www.census.gov/newsroom/press-releases/2015/cb15-185.html.

U.S. Congress. 2016. H.R. 1831. Available from https://www.govtrack.us/congress/bills/114/hr1831/text.

U.S. Government Publishing Office. 2016. *Budget of the United States government*. Available from https://www.gpo.gov/fdsys/browse/collection.action?collectionCode=BUDGET&browsePath=Fiscal+Year+2017&isCollapsed=false&leafLevelBrowse=false&isDocumentResults=true&ycord=931.

Wu, Fei, and Max Stevens. 2016. *The services homeless single adults use and their associated costs*. Los Angeles, CA: Chief Executive Office Service Integration Branch Research and Evaluation Services Unit. Available from http://www.aisp.upenn.edu/wp-content/uploads/2015/03/LACountyHomelessness2016.pdf.

Wulczyn, Fred, Richard Clinch, Claudia Coulton, Sallie Keller, James Moore, Clara Muschkin, Andrew Nicklin, Whitney LeBoeuf, and Katie Barghaus. 2017. *Recommended minimum data for integrated data systems expert panel report*. Philadelphia, PA: Actionable Intelligence for Social Policy, University of Pennsylvania.

Building an Infrastructure to Support the Use of Government Administrative Data for Program Performance and Social Science Research

By
JULIA LANE

This article provides an overview of the elements necessary to build a sustainable research data infrastructure. I argue that it needs the financial and intellectual engagement of a community of practice. Most attention has been paid to researchers and policy-makers, but a third group—government programmatic agencies—must be a focal point since they act as both data producers and as policy implementers. I also discuss possible business models that are both consistent with serving the needs of multiple stakeholders and that are not completely dependent on the largesse of the public purse.

Keywords: data infrastructure; linked data; evidence-based policy

There is a new opportunity to link administrative data across agencies at all levels of government—federal, state, and local areas of all sizes. There is clear interest in data-driven research and policy as evidenced by the push toward open data (Catlett et al. 2014) and the proliferation of government chief data officers (Pardo 2014), the establishment of the Evidence-Based Policymaking Commission, and the active engagement of many important private foundations in supporting linked data systems. It is fair to say that there is now the potential for the evolution of a new research infrastructure that joins

Julia Lane is an elected fellow of the American Association for the Advancement of Science, the International Statistical Institute, and the American Statistical Association. She cofounded such data infrastructures as the LEHD program at the Census Bureau, Patentsview at the Patent and Trademark Office, the NORC/University of Chicago Remote Access Data Enclave, and the Institute for Research on Innovation and Science.

NOTE: Many thanks for very useful comments from Erica Groshen, Danny Goroff, David Ellwood, Mark Lowenstein, Sarah Dale, Kristen Monaco, Scott Fricker, and Andrew Reamer.

Correspondence: Julia.lane@nyu.edu

DOI: 10.1177/0002716217746652

datasets across federal and local agencies and enhances decision-making. Building such an infrastructure will require a thoughtful balancing of costs and benefits, documented value, and the engagement of the full community.

The potential value is immense. If the infrastructure is well designed, agencies can manage their programs better. Respondent burden could be reduced if statistical agencies used administrative records to replace or enhance survey questions. Operational costs could also be reduced to save taxpayer dollars. For example, the current cost estimate for the 2020 Decennial Census of $15.5 billion—or approximately $107 per man, woman, and child in the United States—could be reduced by about $1.5 billion.[1] Better policy interventions could be designed—just as early uses have led to the development of permanent supportive housing for the homeless, the design of effective training programs for dislocated workers, or the implementation of school curricula that really change the way in which children view drug use.[2] In the most forward-looking sense, social science research could be galvanized by access to new sources of high-quality data. For example, work by Raj Chetty using tax records has documented that intergenerational mobility is declining, and the American Dream is less robust than previously thought.[3]

The potential risks of massive integrated data systems are high as well, though. Poorly designed infrastructure could lead to security breaches that could harm vulnerable populations—imagine the effect of an Equifax-style breach on data that pertained to immigrant populations. Poorly documented or intermittently available datasets could result in higher, not lower, costs to statistical agencies as staff struggle to reconcile changing classification systems, or fill in gaps that occur because data providers went out of business. Imagine, for example, if the Bureau of Labor Statistics came to rely on ADP employment data to measure employment, and ADP[4] simply stopped providing information or decided to triple prices for that information.

It is critical to move from hypothetical to actual value and to demonstrate that confidentiality can be protected (Abowd, Haltiwanger, and Lane 2004, 224–29). Many agencies are not legally permitted to share data for research unless the work that is to be done is consistent with the agency mission. For example, the success of the Longitudinal Employer Household Dynamics (LEHD) program is at least partly due to the development of the Quarterly Workforce Indicators and the "On the Map" program, which generated value for both statistical and programmatic agencies while protecting confidentiality.[5]

The success of LEHD (and other similar efforts) was also made possible because it could be embedded in a strong research infrastructure: the Center for Economic Studies at the U.S. Census Bureau, which enabled the linkage activities to be institutionalized and professionalized, in essence, creating a "coral reef" of data.

What precisely is a research infrastructure? Funding agencies tend to define it by its operational characteristics. The European Commission says, "The term 'research infrastructure' refers to facilities, resources and related services used by the scientific community to conduct top-level research in their respective fields, ranging from social sciences to astronomy, genomics to nanotechnologies."[6] In the United States, the National Science Foundation's Major Research Instrumentation Program (MRI) says a research infrastructure "serves to increase access to shared scientific and engineering instruments for research and research training in our Nation's institutions of higher education, not-for-profit museums, science centers and scientific/engineering research organizations."[7] The National Institutes of Health does not precisely define research infrastructures, but says that it "includes the physical, intellectual and human resources that advance biomedical research at the NIH."[8]

   In this article, I argue that the real mark of a good data infrastructure is that it is sustainable, and that its results are valued by the broad community that it serves. Without that value, there will be no long-term sustainability. In other words, an infrastructure needs the financial and intellectual engagement of a community of practice. In terms of developing a new infrastructure for the use of administrative data, most attention has been paid to researchers and policy-makers, but a third group—government programmatic agencies—must be a focal point since they act as both data producers and as policy implementers.[9] I argue that the provision of technical solutions to housing safe data is a fundamental and necessary step to get data providers to contribute data. However, technical solutions, while necessary, are not sufficient to ensure that data are made available for operational and research purposes. I thus also describe the core organizational features necessary for all stakeholders to participate in the establishment of a new intra-agency data infrastructure: reputation, reciprocity, and trust (Ostrom 1998, 1–22). I describe the complex motivations of the different stakeholder groups and argue that there should not be a "one size fits all" approach to designing a successful institutional framework (Ostrom 2010), though ultimately some core elements of technology, law, and privacy protection can move toward a much greater degree of standardization. I conclude with a discussion of possible business models that are both consistent with serving the needs of multiple stakeholders and that are not completely dependent on the largesse of the public purse.

Infrastructure

Merriam-Webster defines an *infrastructure* as the basic equipment and structures that are needed for an economy or an organization to function properly.[10] This volume documents in extensive detail the extent to which an administrative data infrastructure will make the country function better through accessing and using data. The operational aspects are obvious: there are many data uses, such as being used to track program participants across programmatic agencies and across time and space, which simply make programs more efficient. Research is equally important: determining what works and what does not enables better use of taxpayer dollars. Researchers, policy-makers, and government agencies (in their twin roles as data producers and policy implementers) need to work together for the country to be served well by a data infrastructure. For example, institutions such as the University of Chicago's Chapin Hall[11] have worked with all three stakeholders to combine administrative data on children from many sources and have been a remarkable resource for evidence to Illinois policy-makers and communities for more than 50 years. The challenge before us is to determine the institutional characteristics necessary to engage stakeholders at a national scale.

One challenge to building a sustainable model is dealing with mission divergence among stakeholders. University scholars are motivated by research that takes years and is aimed at peer-reviewed journals. Policy-makers have short time frames to make a difference. Agencies, in their role of providing support to policy-makers, are focused on concrete service improvements for citizens. Agencies in their role of data provider must both protect data and ensure that data access is granted for mission specific purposes.

The work of Nobel Laureate Elinor Ostrom is extremely instructive in designing a sustainable data infrastructure. She has described in detail how her empirical study of different institutional structures led her to identify three key features of these structures: reputation, reciprocity, and trust. She emphasized the importance of small groups, face-to-face communications, and the development of shared norms in developing those three features. Ostrom also made it clear that there are multiple (seven) types of rules that govern behavior but "gave up on the idea that [there were] specific rules that were associated with [a] successful case"; in other words, she was against one monolithic approach (Ostrom 2010, 652). She argues for the facilitation of institutional development that brings out the best in humans and deals with the inherent complexity of human dynamics, what she calls a *polycentric approach*. Such a polycentric approach should sit at the core of the development of a data infrastructure. The human dimension, which brings together the three groups of stakeholders, should be as carefully thought through and made as central to the design as the technical dimension. The following describes each of their interests in turn.

Stakeholders

Policy-makers

Policy-makers can better design effective operations and policy with administrative data. Administrative data are often of higher quality than survey data in key dimensions. In particular, administrative data are, by definition, better at capturing the population of participants in government programs than are surveys. This is important, since if participation is underestimated, particularly for particular groups, the structure of the interventions will be biased. In a series of high impact and thoughtful papers, Bruce Meyer and coauthors have shown that survey data suffer from nonresponse both at the unit and item level, as well as response measurement error. They documented that using administrative data can significantly increase quality (Meyer, Mok, and Sullivan 2009, 2015; Meyer and George 2011).

Administrative data can be structured to be longitudinal, with typically less attrition than that which is exhibited by surveys. Such data can permit the examination of the effect of interventions. In the educational arena, for example, longitudinal administrative data make it possible to examine the returns to pre-school education or No Child Left Behind. As Figlio, Karbownik, and Salvanes (2015) point out:

> Registry data have been used to study the introduction of new technologies to schools in England (Machin, McNally, and Silva 2007), experimental evidence on schools' influence on parents' involvement in education in France (Avvisati et al. 2014), experimental evidence on gender differences in competitiveness and its consequences for educational choices in the Netherlands (Buser, Niederle, and Oosterbeek 2014), the role of school quality in Romania (Pop-Elches and Urquiola 2013), experimental evidence on learning incentives in Mexico (Behrman et al. 2015), perceived effects of school quality on the housing market (Figlio and Lucas 2004), the role of peer effects utilizing student reshuffling due to extreme events (Imberman, Kugler, and Sacerdote 2012), and the ability of principals to recognize effective teachers (Jacob and Lefgren 2008).

Of course, there are negatives to linking data that policy-makers also need to recognize. Administrative records are collected for the purposes of administering programs, so their coverage and applicability depends on the nature of the program for which the data were collected. It may be difficult to generalize conclusions from one population to another.

Government agencies

Government programmatic agencies are being forced by Congress and budgetary expediency to use new technology and approaches to make better use of existing data. At the state and local levels, agencies have created a new job title, "chief data officer" and built dashboards and initiated predictive analytic and smart sensor projects in the name of better efficiency, accountability, and improved community engagement (President's Council of Advisors on Science and Technology 2016). Local government organizations (e.g., U.S. Conference of Mayors, National League of Cities and the International City/County Management Association) have launched data initiatives.

There are similar pressures on government statistical agencies. The declining response rate and quality of surveys has caused widespread concern (Meyer, Mok, and Sullivan 2015; Meyer and George 2011). In response, the Office of Management and Budget's Interagency Committee on Statistical Policy has encouraged a set of system-wide pilot projects to advance the statistical uses of administrative data (Smith 2014).

There are many reasons to link datasets. By linking to an existing source of data instead of implementing a new survey, there is a cost savings (and almost certainly a time savings as well). For some research questions (e.g., a survey of the reasons for death of a longitudinal cohort of individuals), a new survey may not be possible. In the case of administrative data or other automatically generated data, the sample size is much greater than would be possible from a survey.

And once links are made to one dataset, there may be an opportunity to vastly expand links in the future.

There are also, however, multiple challenges for agencies to provide and link data—there are many legal and technical hurdles to clear and few prototype successes to point to. As some white papers have pointed out, the legal framework varies from agency to agency, and negotiations between lawyers and analysts can take many months of staff time. In addition, the pressures to meet existing program needs make it difficult for agencies to allocate staff time to try something new and create pipelines for new products. There can also be serious downsides to allowing access to data, either because of the potential for breaches or poor-quality analysis that results in agency embarrassment. In addition, government salary structures often make it difficult to hire and retain enough in-house data analysts, so agencies do not have the capacity to work with new linked data. The lack of workforce capacity is a binding constraint, because agencies often do not have the mechanisms and resources to share data and build the linked datasets. They also do not have the resources to develop new products in their own right. And while some federal agencies have professional development funds for staff, some do not.

The research community

The value to researchers of using administrative data has been well established (Card et al. 2011; Jarmin and O'Hara 2016). Indeed, the use of administrative data by researchers has increased substantially over the past 30 years (see Figure 1). There are many reasons for this. The coverage is broad and the sample size large. This means that it is possible to study rare events and small segments of the population. Since much of the economic and social activity of interest is concentrated in a small segment of the distribution—such as health care costs or job creation—it is critical to have sufficient data to study outliers. So, for example, business dynamics, which are heavily skewed, can only be studied using administrative data (Decker et al. 2016). One important finding has been the decline of transformational entrepreneurial firms—those that introduce major innovations and make substantial contributions to growth—particularly in the high-tech sector. On the human dimension, a small number of individuals disproportionately contribute to crime incidents, a small number disproportionately contribute to health care costs, and a small number disproportionately contribute to welfare costs. The study of the behavior of such groups, and designing appropriate interventions, is made possible by large-scale administrative data.

There are a number of barriers to accessing administrative data—many of which can substantially reduce the willingness of researchers, particularly junior researchers, to work with administrative records. A major issue is simply getting access to data. There are substantial legal restrictions on data use and access. Researchers need to first identify champions within an agency who are willing to take the time to work with them. They must then identify what data are available, develop projects that are consistent with the agency mission, and develop detailed data management and security plans. If a researcher wants to link data

FIGURE 1
The Use of Administrative Data

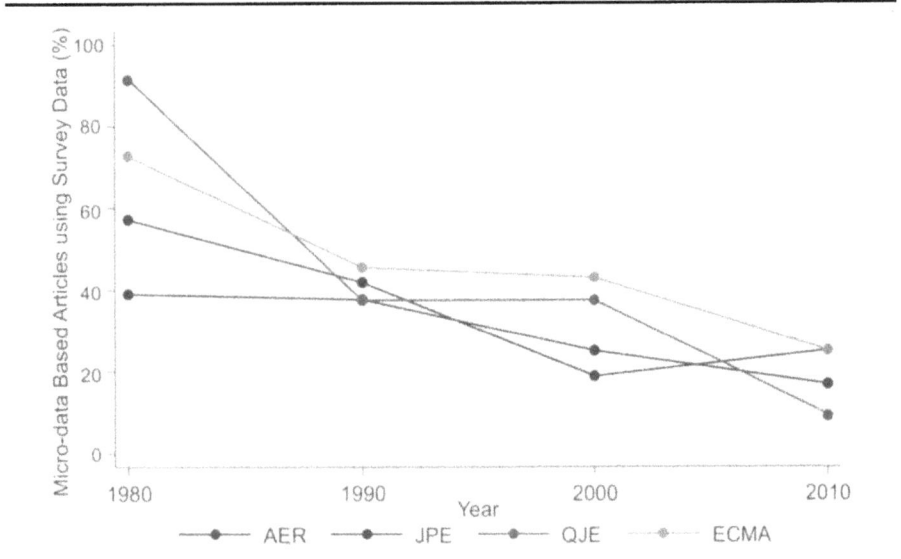

SOURCE: Raj Chetty.

across agencies, she or he must work with the agencies to develop memoranda of understanding or interagency agreements, common access protocols, and research review requirements. This process can take years, which a junior researcher, wanting tenure, simply does not have. However, these barriers should not be completely eliminated. Access to confidential micro data is a privilege, not a right. And some difficulty is necessary so that the researcher is constantly reminded that she or he is working with data that deal with human subjects (Ohm 2014).

The incentive structure for the hard work of building widely useable data infrastructures is also lacking. There are many academic rewards for publishing. There are few rewards for building and documenting data infrastructure efforts. It is also much easier to get funding for projects that promise publications; there are few initiatives that fund infrastructure development.[12]

General barriers for all stakeholders

A major issue with linked data, although difficult to quantify, is dealing with turf battles, both internal and external, to the pertinent agency. I experienced a turf battle when I worked with an internal champion in a major governmental agency to develop a researcher access program that provided access to extremely sensitive microdata. That program was established and is now extremely successful. However, the internal champion had to be creative within his agency to move things forward; once he was uncovered, he was sidelined and subsequently retired. There were similarly many external turf battles in the establishment of the Longitudinal Employer-Household Dynamics (LEHD) program; dealing with those challenges took more time than dealing with the technical issues.

Building a Business Model

Infrastructure development should explicitly address how to develop reputation, reciprocity, and trust between agencies and the research community. Given the complexities of the different agencies and policy issues, the infrastructure should draw on common standards, while customizing some elements—as Ostrom pointed out, one size should not fit all. Indeed, Ostrom identified some key mechanisms in building successful institutions: reliance on small to medium-size organizations to ensure flexibility, voluntary participation to ensure that the needs of stakeholders are met on an ongoing basis, and multiple service providers to ensure responsiveness (Ostrom 1990).

An example from personal experience—building a training program for government agencies—might serve to fix ideas and show how such centers can work with sufficient initial investments. New York University was tasked by the Census Bureau to build an Administrative Records Research Facility to inform the decision-making of the Commission on Evidence-Based Policymaking. The goal of that facility was to build and support an infrastructure that will expedite the acquisition of federal and federally sponsored administrative data; sources for program evaluation; improve data documentation and linkage techniques; and leverage and extend existing systems for governance, privacy protection, and secure access to these data. That facility thus was designed to address the technical problem of security and access. However, because of the ADRN UK experience, which struggled to gain agency acceptance and data, it was clear that it was critical to also build an agency engagement strategy. I worked with Rayid Ghani, a computer scientist at the University of Chicago, Bob Goerge at Chapin Hall at the University of Chicago, and Frauke Kreuter, a statistician at the University of Maryland (UMD) to develop training classes centered on empirical policy issues (Foster et al. 2016). These training classes have been a huge success. They address the key agency challenges: workforce capacity and the need to serve agency missions. The classes are designed to build new products through linking data, using modern technology, and applying active learning techniques in a sandbox environment. It (1) creates a pipeline of new prototype products central to an agency's mission as defined by senior management, (2) develops teams of practitioners who can demonstrate the value of the new types of data for solving real-world practical problems and who become embedded in their organizations, and (3) makes new linked data available on an ongoing basis. This framework builds trust, reputation, and as it is repeated, reciprocity—the features that Ostrom identified as critical.

Our initial experience has been extremely positive. We have engagement in two key policy areas of interest: the labor market outcomes of ex-offenders and

FIGURE 2
Canonical Example of Linked Data for Policy

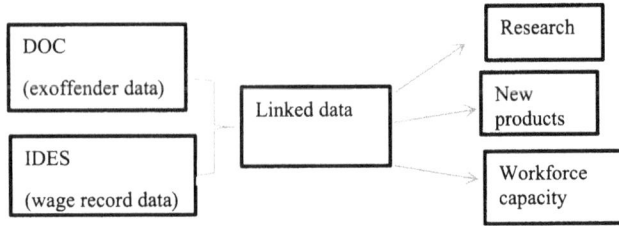

the labor market outcomes of welfare recipients. By providing incentives to provide data, resources to work on high-priority problems and demonstrated value in sharing data across agency lines, we demonstrate the value of linked data by engaging staff from multiple agencies to work on cross-agency problems. The classes are not structured as lectures but rather are inquiry based and modular. We engage agency staff in a lab in which participants implement skills to produce actionable analyses (Handelsman et al. 2004). Our strategy has been to build ongoing agency use of linked administrative records and other sources of data for program evaluation by demonstrating value to the agency.

For each project, the NYU/Chicago/UMD teams build the core linked dataset that can be modified and expanded as engagement increases (see Figure 2). That infrastructure makes use of new technology (Granger 2015; Pérez and Granger 2007, 21–29), with specific examples and code developed through the notebooks and the companion book (Foster et al. 2016) so that participants can have direct, replicable, and high-value interaction with the data and with each other. The expectation is that networks will be formed, new data assets will be created, and useful reports and analyses will be generated (Figure 2). We have well over 175 students signed up from almost sixty government agencies. Agencies are providing data to be linked—across state, local, and federal agencies—since the activity serves their missions.

The role of external funding was critical. The Census Bureau and the Laura and John Arnold Foundation were critical to the success of our initiative. The Census Bureau provided initial funding for a remote access data facility; the Arnold Foundation provided scholarships for the test cases.

This approach is one example of how financial sustainability can be developed, once initial startup funding is made available. There are multiple options to revenue generation. Class tuition is certainly one, but it is also possible to build a membership model jointly with city agencies to study topics of cross-cutting interest. If the linked data are built on—using a "coral reef" approach—the university centers could partner with government agencies to develop customized reports; such an approach has been successful in other contexts.[13] There is already some interest in the classes being used as the basis for developing long-term state and local government and federal statistical agency data exchange partnerships.

Of course, there have been many other models in the past where universities have partnered with key communities of interest; the agricultural extension program is one example (McDowell 2003a, 2003b; Cash 2001). There are certainly a number of centers that have been successful in their own right, as Dennis Culhane and Bob Goerge have demonstrated in their contributions to this volume. The question is how to scale to a national model. The role of private foundations could be critical here. The Alfred P. Sloan Foundation's call for a network of research facilities, and the Laura and John Arnold Foundation's substantial investments in research centers have led the way in building that mass. Scaling and building on the existing polycentric communities would seem natural, given that universities have both research and education missions, and agencies need both research and workforce training. We should note the importance of entry and exit in shaping the infrastructure (also identified by Ostrom 1990). In our model, successful activities (such as classes), aimed at serving the interests of researchers, policy-makers, and government agencies, would grow and expand; those that were not as focused on stakeholder interests should be allowed to die.

Infrastructure is long term in nature. Thus, attention must be paid to financial sustainability and to building a vibrant community of practice. There are some major investments that must be made to lower fixed costs so that more researchers become involved and more agencies provide data. For example, developing common agreed-upon legal and technical standards would likely create both a safer and more interoperable environment, while maintaining some flexibility. The articles by Petrila, Culhane, and Goerge have addressed the importance of establishing a coherent legal framework with standards for privacy protection, including memoranda of understanding and nondisclosure agreements; conflicting and confusing rules add risk and cost to data providers and cost and burden to researchers. The development of such frameworks can draw on the expertise of legal scholars, and ideally be the basis for standard-setting legislation. In this volume, Foster and Culhane have addressed the importance of providing a template for technically safe environments, so that resources are not wasted by duplicating technical efforts. The federal investment in the Federal Risk and Authorization Management Program, or FedRAMP, standards is illustrative of the value of established standards in promoting access.[14] The development of standardized environments can draw on the considerable expertise of computer scientists.

The startup costs for building infrastructure are high. Private foundations could play a fundamental initial role. Private foundations could invest in providing support for developing and disseminating best practices for the technical security of data facilities, as well as disseminating information about disclosure limitation techniques. They could identify key policy foci—whether they be pathways out of poverty, improving community services, or stimulating entrepreneurship—and pay for scholarships or initial projects for the development of classes in these areas. New ideas could be generated by annual workshops that bring together experts on the many facets of the community. They would include data providers, policy-makers, and researchers (social scientists and computer scientists).

Where to Go from Here

This article has argued that the development of a new administrative data infrastructure has to be informed by thoughtful and deliberate engagement with appropriate stakeholders. Because of the legal and technical barriers associated with providing data access, serious resources must be devoted to reducing those barriers. Building an operational business model requires that stakeholders be engaged in a mechanism that builds reciprocity, reputation, and trust and that there are sufficient resources—financial, technical, and human—to make it all happen (Pardo 2014). The current person-by-person and ad hoc links between individual data producers and a few scholars are not sustainable over the long term.

A scalable and sustainable approach could involve developing a network of city/organizational partnerships where data producers, scholars, and policymakers come together to work. One possible starting point is to build those partnerships around executive education–style classes. In those classes, agency staff could work together in secure state-of-the-art neutral data repositories, working to produce useful projects and research that are mutually beneficial. If all projects made use of a common interoperable data infrastructure that served as the backbone for the safe use of linked administrative data across governmental units, it would both assure data providers that their data are being accessed in a secure and safe environment and reduce onerous, time-consuming, and costly startup time.

A natural place for this to occur is at universities. If a group of universities in collaboration with governments built safe, credible high-service data centers that specialized in data linkage, usage, and dissemination and demonstrated their operational and policy value through training programs targeted at agencies' workforces, the world might beat a path to their door. We have seen how university-based centers can support themselves and provide good operational policy analysis. Two illustrative examples are the Institute for Research on Innovation and Science at the University of Michigan, which is almost completely funded by member universities, and Tulsa's MHealth network, which now includes more than four thousand providers and their patients, and demonstrated significant cost reductions and shown improvement in health outcomes.

While each center is different, some core lessons are surprisingly similar. Each group started by focusing on a core problem. Integrated data and technology was treated as a tool to help solve the problem, not the primary goal in and of itself. The effort had strong and visionary leadership, which convened and engaged key stakeholders around the problem and created an effective governance system that ensured each had a voice and a strong stake in the work. That leadership did see a sustainable system for data integration as an essential goal of the work, but it was always described as serving the large goals of health and efficiency. And the project started with demonstration support, while ultimately creating a system that was self-sustaining because of the demonstrated benefits to the producers themselves.

A massive step forward could be made if a consortium of foundations made major similar investments that would be competitively allocated across multiple centers. Such a consortium could create a mechanism for local governments to connect to national efforts to link data for the purposes of designing cutting edge policy/program pilots combined with proven and developing technologies for data access. Since technical solutions are necessary, but not sufficient, to ensure sustainability, the approach should include the building of community data skills and associated human capital, which has the added benefit of ensuring sustainability if the project focus is in demand.

Notes

1. http://www.gao.gov/highrisk/2020_decennial_census/why_did_study; http://www.washingtonexaminer.com/2020-census-to-cost-107-per-household-156-billion-most-ever/article/2639061.

2. Commission on Evidence-Based Policymaking Final Report (pp. 9–10); see https://www.cep.gov/content/dam/cep/report/cep-final-report.pdf.

3. http://www.mobilitypartnership.org/blog/intergenerational-mobilitys-downward-trend.

4. https://www.adpemploymentreport.com/2017/June/NER/NER-June-2017.aspx.

5. See https://lehd.ces.census.gov/doc/LEDonepager_2017.pdf.

6. https://ec.europa.eu/research/infrastructures/index_en.cfm?pg=what; EU support for Research Infrastructures (RIs) in the context of its Framework Programmes (FPs) began with FP2 (1987–1991) when it had a budget of about €30 million. From these relatively humble beginnings, FP7 (2007–2013) earmarked €1.85 billion for RIs between 2007 and 2013 and the Horizon 2020 Programme will support research infrastructures with about €2.5 billion between 2014 and 2020.

7. https://nsf.gov/funding/pgm_summ.jsp?pims_id=5260&org=OIA&from=home.

8. https://dpcpsi.nih.gov/sites/default/files/ORIP%20Strategic%20Plan%20Final-%20April%202016.pdf.

9. Private data providers should, of course, be part of a broader conversation.

10. https://www.merriam-webster.com/dictionary/infrastructure.

11. http://www.chapinhall.org/.

12. There are notable exceptions.

13. See, for example, the model developed by the Institute for Research on Innovation and Science (iris.isr.umich.edu).

14. www.fedramp.gov.

References

Abowd, John J., John Haltiwanger, and Julia Lane. 2004. Integrated longitudinal employer- employee data for the united states. *American Economic Review* 94:224–29.

Card, David, Raj Chetty, Martin Feldstein, and Emmanuel Saez. 2011. *Expanding access to administrative data for research in the United States.* Available from http://emlab.berkeley.edu/~saez/card-chetty-feldsteinsaezNSF10dataaccess.pdf.

Cash, David W. 2001. In order to aid in diffusing useful and practical information: Agricultural extension and boundary organizations. *Science Technology Human Values* 26:431–53.

Catlett, Charlie, Tanu Malik, Brett Goldstein, and Ian Foster. 2014. Plenario: An open data discovery and exploration platform for urban science. *Bulletin of the IEEE Computer Society Technical Committee on Data Engineering* 37 (4): 27–42.

Decker, Ryan, John Haltiwanger, Ron Jarmin, and Javier Miranda. 19 March 2016. The decline of high-growth entrepreneurship. *Vox.*

Figlio, David N., Krzysztof Karbownik, and Kjell G. Salvanes. 2015. Education research and administrative data. National Bureau of Economic Research Working Paper, Cambridge, MA. Available from http://www.nber.org/papers/w21592.

Foster, Ian, Rayid Ghani, Ron S. Jarmin, Frauke Kreuter, and Julia I. Lane. 2016. *Big data and social science: A practical guide to methods and tools*. New York, NY: Taylor & Francis Group.

Granger, Brian E. 2015. Jupyter and JupyterHub. Available from https://jupyter.org/.

Handelsman, Jo, Diane Ebert-May, Robert Beichner, and Peter Bruns. 2004. Scientific teaching. *Science* 304 (5670): 521–22.

Jarmin, Ron S., and Amy O'Hara. 2016. Big data and the transformation of public policy analysis. *Journal of Policy Analysis Management* 35 (3): 715–21.

McDowell, George R. 2003a. Engaged universities: Lessons from the land-grant universities and extension. *The ANNALS of the American Academy of Political and Social Science* 585:31–50.

McDowell, George R. 2003b. *Land-grant universities and extension into the 21st century: Renegotiating or abandoning a social contract*. Iowa City, IA: Iowa State University Press. Available from https://eric.ed.gov/?id=ED462043.

Meyer, Bruce D., and Robert M. Goerge. 2011. *Errors in survey reporting and imputation and their effects on estimates of food stamp program participation*. Washington, DC: Food Assistance and Nutrition Research Program.

Meyer, Bruce D., Wallace K. C. Mok, and James X. Sullivan. 2009. The under-reporting of transfers in household surveys: its nature and consequences. National Bureau of Economic Research Working Paper, Cambridge, MA. Available from http://www.nber.org/papers/w15181.

Meyer, Bruce D., Wallace K. C. Mok, and James X. Sullivan. 2015. Household surveys in crisis. *Journal of Economic Perspectives* 29:199–226.

Ohm, Paul. 2014. Changing the rules: General principles for data use and analysis. In Privacy, big data, and the public good: Frameworks for engagement, eds. Julia Lane, Victoria Stodden, Helen Nissenbaum, and Stefan Bender, 96–111. New York, NY: Cambridge University Press.

Ostrom, Elinor. 1990. *Governing the commons: The evolution of institutions for collective action*. Cambridge: Cambridge University Press.

Ostrom, Elinor. 1998. A behavioral approach to the rational choice theory of collective action: Presidential address. *American Political Science Review* 92:1–22.

Ostrom, Elinor. 2010. Beyond markets and states: Polycentric governance of complex economic systems. *American Economic Review* 100:641–72.

Pardo, Theresa. 2014. *Making data more available and usable: A getting started guide for public officials*. Available from http://cusp.nyu.edu/wp-content/uploads/2014/07/Pardo.pdf.

Pérez, Fernando, and Brian E. Granger. 2007. IPython: A system for interactive scientific computing. *Computer Science & Engineering* 9:21–29.

President's Council of Advisors on Science and Technology. 2016. *Technology and the future of cities*. Washington, DC: President's Council of Advisors on Science and Technology, Executive Office of the President.

Smith, Kitty. 2014. *Increasing researcher access to federal administrative data: A project of the council of professional associations on federal statistics*. Available from http://www.copafs.org/UserFiles/file/IncreasingAccesstoFederalAdministrativeDataProject.pdf.

www.ingramcontent.com/pod-product-compliance
Lightning Source LLC
Chambersburg PA
CBHW070803300326
41914CB00052B/610